PRECIOUS WOMEN

PRECIOUS WOMEN

BY

Dorothy Anne Liot Backer

Basic Books, Inc., Publishers NEW YORK

I wish to acknowledge the patience, kindness, and friendship of Professor William H. Barber, of Birkbeck College
at the University of London, whose encouragement over
several years made this book possible.

For Eric
and my two Annas

La pretieuse de soy n'a
point de définition; les
termes sont trop grossiers
pour bien exprimer une
chose si spirituelle.

—Abbé de Pure,
La Pretieuse

Contents

I

Rambouillet

II

The Precious Decade

III
Grandes Mondaines

Illustrations

PRECIOUS WOMEN

Euphémie (I)

It is Wednesday afternoon and Euphémie is receiving. She lies on her bed fully dressed, propped up on cushions. The bedspread is tucked in around her like a cocoon, but the upper half of her dress is visible to her guests in the discreet light, softened by the bed-hangings. She is wearing a gown of green velvet, whose sleeves are stiff balloons slashed to reveal layers of white satin underneath. These sleeves harbor mysteries, their patterned shell invites concentration on the loopholes, but all that is offered to the eye is more fabric. Somewhere under there, beneath all that workmanship, are arms.

The sleeves are so stiff and round that they prevent the elbows from touching the body. Above them the sloping shoulders and the round nape of Euphémie are weighed down by the heavy velvet. The bodice of the dress, stiff and tubular, further immobilizes her body. Perhaps she is made of something other than flesh. Marble, say, cold, polished, and pink. Or crystal, immensely fragile. Euphémie lies very still. Her gestures are limited to the hands and face. She never makes an involuntary move.

Her hair is flattened with pomade on top, with bunches of curls at the sides. Like the body, it has been transformed into some other material, some precious metal spun into lace.

Euphémie is delicate. She has been delicate ever since her father married her, in her thirteenth year, to an army hero who had already buried two wives. After three painful and bloody occasions when she delivered sons to him, thus securing his name, she fell into a strange weakness. Fortunately, every year, as soon as the crocuses appeared, he would mount his horse and go off to war, not to return again until the first frosts of November. At last he was blown up in a border skirmish in Germany. Euphémie, now a

3

widow, still has headaches and keeps to her bed. But with the release of her dowry she has achieved all the independence and security that a lady needs, and does not plan to remarry. Her money is her own. Her heart is unengaged. She reclines serenely on this Wednesday in May 1657, in her house in Paris, and listens to the murmuring voices of her guests.

They are gathered around her on stools and armchairs. The room is small, the smallest and last box in a narrowing series of reception areas, a *réduit*, a snug dark spot. The ladies are engaged in the highest and noblest of all human activities, the most challenging, the most fulfilling, the most serious, the most precious, the most joyful: conversation.

What is there to talk about? M. Corneille's tragedy, *Timocrate*, must be disposed of, and those anonymous Jansenist letters touched on—only touched. The latest thing, M. Benserade's new madrigal, must be introduced and compared to M. Voiture's. And the terrible abbé d'Aubignac, who has drawn a map of the Land of Flirts, must be denounced.

Doralie can be depended on to whisper her husband's most recent bestiality. Agaride will foam at the mouth about trial marriage, free love, divorce on demand, and other wild notions. Bélise will bemoan her pregnancy which is spoiling her waist already. Caliste will wring her vocabulary dry for a new way to say the ugly word *skin*—"dermal carapace" perhaps, or "living garment," or, yes! "self's sleeve"! And then back to the reality of Doralie and her husband's unspeakable brutalities. But that is such an old story. We have whispered it, heard it, and felt it so many times.

On a hard bench by the window, as far as possible from the hostess, sits Cathos, Euphémie's niece. She arrived yesterday, "from Nantes or Troies," whispers Euphémie, "I can never remember which." From her limbo by the window Cathos can see that those nearest to the hostess are the dearest. There is a dumpy little mouse who seems to be the star. But Cathos cannot see why. Sophie is far more plainly dressed than the other ladies, and hardly ever speaks at all.

Three men are hovering around the hostess. The pretty, sweet-smelling abbé Rodolphe, about the size of a large poodle, and just as curly, sits by the bed reciting an acrostic sonnet he has just dashed off. It reads vertically: "Euph / émie / a ma / vie."

Cathos leans forward to hear and knocks over a stuffed parrot

Une ruelle by Abraham Bosse

which explodes in a flurry of dusty feathers. In her confusion she exclaims a peasant oath.

"Your niece is charming," murmurs Rodolphe.

"Oh, don't be beastly," replies Euphémie. "What in heaven am I to do with her?"

"Marry her to Florizel, evidently," he replies maliciously. For Cathos has been gazing in blatant fascination at a beautiful blond gentleman in grey satin, who sits closest of all to Euphémie, in the *ruelle*—the little corridor between bed and wall—and who is called Florizel. Euphémie lays her hand on the bedspread, the two middle fingers together, poised below the heavy sleeve. Florizel gazes at this hand as though it were an edible delicacy for his famished heart. But he does not touch it. It is a gift for his eyes only.

And there is Amidon, an Academician famous for his translation of the *Iliad*, in madrigal form, suitably edited for ladies. His threadbare doublet smells faintly of mold, for he has grown old and poor in the service of the Muses. He has just drawn from his pocket twelve wrinkled pages.

"Dear lady, I promised you I would compose your portrait, and with the permission of your charming guests—"

There is a ripple of sighs and groans. Euphémie nods, smiling. The ladies wait until Caliste has finished telling of the *newly shaven dog* which crossed her path in the street today, and made her *faint* with *shame*. Then Amidon, after a honk into his handkerchief, begins:

"Euphémie—Euphémie is always the same." Dramatic pause. "A rich cascade of gold falls in tender torrents on her lovely head, where two small shells are fleetingly glimpsed." Pause. "On Euphémie's cheek the roses and the lilies are at war—"

Some of the ladies are fidgeting. Doralie resumes in a whisper to Agaride the tale of her marital misery. And Corinne—ah! Corinne of the low neckline, Corinne of the fiery black eyes under long lashes—is casting sidelong glances at Florizel. But Amidon drones on, working his way down from the eyes of Euphémie, "deep pools of innocent treachery into which an unsuspecting admirer might fall and be drowned forever," to the mouth, "the pearls of the deep were chosen to be the pillars of this enchanting grotto," to the neck, "the buried towers of Ilion never stood in their glory so erect and proud," to further delights, "but no one dare describe those marvels hidden forever from the curious eye, for Euphémie is as chaste as she is beautiful. I pass then to Euphémie's moral portrait—"

Euphémie gazes out to the garden. Always the same? Always the same as what?

The ladies are heavy-lidded. Euphémie's eyes turn to Rodolphe in supplication.

"My dear confrère," says Rodolphe, whose shapely legs, crossed in their black silk hose, almost touch the stout ankles of Amidon in their patched brown lisle. "You are turning the lady's head—and perhaps giving her a headache as well. I have another entertainment to propose. A *question d'amour!*"

All the ladies twitter and rustle with approval. Euphémie is asked to name the question.

The lady in the bed, with all eyes upon her, surveys the farther reaches of the garden through the partly shrouded windows. It is almost twilight, that velvety hour when all colors are imprecise, the candles not yet lit, the day drawing in. It is that enclosed, sheltered hour, the most priceless hour of the day.

Euphémie speaks softly, looking out to the garden. "Which is better, to be loved because one is always the same, or in spite of it?"

Who is Euphémie? She is a *précieuse*, a delicate pressed flower under glass, one of the exquisite Parisian ladies who first discovered the infinite world of social intercourse, full of rich treasures hiding in labyrinths of words, and invented politeness as a means of exploring it.

Euphémie is buried in history. She and her friends have sunk into something worse than obscurity. They are remembered only for their foolishness.

When I think how these ladies occupied the attention of the gossips of their day, how their clothes, their ideas, their *bons mots* were studied and repeated, how they believed in progress and science and women's possibilities and freedom, even as they fluttered their fans and sighed over the worst poetry ever written—it seems extraordinary that they fared so badly. For in their very prime, and to their great surprise and confusion, instead of being consecrated as the ultimate in superior womanhood, sensitivity, and wit, the précieuses were laughed out of countenance forever. By an unknown upstart named Molière, in a little curtain-raiser, *Les Précieuses ridicules*, in 1659.

But that is another story. What we want to describe here is what these ladies were like in their heyday, before the cynics cut them down.

Introduction:
Who Were
the Précieuses?

A T FIRST they were the precious few of their time, a group of favored ladies who gathered in private houses and learned to make conversation artfully. They were the magical secret feminine center of early seventeenth-century society, a society launched by the marvelous Marquise de Rambouillet, the first, the greatest, the archetypal hostess. And their aim in life was nothing less than the creation of worldliness, the imposition of form and ritual on a community that was wallowing in lust, blood, and dirt.

But they succeeded, and became the many, so many that their secret precious style ended up a public joke.

All we have left of the précieuse is the cultural stereotype Molière gave us, the pretentious lady whose pedigree is in doubt and whose intellect is small, but who claims to know everybody and everything. She sets a high price on her person; she is an absurd narcissist, sitting up in bed to entertain—let others come to her, she is too fragile to go out in the cold—and will talk only of poetry and beauty-aids. She is supercilious; she cannot say "teeth"; it has to be the "furniture of the mouth." She is the acme of irresponsible and shallow womankind, a pampered, frigid doll.

The word *précieuse* was not always such a rebuke, although there is something inherently vulnerable in it. It was a shrill cry of self-definition, and it was bound to be put to scorn by a newer breed of worldlings who came to take her place. The précieuse did indeed set a high price on herself. This in itself was not new. Her earliest

9

ancestor, the medieval *belle dame sans merci*—discovered by the poets and set in front of them on an altar—had already done so. But that ancestor was simply a lady too good for the poet who sang of her beauty. Her self-importance had no literary tinge. She gave men pain, but she did not compete with them; she was, after all, their creation. She remained passive and inscrutable, a needle in the poet's heart.

But the seventeenth-century précieuse was a new kind of woman. No longer content to be the passive object of masculine sentiments, she wished to experience and express feelings of her own. She would take hold of her environment and make it habitable; she would go further and reshape her own identity therein and force it on the world.

This shocking program was a long time in preparation before it became visible. It began with the dawn of the century and Mme. de Rambouillet. But this lady took years to transform French society, and once she gained control of her circle she was content to stay put. The decades of the reign of Louis XIII (1610–1643) are a kind of bronze age of worldliness, when the new myths and patterns of feminine behavior were slowly being formed and set. A second generation of ladies, who inherited the marquise's style, found their own social aspirations interrupted by the war of the Fronde. It was not until peace returned in 1653 that the way was finally clear for any and all women who had a minimum of funds and leisure to seize their freedom and create themselves. The *précieux* style became a "movement" at last, and *préciosité* reached its brief but stunning climax.

There was a moment in the 1650s when virtually every literate woman in France was in some wise a précieuse. Princesses, duchesses, bourgeoises, provincial and Parisian women, prudes and coquettes, nuns and actresses and kitchenmaids shared a heroic restlessness, a set of confused demands for social and civil equality with men, a yearning for distinction and private value. Once the movement was *named*, there was a scramble for further distinctions within it. There were successful précieuses and poor copy-cats, some who were admired by everyone, others who were called "précieuses" with a sneer. This internal disunity certainly helped to hasten the downfall of all. Yet the ladies had too much in common to disperse immediately. Their painful secret bond was the curse of being a woman, the trap of sex, their bundle of feminine liabilities and grievances. They were far from what we would call "sisterhood" today. But they did have a sort of solidarity against the common enemy: men, philistinism, vulgarity, ordinariness, or just the monotony of life. The real enemy was their bodies, so easily crippled, so soon spoiled. In their day, anatomy was more than destiny; it was doom.

Sometimes the doings of the précieuses remind us of our own "consciousness raising" feminist circles. Their crisis of self-discovery has obvious parallels with that of women today. Yet we will not insist too much on these parallels. They lived in a different world, a world of marriage contracts, dowries, rank, titles, primogeniture, childbed fever, plague, smallpox, and violent death. They did not dream of the scope and freedom that women take for granted today. The *précieux* phenomenon was a "women's movement" of its own time. And it was, more than that, an aesthetic and moral adventure. Not a revolution—revolution was unthinkable in France in the seventeenth century—but an experiment in civilization. An experiment serious enough to be qualified as one short-lived victory for humanity, buried though it has been under centuries of laughter.

Worldliness does not exist without a sense of class and exclusivity. The seventeenth century saw, alongside the development of women's rights, the rise of a new class, the very rich bourgeoisie, eager to climb the ladder into the nobility and to shrug off the "filth" of its commoner status. This irresistible upward drive of the rich is perhaps the most important fact of the social history of France in that century. It is easy to lose sight of it. We are dazzled by the panoply of lords and ladies at the court of Louis xiv, and by the artistic pinnacle of French classical literature, both of which, of course, occupy the latter half of the century. In our fascination for political and aesthetic absolutism, supported as they were by the most hieratic and rigid of class systems, we hardly notice that an inexorable social progress had already begun, in keeping with the movement away from feudalism and toward a mercantile economy, a progress which the Sun King himself was to favor constantly, using commoners like Colbert to implement his designs.

The nobility was already functioning on at least two levels: a *noblesse d'épée*, the old feudal, racial aristocracy which owned the land and fought the wars; and a newer *noblesse de robe*, consisting of magistrates, financial experts, lawyers, who had been ennobled for their work, or bought their offices and titles for money.

11

The robe was still socially inferior to the sword. But it was a very respectable goal in the elevation of the commoner to the level of his betters.

Préciosité was a factor in this social evolution toward money and away from land. The worldly conventions were of course utterly reactionary and did not admit this. Everyone knew you had to have heraldic credentials to get into Mme. de Rambouillet's blue room. But the reality was something else, as we shall see.

When we look beyond Mme. de Rambouillet and the Fronde to the final stage of the history of the précieuses, in the 1650s, we find such a confused mixture of noble and common women, such a muddling of class barriers, that we can actually speak of a leveling spirit as one of the characteristics of *préciosité*.

The means to this leveling was literature, the favorite hobby of the précieuses. Any woman with the literary sensitivity, talent, queerness, bravery, or reading habits of a précieuse belonged to the freemasonry, regardless of her class. We turn to the literature they admired in the hope of getting closer to these ladies (for do not the poets speak across the centuries and bind the past to us?). But we are in for a disappointment. Their poetry is witty but thin and trivial, and often tasteless as well. It is heavy with hyperbole, overstrained images, false sentiments. We may say that they got lost in the labyrinth of language, for they tried to make literature work for them, rather than express significant truth. They had rules of a sort, to guide them, but these have long since been discarded, and we cannot bring them back. If those rules had meanings for them, we have to allow that they were good, but they certainly are not ours.

And alas, the best writers of the century, who came on the heels of the précieuses, did not tolerate their literary game either. After Molière came Boileau, who despised the précieuses as the worst of all subdivisions of an unredeemed and hopeless sex. La Fontaine simply abandoned the précieuse he found he had married, and cunningly ran the species down ever after. Finally, La Bruyère immortalized their faults in a few deft portraits. They could not survive such talented predators.[1] The poor ladies had their enthusiasts as well, but these were fifth-rate hacks, justly forgotten today: who has ever heard of Somaize, Pure, Saint-Gabriel, Beauchasteau, La Forge?[2] Between such flunkies and the famous misogynists, the true précieuses are not easy to see.

The précieuses were in fact victims of both their defenders and their detractors. Well before the arrival of the great writers we call classical, our ladies were being praised to the skies by admirers and laughed at by cynics. A set of flatterers and scoffers, extremists of the ideal and the real, have left behind for us the two styles of testimonial that describe these ladies, and we are forced to pick our way between them with caution. It almost seems as if Baudeau de Somaize (flatterer) and Tallemant des Réaux [3] (scoffer) were talking about two different sets of women when they wrote about the précieuses. And in a sense they were, for the one addressed himself to the frozen smile of the official lady, while the other was looking at her unposed, unwitting self, the woman behind the précieuse.

Consider Mme. Anne Paget.[4] Somaize calls her by the resounding name of "Polénie":

Polénie is a most witty précieuse of exceptional merit, who sees a great many intelligent people of both sexes. Barsamon [the poet-abbé Boisrobert] is one of her dearest friends, and there are very few authors who do not seek to be in her good graces.

This description lifts Mme. Paget out of her class, her marriage, her personal problems, and transforms her into the lady she would like to be. But what does Tallemant say? He simply jots down what he has lately heard about a meeting between the middle-class matron Paget and the courtesan Ninon de Lenclos—in church. Between genuflections Mme. Paget has struck up a conversation with this attractive girl who is unknown to her. She complains to the girl that her good friend Boisrobert has left her neighborhood to go and live near a certain Ninon, a vulgar, loose woman. Ninon replies, "Ah Madam, you mustn't believe all you hear. She may be a perfectly honest girl. They could be saying the same thing about you and me. Gossip spares nobody." At this point Tallemant informs us that Mme. Paget has a reputation for flirtatiousness too. Later Boisrobert revealed to Mme. Paget the name of her new girlfriend. The lady's first reaction was stupid annoyance, but eventually she accepted the joke on herself, and even became friendly with Ninon, charmed like everyone else by her civilized wit. Thus the bland image presented by Somaize is foiled by Tallemant's zest for facts. Polénie turns out to be a real human being. We know her better and may even like her more.

This Anne Paget was a beautiful and rich lady who had married a magistrate. Her husband, if not of the best quality, was a respectable gentleman of the robe, good enough to launch her in the upper circles of bourgeois Paris, from whence she was able to hoist herself farther up into the rarefied air breathed by princesses. How did she do this? By spending money, by exploiting her social chances, but above all by a preoccupation with literature and the arts which earned her a place in each of the published directories of well-known précieuses. "An ecstatic beauty; the delight of all eyes that contemplate her" (Saint-Gabriel). But the most valued tribute of all was a profile in the *Galerie des portraits* compiled in 1659 from the portraits written by the ladies who frequented the great virgin princess Mademoiselle de Montpensier. Mme. Paget appears there with her son under the names of Venus and Love. After praising her alabaster bosom and pearly teeth, the portrait goes on:

Her speech was rather curt, but that is more agreeable than the listless style sometimes attributed mockingly to the précieuses of our times, and which is not usually that of a person of quality. Besides, she was quite at ease in the houses of princesses and belonged to the inner circle. She was allowed to stand in the presence of the queen. The honorable positions of her husband in the legal profession and in the Council of State have made her divide her time between the court and the town. But she has so tactfully conducted herself in both places that, although she prefers the ladies of the court, she has never shown any contempt for the others, at least not openly. She was esteemed for two things: dancing and singing.

This portrait is the consecration of a lifelong ambition crowned with success. Mme. Paget could confidently expect to be known to all the ages as a lady of surpassing merit and supreme connections. She is even more than an eminent précieuse; she is a "person of quality, at ease in the houses of princesses."

But there is a shabby underside to all this. If Anne Paget is the "Polénie" of a circle of refined ladies, her husband Jacques is the "Crispin" of a less reputable crowd, a gang of profligate noblemen who despised him even as they caroused with him and drank his wine. The Marquis de Bussy-Rabutin describes in pitiless detail the financial arrangements by which Paget became the principal paying lover of a lady of notorious promiscuity, Mme. d'Olonne, who used his money to entertain other lovers of more illustrious birth. This sordid transaction came to light in Bussy's *Histoire amoureuse des Gaules*, a stylishly written work which—unfortunately for Polénie—has had far more readers down through the centuries than the *Galerie des portraits*.

The contrast between the facelessness of the official portraits and the pockmarked grimace of the underground tittle-tattle is remarkable. The one blows a bubble around the lady, her *précieux* reputation. The other pricks the bubble. The purer the heart of a lady in the eyes of Saint-Gabriel, the worse slut she becomes in the *Alléluias* of Bussy.

We tend to trust the scoffers more. They are interested in plain facts. Some were unprintable in their own day, and it is perhaps these that we trust the most. Their harsh libertine realism seems less inartistic and more reliable to us now, for we have grown impatient of the sort of sterilized truth which most seventeenth-century writers aimed for when they were writing for the polite public. Even works of art like the *Caractères* of La Bruyère tell us as little about specific persons as the socialite cameos of the *Galerie des portraits,* for they look beyond the accidental elements of a life, to present an abstract version of it, valid for eternity.

But luckily not everyone was writing for eternity. The letters and diaries and ribald street songs crept back with the facts; they were a revenge on the unrelieved euphemism of the published works, a secret loosening of the corset of *bienséance.*

We have such uncorseted writers as Tallemant to thank for most of what we know about Mme. Paget. The unique dreams of a particular bourgeois housewife, in an age of upper-class focus and literary decorum, just did not get into the plays of Racine, or even of Molière for that matter. He too was in search of archetypes behind the visible surface of life. We will look for Mme. Paget therefore in the tart gossip of casual observers less concerned for high comedy.

And yet, Polénie is the one we are after. And we can see this lady dimly in the panegyrics of her sycophants, for if they do not tell the truth about her, they at least reveal the person she wanted to be. Tallemant and Somaize together show us the two halves of her, the real and the ideal Mme. Paget.

Of all the gallant champions of the précieuses, Baudeau de Somaize was the most eager. A writer of small merit, living precariously on the fringes of the theatrical world, he was nevertheless astute enough to set himself up as a historian of the ladies, famous and obscure, of his time. Somaize had no dramatic talent; he turned from the cutthroat world of the stage to the soft, protective semidarkness of the middle-class *ruelles,* where there was scope for the play of ambiguities, where insufficiencies of purse or wit could be glazed over with a pretty compliment, and a young man could make his fortune out of the vague, bittersweet longings of women. Somaize wrote a large compendium of names of ladies,[5] with descriptive notes to immortalize their virtues (and a few of their vices). He knew, or claimed to know, more than three hundred précieuses. His roster is alarmingly varied, and includes almost every lady in the public eye and many others we have never heard of elsewhere. Such catholicity could make the word meaningless by destroying the very exclusivity and precision of outline that the ladies were seeking; and in fact this is what went wrong, in the end, with *préciosité.* For when every lady is remarkable, then all are ordinary. Not everyone can be at the top of a pyramid. The style setters, the Rambouillets and Scudérys, were copied by hordes of ladies whose "distinction" failed because they were all doing it.

Not every lady Somaize mentions was *précieuse* all the time, but most of the ones we know dabbled in it seriously enough to be reasonably included on his list. If we think of the style of the précieuse as a mask worn on occasion but not defining the lady's whole self, we can see how it became virtually universal in Paris, and widespread throughout the provinces. But it also had a certain speciousness; it did not engage the whole person. It was an attitude that could be laid aside. The précieuses were composing an image of themselves, which they hoped was in correspondence with the inner truth of their being. But they could shrug it off when it became an obstacle to reality.

Somaize defines the précieuse by classifying all women in four categories.[6] The first and lowest are completely ignorant about poetry and the use of words, and cannot express themselves coherently. The second are equally illiterate but have natural gifts of intelligence and can articulate their simple native ideas. This is the woman we mean when we speak of *"un esprit de femme,"* a woman who owes her wit to nature, not art.

The third kind of woman, prettier or wittier than the others, tries to lift herself above the common herd. She reads novels and *"poésie galante"* and receives many visitors. As she tries to express more complex and refined ideas she often uses new words and phrases, and the result can be extraordinary and clever. Her mirror becomes the "counselor of her graces," her comb a "Dedalus" finding its way through the labyrinth of her locks.

But the fourth and best group comprises the truly learned and cultivated ladies, the *femmes illustres* who know as much about books
as the authors they meet, who speak several languages and can write
"in prose and verse." These ladies have a composure, a delicacy, a
sense of proportion to match their talents and learning.

It is only the last *two* of these four types which Somaize acknowledges as précieuses. Of these two types, the lower are the
"précieuses galantes," coquettish second-raters by comparison with
the last, supreme type, the *"véritables précieuses,"* the ultimate in
self-possessed womanhood.

Very well. But when we leaf through Somaize's *Dictionnaire* we
find among these three hundred women many who cannot pass his
own test of *préciosité*. Some are merely pretty or well-connected, or
have had some adventure worth reporting. Somaize could not formulate all the aspects of *préciosité*: the field was too rich, the variety
bewildering. A number of sweet young things get on to his list
and sparkle there alongside princesses. The effect is of an ill-
assorted crowd, not all sleek and self-assured, many of whom only
aspired vaguely to the condition they thought might be *précieuse*.
There is an endearing would-be quality to these unknown ladies.
They are précieuses only by virtue of their desire to be. They have
not yet arrived.

Perhaps the abbé de Pure was wiser than Somaize; he refused to
pin down the butterfly, but contented himself with contemplating
it, in a long, spongy novel, *La Pretieuse, ou le mystère des ruelles*.
He portrays the typical précieuse in her shadowed retreat, spinning
out her conversations, discussing her womanly problems with her
friends. This mysterious woman has no past or future. She is the
persona of the précieuse, the paragon for all the girls in Somaize's
Dictionnaire to emulate.

But the précieuse was a more substantial being than these industrious
publicists knew. Reading Somaize and Pure with the corrective of
Tallemant's revelations, we can see her as a real person in search of an
identity. Somaize and Pure, in trying to provide one, only increased the confusion.

The précieuse was clearly tired of being a woman. The trauma
of childbirth, the sexual contempt of men, the legal disabilities
turned her against marriage, against sex, against love itself, in the
famous *refus de l'amour*. Some women left their husbands; some be-

trayed them with other men, for the itch was still there, even when they blamed it for all their troubles. Most of them practiced, or pretended to practice, a ferocious virtue that gave them moral leverage in the battle of the sexes.

Another lever was their distinction. The précieuses wanted to be just that: priceless, unique, each a rich jewel on a velvet cushion, each an island in the middle of a small universe. They experimented in startling dress and behavior, bizarre speech, extreme ideas. They read poetry to keep in their minds the picture of themselves they were composing. They wrote poetry to show that they had thoughts and feelings which men were unable to communicate.

The précieuses were groupy. There was no self-definition in solitude or seclusion. One had to find one's being in a social setting. Conscious of their weakness in a man's world, they banded together; yet this collective instinct was counteracted by the exclusivity natural to a class-conscious world, and to worldliness itself. Coteries sprang up which despised other coteries. There was a great desire to belong, but the only way to enjoy one's membership was to keep others out. Prudish women excluded coquettes. Learned women kept out fools. Lower-class women were democratic until they arrived upstairs; then they were as contemptuous of their inferiors as anyone. Snobbery almost always won out over sisterhood.

When women discovered literature they also discovered language. A curiosity of the *précieux* movement is their "mysterious" speech mannerisms, which have come down to us mainly in the distorted forms ridiculed by their critics. But these affectations were not mere pathetic efforts to achieve instant elegance, as Molière would have us believe. They were more like passwords, constantly changing in-group signals. They were part of the arcana of the coterie. And they were fun to make up. Calling sighs "the children of the air" was *préciosité* at play.

Their approach to poetry was straightforwardly utilitarian. It had to entertain them, make them feel important, give them hope of happiness. The poetry they got was cold food for their vanity—insincere wit-writing, hard, crystalline verse that cut them to the bone while it promised eternal devotion. But they did not expect real sentiments. Theirs was a rough world, where all children were beaten to educate them, where nearly all the natural pleasures of life, the immediate, spontaneous ones, were still associated with sin.

Civilization was a cruel training for this world. Their artificial art was an escape from the unendurable plight of real life.

And yet, though their poetry was heartless, the main topic of the précieuses was the heart. They examined the forms of love with the minutest attention, subdividing its categories inexhaustibly, never tiring of the intricacies and paradoxes of a feeling they were starving for.

And dimly, through all the posturing and rhetoric of their style, they were looking for something new, an undiscovered continent of the future, limitless and full of joy. They were modernists, futurists, optimists; they believed in change and the pursuit of happiness.

The whole artistic trend of their century was toward pessimism, defeat, and acquiescence in the way things are. They bravely and thoughtlessly set themselves against it.

This book will introduce the real and ideal personalities of only a few of the hundreds of women who were précieuses in one way or another. They are a mixed lot, each trying to achieve distinction in a narrow field. Some even claimed to be antiprécieuses and dissociated themselves from all the others, in an effort to be still more distinct. But they all shared the self-consciousness, the grievances, the crisis of their sexuality, the refuge of poetry, the yearning for something better.

The pitiless anecdotes of the scoffers and the fulsome rhapsodies of the flatterers that made them prominent in their own time are the keys that we hope will open the way into the distant world of the précieuses. To find our way we must go back to the early decades of the seventeenth century, to the reigns of Henri IV and Louis XIII, and the quiet social upheaval produced by the Marquise de Rambouillet, in whose drawing room an atmosphere was first composed which the précieuses could breathe.

The dirty linen of royal households, the controversies of learned mystics, wars, medical practices, the treatment of servants and children, all these add substance to our own *Galerie des portraits*.

For the précieuses are truly very far away from us, wrapped in their own age and culture as snugly as we in ours. To reach them, we have to burst our technological cocoon and conjure up

Introduction

textures and smells that have all but vanished from the earth. The feel of starched linen, the odor of tallow, the sharpness of cries in a background of real silence, a blanket of animal droppings on a shaky wooden bridge in the center of the most elegant city of Europe—these perceptions are in such contrast to our steel and neon and laminated surfaces, our chemical envelope in which we gasp for life but live much longer, that it is a delight to dwell on this sensory aspect of the past, peering down through the centuries into their dim candlelit rooms, listening for their sedate music, fondling their stiff damask.

And not only technology separates us from the précieuses. We must adjust our intellectual focus, peel off many layers of subsequent thought, go back beyond Freud, Marx, Rousseau, Montesquieu, to a day when there were no formulated economic systems, no clinical psychology, no theories of history, no sentimental humanitarianism, no tolerance or democracy. The précieuses and their contemporaries had a full set of prejudices of their own, just as complex as ours and filling their lives completely. But they were oblivious to history, innocent of economics, unconscious of the unconscious. For them there was no common man, but neither was there an "individual" in our civic sense. Their world had far fewer people in it, and their population problem was the exact reverse of ours. Infant mortality was the universal curse of their time. In such a world, where human beings are scarce, the value of a single one of them must surely, we imagine, be greater than on our overpopulated earth. Yet it often appears to have been less. This paradox haunts us. Can we ever really know how they felt?

Certainly the précieuses had to be a lot more thick-skinned and robust than we are, to survive at all in that remote and brutal dawn of the modern world. Could it be that they sometimes experienced even more intensely than we do the common facts of their condition, loved and hated, ate and laughed with more zest? Felt death more bitterly?

We wish we could know all that they knew, imagine as they imagined, dream their dreams, move about familiarly as they did in their world of symbolic objects and notions. They did not foresee the literary fashions, the philosophies, the technology that were going to supersede them and hide them from the future. They did not even know their very hair styles were going to look dreadful in another ten years. They visualized a future of their own choosing

20

beyond their cramped horizon, and we wish we could see into it from their vantage point. We may pity them, laugh at them from our safe distance in the twentieth century, but if we hope to understand them we must somehow try to enter the continuum they lived in and become précieuses. This is impossible, and our history, born of a passion for intimacy with what is gone forever, will fall far short of our desire.

NOTES

1. See, for example, Boileau, *Oeuvres complètes,* ed. A. Adam (Pléiade, 1966), "Satire X," pp. 63–80, first published in 1694 but circulated in manuscript for perhaps twenty years before that; La Fontaine, *Fables Contes et Nouvelles,* ed. Pilon and Groos (Pléiade, 1954), "La Chatte métamorphosée en femme," p. 67; and La Bruyère, *Les Caractères,* ed. Garapon (Garnier, 1962), "Des Femmes," pp. 112–51.

2. Somaize, our most important source of favorable commentary on the précieuses, is referred to throughout this study with page references to the Bibliothèque Elzevirienne edition of his collected works, ed. Ch.-L. Livet (Jannet, 1856), 2 vols. This edition contains two plays, *Les Veritables pretieuses* (1660) and *Le Procez des pretieuses* (1660), as well as *Le Grand Dictionnaire des Pretieuses on la Clef de la langue des ruelles* (1660) and *Le Grand Dictionnaire des Pretieuses Historique, Poetique, Geographique, Cosmographique, Cronologique et Armoirique* (1661). It is the last of these works which is referred to hereafter as *Dictionnaire.*

The abbé de Pure (*La Pretieuse,* 1656), referred to hereafter in the edition by E. Magne (Droz, 1938–39), is a more ambiguous flatterer. He often seems to be admiring the précieuses with tongue in cheek. But Saint-Gabriel (*Le Merite des dames,* 1657), the boy-poet Chastelet de Beauchasteau (*La Lyre du jeune Apollon,* 1659), and Jean de la Forge (*Le Cercle des femmes savantes,* 1660) are relentless grovelers before their subject.

3. Tallemant des Réaux, a great gossip and memorialist, and our principal source of facts, is referred to throughout this study in the most recent edition of his *Historiettes* with its voluminous notes by M. Antoine Adam (Pléiade, 1960–61), 2 vols. I gladly acknowledge a huge debt to Adam, as well as to Tallemant.

4. On Anne Paget, see Tallemant, *Historiettes,* I, pp. 409, 416, n. 1065; II, p. 445, n. 1285–86, et passim; Saint-Gabriel, *Le Merite des dames,* p. 345; Boisrobert, *Epîtres en vers,* ed. M. Cauchie (Hachette, 1921–27), I, p. 232; *La Galerie des portraits de Mlle de Montpensier,* ed. E. Barthélemy (Didier, 1860), pp. 209–13; Bussy-Rabutin, *Histoire amoureuse des Gaules,* ed. G. Mongrédien (Garnier, 1930), I, pp. 7–10; Somaize, *Dictionnaire,* I, pp. 194, 206.

5. The *Dictionnaire* mentioned in note 2 above.

6. Somaize, *Dictionnaire,* I, pp. 8–9.

I

Rambouillet

Catherine *1600–1610*

IN 1600 a beautiful twelve-year-old girl named Catherine de Vivonne-Savelli married a handsome gentleman of the French court. The bridegroom, Charles d'Angennes, twenty-three and already promising to become an influential diplomat, had elegant manners, and spoke Spanish fluently. He was myopic, which only increased his ceremonious charm. He spent his money with abandon, as a gentleman should. He drove around Paris in a real carriage, a novelty that nobody but the king could match. He adored Catherine. Catherine looked upon him with solemn respect as an adult, for he was twice her age.[1]

We see this little bride standing doll-like in a costume appropriate to her station: stiff-boned bodice flattening her chest, rigid fluted ruff to frame her face, tight sleeves which stand up at the shoulders. The materials are heavy and rich and intricately worked; she has to move slowly in them, up the aisle of the dark church where candles flicker on the faces of her relatives; and no one in her world, not even herself, thinks there is anything strange about a little girl in a grown-up dress, who might be playing a game of make-believe but is in fact getting married, forever, to a young man of the court of France.

The bridegroom's name was two hundred years old, and Charles would eventually inherit the family title of Marquis de Rambouillet. But this did not impress the bride especially. His lineage was nothing to compare with hers. The Savellis counted two popes among their ancestors in Rome as far back as the thirteenth century. Her genealogical tree was heavy with Strozzis and Medicis.

Indeed, her background was so steeped in the blood and politics of the Italian Renaissance that the presence of this young girl in Parisian rather than Roman society needs some explaining. The explanation goes back to before she was born, as far back as 1578 when another Catherine, Catherine of Medici, dowager queen of France, was looking for a young lady of the right noble extraction whom she could import from Italy to the French court. The old queen was a transplanted Italian herself and wanted to hear the music of her native tongue in her declining years. Giulia Savelli, our Catherine's mother, was a suitably unattached girl, being then a childless widow.[2] She was accordingly married to an old French diplomat, the Marquis de Vivonne, who was serving in Rome as ambassador to the pope. It was understood that Vivonne would bring his wife back to the French court, to take her place among the handmaidens of the queen.

But before that could happen, Giulia produced a baby daughter, our Catherine de Vivonne-Savelli. And then Catherine de Medici died. The Marquis de Vivonne returned to Paris permanently in 1590 leaving Giulia in Rome with the baby, and did not see his wife and daughter again for five more years.

It is understandable that Vivonne preferred not to bring his family to France just then. These years, the 1590s, were times of war and anarchy in that country: Catholic and Protestant were still at each other's throats. There was no king in the Louvre, for although Henri of Navarre had been calling himself Henri IV since 1589, he was still fighting the remnants of the old Catholic Ligue and trying to impose his authority on a deeply divided and exhausted country. The Marquis de Vivonne had to make a choice. He decided to throw in his lot with Henri. Although over sixty, he put on his sword and fought bravely for the king in the last wars of the Ligue. His courage earned him the command of the best troops in Henri's army: the Cornette Blanche. It also earned him exclusion from the Papal States, for the pope was bitterly opposed to the Protestant French king who had made what looked like a phony conversion (*"Paris vaut bien une messe"*) in order to seize power. Vivonne could not go back to Rome.

But when at last Henri secured his right to the French crown and peace came, the loyal marquis was rewarded with a good job at court. He could now send for Giulia. The lady set off from Rome with her seven-year-old daughter Catherine in 1595. She had carefully seen to it that the girl spoke French as well as Italian.[3]

Catherine arrived in Paris to find herself in a rude city of soldiers and rain and dilapidated Gothic walls. The spacious façades of her native Rome, bathed in sunlight, singing with fountains, were nowhere to be seen. Paris was gloomy and gray. The Louvre, with its one tight courtyard of chiseled stone, was a bedlam of untidiness and confusion.

Her father's new post was that of tutor to the heir apparent of France. This appointment had nothing to do with any pedagogical talents he might have possessed, but showed the immense trust which the king placed in the faithful old soldier. His pupil was a little boy of exactly Catherine's age, the Prince de Condé, son of the king's first cousin. The boy became Catherine's playmate. *"Monsieur le Prince"* already gave evidence of being headstrong and arrogant, thinking himself beyond the reach of discipline, and one day, when they were eight, the prince suddenly grabbed Catherine by the hair and kissed her. This came to the ears of the marquis, who thrashed the boy severely ("for princes are like animals and escape punishment too often," says Tallemant, who was clearly of the opinion that the irate tutor was doing the right thing). We remark that the tutor was also the girl's father. Was he overreacting to what might be a small boy's impulsive bid for affection? We have an inkling of the consequences: little Catherine was teased about this fatal kiss, and even playfully blamed later for the fact that *Monsieur le Prince* turned out to be a notorious woman-hater. Now the punishment for one kiss was hardly enough to drive Condé toward the deviant behavior he later became famous for. But observers like Tallemant could dimly sense the traumatic effect of such childhood incidents, not only for the boy who later refused to become a man, but also for the girl who was to create the new virtue of seemliness, and raise it above all others.

For another four years Catherine lived in her parents' home near the Louvre. And then her brief childhood was over and she became Mme. d'Angennes.

Twelve was a fairly normal age for a young lady to enter into an upper-class arranged marriage. Fourteen or fifteen were more common, but nobody thought of Catherine as a child bride or bothered to find out if she was ready. High-born ladies were married young, much younger than commoners, to secure their families' fortunes and lineage. And anyway, women's primary functions were soon learned: their formal education was rudimentary or nonexistent, since they were not apt pupils of Latin and of course could not share in the military training of their brothers. Girls were seen to be not only intellectually and physically weaker than boys, but also morally frail; it was well to establish them early. The Duc de Sully, Henri's prime minister, certainly thought so. After spanking his daughter Marguerite on her bare bottom and sampling the odor of her private parts to see if she would make a good wife, he married her off at age ten to the Duc de Rohan. She was a mother at eleven.[4]

Questions about the sexual maturity of young girls in the seventeenth century spring to mind. How many girls could become mothers at eleven or twelve? If many such marriages were premature, what was the effect on the women?

Of course, statistical information about such matters in that century is nonexistent. Our usable facts go back only about a hundred years. We do know that the average age of the onset of puberty in girls has been falling significantly in recent decades in Europe. Where it is now eleven it was thirteen or fourteen a hundred years ago. Beyond that we cannot go, and we are reduced to wondering in the dark about Catherine's case. She had no children until age nineteen but we do not know why, simply because this sort of information did not interest the memorialists, gossips, or even doctors who wrote about women. Such writers provide us with plenty of idle speculation about feminine psychology, but few clues to feed our more technical hypotheses. We have to make do with what they did give us—that is, their uncritical assumption that it was all right to dispose of a daughter, without regard to her maturity, as soon as an appropriate match presented itself.

Catherine's parents were not as callous as some, and she had her Italian heritage to modify the brutal French manners of her time. But the prejudices of many centuries about the mental and moral capacities of women were still in force all over Europe. A hot debate on the relative merits of the sexes had been going on for decades, the famous "querelle des femmes." They called on Plato: "Monkeys will always be monkeys, and women, no matter what role they assume, will always be women, that is, stupid and flighty."[5] Anyone could see that woman was a gross, materialistic domestic animal, a necessary evil, devoted to the physical body and therefore only useful to the physical body. Was she not formed from Adam's rib? She must certainly be kept at her spinning and breeding, and never allowed to venture beyond her depth into intellectual pursuits. Men, on the other hand, were endowed with higher yearnings, intellectual possibilities that led them to the finer sentiments of friendship and unselfish love, free of the dross of brute nature.

Marie de Medici arriving at Marseille
COURTESY OF MUSÉE DU LOUVRE

This was only one side of the argument. The other side saw women as not equal to but completely different from men, both morally and intellectually. On this view the best women were the ones who possessed the womanly virtues. Woman was the inspiration, not the creator, of civilization, for a woman could appreciate, even though she may never be able to perform, the deeds of men. To the cultivated male, she was a mysterious object upon which he could fix his passions, to whom he could address sonnets, for whom he could perform exploits. The Beatrice of Dante, the Laura of Petrarch, the queenly virgin of the troubadors of Provence were the models for this idealized woman. Woman was promoted from a beast to an idol. The womanly virtues were chastity, tranquillity, reserve. They were all related to her beneficial effect on men.

A popular book of conversations on moral etiquette, *Il Cortegiano* (*The Courtier*) by Baldassare Castiglione, had been circulating in France for half a century. It examines every aspect of the noble life and proposes correct social behavior in all of life's situations. In the company of Castiglione's model gentleman are model ladies who have all the passive virtues of the idol of courtly love, but yet are not remote, icy figments of the poet's mind. They are real gentlewomen. They provide decorative company, stimulating and uplifting for their men, who treat them with infinite consideration.

Catherine intended to provide such company for her husband and expected such consideration in return. She had learned all the negative womanly virtues by the time she got married and knew already that there would be more to her wifely role than breeding. Charles d'Angennes, an amiable booby with no distinct ideas of his own, agreed with his adorable bride.

In the same year, 1600, Catherine's mother Giulia was entrusted with the diplomatic task of traveling to Marseilles to welcome another Italian bride, Marie de Medici, on her journey from Florence to Paris. Giulia had a Medici grandmother, and was therefore distantly related to the Florentine princess. Marie de Medici was the object of another arranged match, performed by proxy before she left home. The go-betweens who had included her in their bargaining wanted to insure the contract against mishap along the way. For Marie was coming to marry Henri iv, the King of France.

Marie's journey to Paris was a highly ceremonial affair, as befitted a lady coming to wear a crown. The reception at Marseilles is recorded in an enormous picture by Rubens, who almost succeeds in concealing the irreparable banality of this woman, propped up by her courtiers like a piece of expensive merchandise in a profusion of satin hangings, gilded ships' timbers, and writhing naked nereids. The reality of her life as queen of France turned out to be very different from this picture, commissioned and executed two decades after the event.[6] The official images of power, in the history of kings, are always more magnificent than the realities. Brought up in the Pitti Palace, Marie had already been considered for various marital deals, which had fallen through. Thus she was rather old—twenty-seven—when Henri IV, who owed money and favors to the Medici family, asked for her hand. He was still married to his first wife, Marguerite de Valois, but she had not produced any royal children. It was an easy matter for Henri to repudiate Marguerite and start a new life with Marie. It was high time. He was forty-seven himself and needed a dauphin. For a king of doubtful legitimacy, the little Prince de Condé was no substitute for a direct heir.

The lives of these two Italian brides, Catherine and Marie, coincided for a while in Paris. Attendance at the Louvre was expected of a lady of Mme. d'Angennes' position, and there was nowhere else to go. But Catherine had never learned to like the Louvre. She could not stand the crush of people, the mobs of evil-smelling musketeers in greasy brocade, the self-important idlers shouting oaths, dueling, spitting, relieving themselves in corners of the royal courtyards, or crudely propositioning the ladies whose rich satin dresses were bedraggled with mud around the hems. Henri himself was a very rough diamond, a soldier-king now trying to wage peace. He ate greedily with his hands, blew his nose on the floor, never changed his doublet. His smell was rank, and he played savage jokes on his courtiers. Looking back on him today in the perspective of progress toward humanitarianism, we can see Henri IV as a man of peace and tolerance, perhaps the first French monarch to have any notion of economics and a conscience about his people. This attractive image of him has some substance: he appointed intelligent, hard-working Protestant statesmen to help re-

31

build the ravaged country. The parsimonious Sully had charge of his treasury and slowly brought back prosperity. But the focus of his political vision was lost on Catherine d'Angennes. She did not measure civilization in terms of industries, waterways, or toleration, of which she knew no more than any lady in the early 1600s. For her a royal court should be a place where private personal relations are infinitely elaborated against a background of music, poetry, and marble. Exactly the atmosphere of the intimate chats of *Il Cortegiano*. The Valois dynasty which preceded Henri would have understood. But Henri balked at paying Malherbe, his official poet, for the sonnets turned out in celebration of Mme. de Verneuil's eyes. He needed the money for his Gobelin tapestry factory.

The Louvre might have been turned into a cultural haven by the Italian queen. Instead, Marie de Medici went about the palace whining over her husband's infidelities, or drew horoscopes with an Italian girlfriend, Leonora Concini, a lady of inferior family and limited culture who had filled the queen's head with occult nonsense. In ten years of marriage Marie did her royal duty and produced several children, of whom five survived, the first two of them males. The continuity of the Bourbon dynasty was assured. Beyond that, the king had little use for his fat wife. He was more interested in her maids of honor, whom he generally bought rather than wooed. The number of illegitimate children fathered by Henri during these ten years exceeds the legitimate total. Royal offspring were produced regularly by Mme. de Verneuil, Mme. de Moret, Mme. des Essarts. They coincided or alternated with those of the queen.

Catherine d'Angennes decided to withdraw from Henri's court. Just before her marriage she had inherited a house in the rue Saint-Thomas-du-Louvre [7] not far from the Louvre. It was the hôtel du Halde, a gloomy old Gothic pile. After some legal delays she got clear title to the property in 1604, whereupon, at the age of sixteen, she had it torn down and rebuilt to her own specifications in Renaissance style. The interior design was entirely her own. She got an idea in a flash: "Quick! some paper! I know exactly what I want!" and drew a plan of the house she would build. This act of artistic vision and engineering competence was the first remarkable achievement of a young girl brought up to smile and submit. The new house, of brick, cut stone, and slate, had beautifully proportioned rooms, smaller than those of the old house but compensating the loss of space by a gain in symmetry, and airy perspectives of the garden from the floor-to-ceiling windows. Above all, the entrance was placed at the side, a daring innovation. It led to a suite of salons, opening out vistas of worldly possibilities, ending in that ultimate sanctuary of gentleness in a rough world, the *chambre bleue*. There were disadvantages to this highly original layout. We would say today that some convenience and privacy had been sacrificed for effect. But the result was worth it. And it started a trend. Marie de Medici, when building her Luxembourg palace fifteen years later, sent her architects to study the hôtel de Rambouillet and copy Catherine's ideas.[8]

To appreciate the enterprise of this teenage matron, we must visualize a city of Paris consisting of a few cold dark palaces and thousands of closely huddled jerry-built wooden firetraps. Narrow unpaved streets. Two wooden bridges across the Seine lined with five-story houses on either side. Virtually no public space, outside the crowded courtyards of the Louvre. The main square, the Place de Grève, a clearing by the Seine in front of the town hall, smelled of tanneries and often displayed a hanging corpse, for it was the place of public execution. Paris had no garbage collection, and the streets were open cesspools running with offal. It is true that Henri IV, who had a fine sense of urban planning, was trying to do something about it. To beautify his city, he had begun to build two lovely unities in brick and cut stone like Catherine's house: the Place Dauphine, a triangle at the prow of the Île de la Cité, and the Place Royale (now the Place des Vosges) in the Marais. During his reign the Pont-Neuf was completed and became the first bridge over the Seine from which the people could look out on the river and admire the view. But these were "public" works, to be enjoyed by all Parisians. Henri was not a noteworthy patron of the indoor arts. Catherine remembered with regret the spacious private palaces of her Roman childhood. She reacted to the living conditions of Paris by moving indoors. She realized that if she wanted to live in an atmosphere of distinction and order, she must make it herself and keep it under her own roof. She added a formal garden, enclosed in walls, at the end of it, to shut out the view of the hospital of the Quinzes-Vingts where paupers went to die.

A twentieth-century sensibility may register some impatience with the exclusive nature of Catherine's design for living and wonder if it was really, as so many people thought, admirable beyond dispute. We admire in the past those movements which we can clearly recognize as leading in the same moral direction as our own positivistic altruism. We like Henri iv's chicken in the pot for every peasant and we do not smell his sweat. By comparison with the bold public works of Sully, Catherine's dislike seems finicky and snobbish. If she was so clever and sensitive, why didn't she see that Paris needed sewers more than palaces? Why didn't she feel guilty about the paupers' hospital on the other side of her garden wall?

Perhaps she did. But we cannot really ask these questions if we picture the larger political and ethical conditions in which this intelligent girl found herself, and which everyone believed were universal and permanent. Violence and privilege were the inescapable basis of the social structure—as of course they still are. But men were frozen in fatalism about it in a way that they no longer are. If they sometimes hoped for change, they did not entertain the kind of cosmic optimism we do today, in our extremity. Things were bad, and would always be bad; they were not cataclysmic. Malherbe could write, in his prayer for the victorious Henri, a moving affirmation of the coming of peace, but it was all based on the iron force of the king's domination:

La terreur de son nom rendra nos villes fortes;
On n'en gardera plus ni les murs ni les portes,
Les veilles cesseront aux sommets de nos tours;
Le fer mieux employé cultivera la terre,
Et le peuple qui tremble aux frayeurs de la guerre,
Si ce n'est pour danser, n'orra plus de tambours.[9]

(The terror of his name will make our cities strong.
There will be no more watchmen on the walls
or at the gates, or on the towers.
Iron will be used only to plow the earth,
and the people who tremble in fear of war
will hear the beat of the drum only for dancing.)

War was more normal, and no one really expected to see the end of it. It was the main occupation of a whole class, Catherine's class. The men she knew had fought for decades in the wars of the Ligue. They would go on fighting forever, in the Thirty Years' War, in the Fronde, in the expansionist wars of Louis xiv. War was their duty, their pleasure, their identity. It involved them, in ways that modern wars have left behind, in hand-to-hand combat. It was omnipresent, not only on faraway battlefields to which sons and husbands disappeared regularly but in the streets of Paris where the same men reenacted it as a sport.

Mme. de Verneuil was the king's mistress at the time Henri IV was negotiating his marriage to Marie de Medici. This French lady, foreseeing that she would lose her hold on the king when he got his Florentine wife, and thinking that the Duc de Bellegarde had instigated the royal match, asked another nobleman, the Duc de Chevreuse, who was in love with her, to kill Bellegarde. Chevreuse went forth promptly to do the deed and wounded his victim on the very doorstep of a house where the king was dining. Bellegarde's men pursued the aggressor and would have killed Chevreuse but for the arrival on the scene of young Charles d'Angennes, a complete stranger to the affair. Now d'Angennes, moved by automatic chivalrous impulses, rushed to the defense of Chevreuse as the weaker party. For his pains he was shot (the bullet went right through his body) by a member of Bellegarde's forces. The king came out of the house and was so angry with Chevreuse that he refused to allow anyone to come to the assistance of his young defender. The boy lay in the street and was bleeding to death when the king's hostess, Mme. Zamet, came forward and insisted on taking him into the house, putting him in her own bed, and binding up his wounds. "Sire, everyone is master in his own house. You are master in yours, and I am mistress here, if you please." On looking into the matter more closely, Henri forgave the boy his innocent intervention. As it was, d'Angennes recuperated very slowly and would have died anyway, but a faithful "surgeon-valet" sucked the pus from his infected wound and saved him. Catherine married this man and lived with this wound, which went on suppurating for years after.[10]

The hierarchy of privilege in which Catherine d'Angennes lived so near the top was just as permanent as violence. It was based on racial myths that everyone took for granted. Money was beginning to count as well; it was already possible and not uncommon for a rich entrepreneur to buy a pedigree. But no one quite believed this was happening. They believed in the natural prerogatives of superior blood.

Poverty was also seen to be permanent and natural; its very prevalence discouraged any thought of relieving it. The visible hardships of the poor might elicit the occasional Christian charity of the rich. But this charity was different from the systematic humanitarian concern that began to develop in the eighteenth century. And of course it was a long way from the economic egalitarianism that our own century likes to avow. Poverty in Mme. d'Angennes' day was not a social scandal. Poverty was dignified, even sanctified. Inequality and social injustice were matters for God to settle in the next world, not the responsibility of human beings in this one. The soul was invisible, the social hierarchy a very visible reality. The absolute civic value of every person in the community was evident to no one in her day but a few crazy levelers of no account. And the inequity and coercion were going to get worse before they got better. Freedom was a secret momentary gift to the lucky few.

Perhaps we should blame Catherine d'Angennes for not having devised a more generous ethic than mere private worldly excellence. After all, a few theoreticians in England were beginning to formulate a philosophical basis for equality. Even charity was becoming less random and casual. François de Sales and Vincent de Paul discovered and loved the poor, and did not close their eyes to the need for some form of organized welfare. But England was a week's journey away. And these good French clerics were saints. That is, they were so rare in virtue that the century found it necessary to fence them off as a separate heavenly species. Mme. d'Angennes' talents were of another order. She was neither a philosopher nor a saint. She had no profession. She was a woman in a man's world. The dragons for her to slay were coarseness, vulgarity, insensitivity in the realm of personal relations. The only way for her to improve the quality of life in a society dominated by violence and privilege was to work on her own being. To be gentle, refined, kindly, detached, and dispassionate—in a word, civilized—was her mission in life.

Having built her house and set a fashion, Catherine d'Angennes gave great care to the interior decor. She was the first to think of having a room done in some other color than the red or brown Cordovan leather paneling of the Renaissance château,[11] and this is why her big reception room came to be called the *chambre bleue.* It was hung with blue tapestry, encrusted with gold and silver. The panels were so stunningly handsome that they were never to be replaced. They remained there, growing old with the marquise, until, half a century later, when they were completely faded and ragged, she died.

Everything she acquired for her new home, the crystal vases, the bibelots, the Venetian mirrors and Oriental rugs, everything was remarkable.[12] She knew she was setting a stage, and the actors when they arrived must know too that they were in an exceptional place and on display before an audience consisting of each other.

It was very expensive. The young couple, though not as rich as they seemed, squandered their money magnificently. Charles gave Catherine free rein in the home. He himself cut a dashing figure transporting pretty ladies around Paris, although carriages, which had just been invented, were an illegal luxury for all but royalty. His poor vision was his pretext for breaking the rule. But he had to keep his carriage out of Henri's sight.

Catherine had brought to the union a dowry of ten thousand écus a year, a very comfortable income which, added to their social position, ought to have assured the young couple of a life of luxury. We would like to be able to give the precise value of this dowry in modern terms, but cash values are impossible to translate across the centuries. Money was not yet, in the lingering twilight of feudalism, the supreme measure of value. Even if we listed all the known prices of commodities to see what could be bought for her dowry, we would be little wiser. Some amenities— the Venetian mirror, say—would seem wildly expensive, while others —a dozen household servants—would be incredibly cheap. Catherine's ten thousand écus represented only one part of her wealth. There were other intangibles. For instance, that valets were hired for a pittance and a room under the eaves is true but not the whole truth. They were also joining a family, coming under the protection of their masters, participating, like extra sons and daughters of inferior status, in the qualities that made a person like Catherine rich and desirable. Their services and respect were not entirely within the reach of money, whose full value they did not yet grasp.[13]

The power of money was not well understood by the gentry either. No one in Catherine's class knew how to earn it or how to put it to work. It was only something to spend. Consequently they grew poorer over the years. But it was a long time before they realized this.

Seven years passed before her first child was born. Whatever the causes of this delay, it gave Catherine a chance to develop. She learned Spanish. She took up drawing: her sketches were compared to those of Michelangelo. She read books: heroic romances like the

Amadis de Gaule, edifying works like the moral epistles of Honoré d'Urfé, a courtly gentleman of Franco-Italian origin like herself. She disdained the new breed of sentimental novel, successful for a few seasons around 1610, wherein sighing lovers expressed their sentiments in preposterous and inept metaphors ("My love takes off its hat to say goodbye to you"). Writers who have been called *précieux* before their time, Nerveze and des Escuteaux, dished up this pablum for the stout, yearning appetities of the women of the middle class. But it would not do for Mme. d'Angennes. She preferred delicate pastoral romances like the *Diane* of Montemayor in Spanish and the *Pastor fido* of Guarini in Italian. The vogue for such pastorals was universal among the aristocracy. In 1607 the best of them all, d'Urfé's *L'Astrée*, began to appear, and very quickly occupied the idle hours of all the cultured nobility who could read. It became "the breviary of the ladies of the court," says Mlle. de Gournay, and even Henri IV had it recited to him in his amorous moments. Its world view was one which Mme. d'Angennes could welcome and appreciate like anyone else. Set in never-never land (the province of Forez in the fourth century), it celebrates the peaceful amusements of a group of shepherds and their sweethearts who have come here to escape the barbarian invasion of the Roman Empire. These rustics do not plow the land or tend any flocks. They are aristocrats disguised in burlap—a burlap which does not itch—living a calm sheltered existence, going on picnics under perpetually blue skies, discussing affairs of the heart, telling love stories, writing verses to each other. Their passions are wordy and platonic. There is no physical need or drive. For five thousand pages the book describes the unrequited adoration of Céladon for Astrée, a beautiful but implacable girl who has banned him from her sight because of a trivial misunderstanding. To fill up the long leisurely pages, Céladon's suit is interrupted with sentimental episodes in the lives of their friends. While he goes off into the forest to weep, we read the adventures of Hylas, a shepherd who refuses to love constantly, and of Sylvandre, who is a defender of fidelity. The oratorical debates of these swains explore the intricacies of the heart in infinite detail. Hylas says: "Love is egotistical. Constancy is the death of love. Women like the unexpected, the uncertain, the lively, the disengaged lover." Sylvandre replies, "Ah no, true love is the death of the self; rebirth in the beloved person." They go on and on, examining all the facets of a theme which has no issue.

This faded work of art was once sharp and bright and meaningful. To Catherine d'Angennes' generation it brought the vicarious pleasure of courtship in a society where marriage came too soon. The author had got the idea for *L'Astrée* from the Spanish pastorals that everyone read. But he had added a little of his own real life to give the story an accent of social truth. For d'Urfé had fallen in love with his sister-in-law, Diane de Châteaumorand, and the long patience of Céladon is just like the ten years' devotion of the author to this lady. However, d'Urfé and Diane were finally free to marry. As happens in real life, but never in pastorals, they soon became disenchanted with one another, fell out of love, and separated. The book was written after this disillusionment but it describes only the illusory premarital sentimental postures of the lovers. Marriage is always the final event of romantic stories, for marriage is too real to be the food of sentimental dreams and yearnings; it can only be the end of them. D'Urfé's novel provided a prolongation of that uncommitted dream world of courtship which was so brief in the life of a lady in Catherine d'Angennes' position, or in most cases nonexistent. Love was to be found only in the imagination. It is because real life was painful and dirty, real human relations brutally elemental, that the life of the shepherds of Forez, bland and sweet and impossibly free, was enjoyed by everyone.

Everyone also enjoyed the *ballets de cour*. Or almost everyone. These were magnificent musical entertainments organized at the Louvre to occupy the leisure of the courtiers, soldiers, and pretty girls who formed the entourage of the royal pair. They were often vulgar and tasteless, for all their pomp. The *Ballet des macquereaux* (ballet of the pimps, or the "ambassadors of love") suggests the tone. Catherine d'Angennes avoided them.

But in January 1609 occurred one such ballet which she could not refuse to attend: the ballet of *Arion*. This production became famous in the annals of the time, not so much for its artistic merits as for what went on behind the scenes. The ballet was staged by Marie de Medici to honor the Spanish ambassador and was held at Sully's home, then repeated at the palace of Marguerite de Valois. (The king's ex-wife lived across the river in full view of the Louvre, and Henri was still on the best of terms with her.) Lingendes and Chevalier, artists of the moment, provided the unmemorable words and music. The story was the usual mythical nonsense: the legend of the demigod Arion, saved from drowning by dolphins charmed by his lyre and his voice. This Arion was a natural child of the sea god Poseidon, who had wooed Demeter when his wife Amphytrite was not looking. Marie de Medici, fatally cast in the role of Amphytrite in the ballet, appeared before her guests on a chariot encrusted with coral, pearls, and seashells, among naiads and tritons blowing into their conches. The sumptuousness, described with innocent wonder in the diary of L'Estoile, must have gladdened Marie's heart. But she was keeping a sharp watch on Henri and sixteen-year-old Charlotte de Montmorency. Charlotte had a singing part in the chorus; the old king had fallen madly in love with her during the rehearsals. In the midst of a quarrel with his wife, he had caught a glimpse of the lovely Charlotte and immediately made peace with Marie, solely in order to be present at these rehearsals. Charlotte was skillfully playing on the king's passion for her while virtuously resisting him.

The day of the performance finally arrived. The king and his guests assembled. The opening tableaux were performed. Suddenly the star of the show appeared, riding a dolphin. This was Arion, an exquisite young body clad only in a thin shift, with golden hair falling down over bare shoulders. She began to sing the title role in a clear, strong voice. The king leaned forward, his attention riveted by this young girl, and it was said that his was not the only mouth that watered.

She was Angélique Paulet, the daughter of one of the king's financial advisors. Of course she stole the show. When her song ended the king rushed forward and kissed Angélique impulsively, having forgotten all about Charlotte de Montmorency. He presented her to the queen in his enthusiasm, and Marie smiled thinly at this new threat to her domestic peace.

Angélique Paulet soon became one of Henri's numerous casual mistresses. She served the purpose of quenching the fires of his unrequited passion for Charlotte. Catherine d'Angennes, witnessing the open wantonness of these royal adventures, decided that she would ban such conduct from her own circle. She never expected that this little opportunist Angélique would one day become her closest friend and the mainstay of her drawing room. Nor that the cunning Charlotte de Montmorency would also feature as a prominent guest of hers. But that was to happen only after the scandals of their adolescence had subsided.

The relations of Henri IV and Charlotte assumed quite heroic proportions, and the story of their unconsummated romance makes a fitting end to this lively reign.

She was the daughter of the Constable of France and far too rich to be bought. And she was so extraordinarily pretty that she had the pick of the court. Her parents began looking over the field when she was four years old. Many people asked for her hand without a dowry, knowing that the girl would eventually catch the eye of the king and that this would redound to the glory and financial advantage of their families. But the proposals were all deflected for one reason or another until the girl was sixteen and rehearsals for that ballet began.

The king decided that the only way to get her was to marry her to someone not likely to present obstacles. He chose the Prince de Condé (the same who as a little boy of eight had tried to kiss Catherine de Vivonne), because "he's only twenty, he prefers hunting to women. She will be the consolation and hobby of my old age which is beginning now." He could not have chosen worse. Condé was not, it is true, very fond of women, but Henri had not reckoned on his sense of property and family honor. The Condés were princes of the blood-royal, the first family in France after the king's. Henri made it very difficult for Condé not to be offended, by openly courting the girl. The king became an impetuous adolescent, wearing new satin doublets and perfuming his grey beard, engaging in exhausting sports like the "*course à la bague*," in which he actually shot his lance through the ring, at full speed on horseback, four times out of eight. He arranged to have Mme. de Condé appear on her balcony with her hair undone one night. She complied: "Good lord, he must be crazy!" But she was pleased to be the favorite, and without having to give anything at all. Her husband felt the affront so badly that he carried her off to Picardy, and then to Brussels, for safekeeping.

Henri was furious. Here was the prettiest girl he had ever wanted, and she was out of reach. He considered taking her by force, which would have involved him in another war—with Spain in Flanders. This middle-aged monarch who had done so much for peace and progress in France was now, at the end of his life, ready to undo it all for the sake of a teenager. The teenager herself, fully aware of the power she wielded, and primed by her ladies-in-waiting (who were in the king's pay), asked for an annulment of her marriage. She was finding Condé a less than ardent husband, and she wanted to go back to Paris. She actually believed that the king would make her his queen if he could get her back. She thoughtlessly ignored the obstacles; to do so he would have had to poison his wife, for his existing marriage had been cemented by male children. Nevertheless, Charlotte did all she could to keep up the king's hopes. The situation reached the level of a serious international problem.

In the meantime, Marie had been invested as future regent for her young son, Louis. This ceremonial appointment meant that if anything happened to Henri, now fifty-seven and about to start a war in Flanders, Marie would be all-powerful in France. Shortly after this investiture, something did happen to Henri. He got into his royal carriage one day in May 1610. He was, they say, taking the Duc de Vendôme, one of his illegitimate sons, to visit Angélique Paulet, in the hope that Angélique's charms would stir up some heterosexual passion in the young man's blood. But he never reached Angélique's house. A traffic jam occurred between the royal coach and a haycart in the rue de la Ferronnerie. The knife of the fanatic Ravaillac found its way into the king's heart.

This assassination left Marie in supreme control of France and a nine-year-old dauphin who disliked his mother.

Catherine d'Angennes now became the Marquise de Rambouillet by another death, that of her father-in-law. Her house was ready. The courtly world began to come to the *chambre bleue*.

NOTES

1. It is Tallemant des Réaux who, listening to her reminiscences many years later, recorded this and other personal confidences about herself and her friends, in his *historiette* of the marquise (*Historiettes*, I, pp. 442–55) and many other references. He was a distant relative of her husband and an assiduous guest at the *chambre bleue* in the 1650s.
Somaize calls Mme. de Rambouillet "Rozelinde" (*Dictionnaire*, I, pp. 61, 80, 205, 209.

2. Giulia's widowhood itself gave her a kind of monstrous distinction. Her husband had been strangled in a Venetian jail for having murdered Vittoria Corombona, the "white devil" of Webster's somber play.

3. Tallemant's remarks on Mme. de Rambouillet's parents are much clarified by Adam, drawing on the *Thuana* and other sources in his notes to the *historiette* of the Marquis de Pisani (I, pp. 19–24, n. pp. 685–91).

4. Tallemant, I, p. 622.

5. Plato's antifeminism may not have been as pointed as the sixteenth-century Platonists could wish, but they felt they could find in him support for their own misogyny. See, for example, the *Phaedrus* and *Timaeus*.

6. The picture forms part of the series of gigantic canvases depicting the events of her life, which Rubens turned out to order in 1622–25.

7. The street ran north-south near the present site of the Arc de Triomphe du Carousel, between the Louvre and the Tuileries. This whole neighborhood disappeared in the urban renewal of the Napoleonic era and the Second Empire.

8. Sauval, in his *Histoire et recherches des antiquités de la ville de Paris* (1724), describes Catherine's new house in detail.

9. Malherbe, *Oeuvres poétiques*, ed. R. Fromilhague and R. Lebègue (Collection des Universités de France: Société des belles lettres, 1968), 2 vols. p. 58.

10. The anecdote is told without surprise by Tallemant (I, pp. 438-39). It also appears in *Les Amours du grand Alcandre*, a novel of unknown authorship about Henri IV.

11. A fine vestige of such leather paneling remains in the queen's apartments at the château de Fontainebleau.

12. The inventory of her possessions, taken at the time of her death, is discussed by E. Magne in *Voiture et l'Hôtel de Rambouillet*, 2 vols.: *Les origines, 1597–1635* (9th ed.), *Les années de gloire, 1635–1648* (6th ed.), (Emile-Paul, 1929–30).

13. Tallemant devotes an *historiette* (I, pp. 543-48), to Mme. de Rambouillet's servants. He is amused by their simplicity, laughs at their malapropisms, and takes their absolute loyalty to the marquise for granted.

Louis *1610–1643*

THEY CAME because with the passing of Henri there was a change in the atmosphere of the Louvre. Henri had never been a very elegant monarch, but he had been a strong one, and a hospitable and cheerful human being. His male magnetism had made the court, if not a decent place, at least a lively one for the women who graced it with their presence. His sudden assassination created a social vacuum.

As soon as she became a widow, Marie de Medici developed a taste for power. But she had no gift to match her desire. The queen surrounded herself with favorites who preyed on her vanity. She disgraced the sensible old Sully and replaced him with a coxcomb, Concini, husband of her Italian girlfriend Leonora. She soon found a pack of greedy noblemen at her door demanding handouts and threatening rebellion. Henri had kept them in check by a combination of soldierly charm and plain tyranny. Marie could think of nothing better than to empty the royal coffers into their pockets.

It is not surprising that this same nobility of La Trémouilles, Montmorencys, and Condés who pillaged the state and plotted with Spain came to the hôtel de Rambouillet for their entertainment. The Rambouillets themselves belonged to the inner circle at court. And though the marquise kept aloof from politics, her husband served as ambassador to Spain on several missions. He was said to be more Spanish than the Spaniards and contributed his influence to an erratic foreign policy which alternated between fighting the Spaniards and marrying them. But he was not a very competent politician or diplomat, and his heart was evidently not in it.

The dauphin Louis did not promise well. This broody, pious boy lacked the warmth of his father. He was secretive and proud, resentful of his mother's authority, and unsure of himself; he occasionally stuttered. The young Louis preferred hunting alone in the swamps around Versailles, where he built himself a small château, to flirting and drinking in the Louvre. The favorite indoor hobby of Louis XIII was repairing guns and clocks by himself in the attic of the palace, or whipping up an omelet for the servants in the kitchen.

Early in his career Rambouillet had bought the post of Master of the King's Wardrobe. This honorary position placed him closer to the king than almost any other courtier. At first he took the job seriously, and conscientiously passed Louis his shirt in the mornings, rather than let a valet do it. The rituals of the king's intimate life must be shared by his liegemen, in the best tradition of chivalry. But Louis' unpleasant jokes irritated the marquis. The king would put out his feet instead of his hands for the sleeves. Once he even presented his behind to the marquis for the royal hat. More seemingly modest and virtuous than Henri had been, Louis was just as vulgar and far less gracious. The marquis surrendered the job when he was able to sell it. As usual, he bungled the bargain, and got only a fraction of the value of the post.

As for the women of Louis' court, those who, like Mme. de Chevreuse and Mme. de Hautefort, found themselves attached to his young queen present an interesting contrast to those who fled to the *chambre bleue* and kept out of the eye of politics. But one and all shared the agitations of an unstable regency and then of a reign that was to be dominated by Richelieu. Society was not so large that anyone could easily hide. Regardless of their private feelings about the quality of life at the Louvre, the fortunes of the Rambouillets were intimately associated with the court.

In an age of kings, the court is the starting point for all social departures. This is why we pause here for a glimpse of Louis XIII, his cardinal, and the women in his world.

Louis was crowned king on his thirteenth birthday. But he had to finish out his childhood under the loveless domination of his mother. Marie arranged the double wedding of her son to the Spanish infanta, Anne of Austria, and of her daughter Elizabeth to Philippe IV of Spain. This royal horse-trade was meant to cement a peace treaty between the two countries, but it did not succeed for long. The struggle between France and Spain for supremacy in Europe ran too deep to be resolved by royal weddings. Such unions only made the conflict more painful for Bourbons and Hapsburgs. It took on the character of an endless civil war.

Louis XIII and the infanta Anne were both fourteen when they married. Thrown together without regard for their personal inclinations, they were an uncomfortable pair from the start. Anne had been raised in the heavy formality of the Spanish court. She was noted for her beautiful hands, but she spoke terrible French and had the jutting underbite of the Hapsburgs. Louis did not like girls anyway. He left her to herself and went hunting.

Meanwhile Marie ruled, by the advice of astrologers and blackmailers, in a kind of disheveled grandeur leading straight to bankruptcy. Louis would have to wrest his royal rights from her by force.

He began by casting about for a friend, and found a certain Luynes among his hunting companions. He made this man a duke and with his help succeeded in having the queen mother's favorite, Concini, murdered on the Pont-Neuf. The corpse was thrown to the rabble of Paris to be mutilated and dragged through the streets until their rage was spent. After this bloody demonstration, Concini's wife Leonora was convicted of sorcery and burnt as a witch.

The queen mother was thus immobilized. Luynes became the king's chief advisor. The ebullient Mme. de Luynes was installed in the Louvre as the young queen's closest friend. This seemed an excellent arrangement; it entertained Anne and freed Louis from his wife's company. But no child came. Clearly the royal couple were not trying very hard; the marriage was never even consummated until they were eighteen, and that by a clever maneuver of the more sophisticated Luynes couple to overcome the king's shyness. But their childlessness was a political liability. In that bundle of mystical beliefs that had been accumulating around the idea of monarchy for centuries, fertility was a major attribute of a good king. The mystique of divine right presupposed that God would bless the royal union with an heir, to assure the continuity of authority which the monarchy must provide. Henri IV had set an abundant example. Malherbe had expressed the joyful hopes of the people for the coming of a golden age: *"Et les fruits passeront la promesse des fleurs."* ("And the fruit will surpass the promise of the flowers.") But Louis' only heir was *"Monsieur,"* his younger brother Gaston

Mme. de Hautefort

d'Orléans, an unstable lad who coveted his crown and was ready to gather up all the malcontents in the realm to oust him.

As for the lady who had been placed beside the young queen, what a duenna! Mme. de Luynes became notorious at seventeen for her lechery and impulsive pranks. She and her husband made a lusty contrast to the uneasy prudery of Louis and Anne. She gave the queen obscene anthologies to read, and once raced Anne up and down the halls of the palace until the queen slipped, fell, and—miscarried.

Luynes died. The king was barely twenty-one. He found himself again at the mercy of his mother, who at once saddled her son with another strong man, this time a cardinal, to rule France on her behalf. But she badly miscalculated the cardinal's aims. His name was Richelieu.

The cardinal simply took the reins of government from her.[1] He then proceeded to crush Anne's fragile hold on her husband. Anne was doubly hateful to the cardinal. She was Spanish. And she had repulsed his advances. Henceforth, until his death, the young queen would live trembling under the shadow of Richelieu's power.

As for Louis, he felt personally reduced by his minister. The cardinal was literate and urbane. He had great successes with women. It was said that he enjoyed the favor of Mme. de Chaulnes, as well as the courtesan Marion de Lorme, and perhaps even of his own niece Mme. de Combalet. No such sexual exploits were ever attached to Louis' name. The king fell in love with one of his wife's ladies-in-waiting, Mme. de Hautefort, an impeccably virtuous girl. Although he took the attitude of a lover, the shy monarch was not enterprising enough to make her his mistress. Their liaison consisted of courtly meetings in the evenings when he described the day's hunting events, to which the lady listened placidly over her embroidery. She was such an irreproachable sweetheart that she remained the queen's friend throughout Louis' "passion" for her.

Though he did not like his minister, Louis needed Richelieu. For pressing in on him still was the perennial wolfpack of nobles, pleading and menacing by turns, forever scheming to get back what they thought was their rightful share of the king's power and wealth. The king's brother, his wife, his girlfriend, his courtiers tried every form of conspiracy to dislodge the cardinal. Plots were formed and exposed, letters written in code and intercepted, political love affairs launched and betrayed.

The plotters paid for their ineptitude. Richelieu exiled them, sent them to the Bastille, burned down their castles, had them decapitated for treason. No one was safe. Even Henri II de Montmorency, head of the most ancient family in France, went to the block (1632). And Cinq-Mars, a charming, foolish protégé of the king's middle age, lost his head (1642).

One of the most exemplary of Richelieu's triumphs was that which concerned François de Montmorency-Bouteville. This young man was typical of his generation. In 1628 he chose to flout Richelieu's latest edict against dueling by fighting his twenty-second duel in broad daylight in the Place Royale. He was going to show the world that he, at least, was not subject to the cardinal's orders.

The incident was important because the duel was a nostalgic symbol of the legendary single combat of feudal times. It had once been an honorable class duty; it had become a class privilege. Blue-blooded layabouts were making a pastime of the "*point d'honneur.*" They spent their time insulting one another and fighting it out. Seconds and witnesses died, too, sometimes six in one encounter, for some trivial personal cause rather than usefully on the battlefield. Dueling reduced the supply of officers for the Thirty Years' War. It also fostered the nobleman's tendency to take the law into his own hands, making him believe he was beyond the reach of the king's justice. Richelieu and Louis decided it was time to outlaw this anarchistic hobby for good.

And so when Montmorency-Bouteville violated the new law, Richelieu acted swiftly. He had him seized, tried, convicted, and decapitated in the Place de Grève, where common thieves and witches were executed. It was an instructive sight for the people of Paris, to see the bloody corpse of the handsome young count lying in the dust like an ordinary criminal.

Mme. de Luynes had been banished from the court when her husband died in 1621, but this troublesome lady came back almost immediately as the Duchesse de Chevreuse.[2] Her marriage to Chevreuse, whose mistress she had already become before Luynes died, was a brilliant tactical move. Louis had to accept her presence again in his wife's entourage.

The history of Mme. de Chevreuse's adventures colors the whole age of Louis XIII. It is a history of everlasting political intrigue, generated by boredom and unused sexual energy. She joined heartily in all the plots against Richelieu. She could weave a plot, but she could never unravel it again. She spread confusion wherever she went. Her intrigue was gratuitous, unmotivated by anything but a desire for fun and romance.

In 1625 the Chevreuses went to England, where Mme. de Chevreuse found a rich field for amorous politics. She had affairs with the Duke of Buckingham and the Earl of Holland. The Bishop of Mende reported back to Richelieu: "I am ashamed and scandalized at the brazen behavior of Mme. de Chevreuse and at the gullibility of the husband."

Mme. de Chevreuse went further. She invited Buckingham to start a long-distance sentimental assault on Anne of Austria. She even enticed the neglected queen to fall in love "by proxy" with the dashing Englishman. This affair never amounted to much, but though the queen's reputation remained technically intact, she had really fallen in love with Buckingham in just a few meetings and one attempted declaration by him in the garden of Compiègne. No political benefit came to anyone from this sentimental affair, but it did drive Louis and Anne farther apart.

Next came the Chalais affair, in 1626. Mme. de Chevreuse masterminded this plot to overthrow Richelieu. When it was discovered, the Comte de Chalais, her lover, paid for it with his head. Another conspirator, the king's brother Gaston, was punished with a forced marriage. Mme. de Chevreuse was merely exiled. She went to Lorraine and immediately launched a new international plot. This, too, came to nothing, but when the dust settled and peace returned, the treaty specified that Mme. de Chevreuse must be allowed back into France. The cardinal resigned himself. Perhaps she would be less dangerous at home, where he could keep an eye on her.

He was mistaken. She began scheming again. She now induced Anne of Austria to establish political contacts in Spain under cover of innocent letters to her family in Madrid. Richelieu put his spies on the queen, and hoped to catch her redhanded. In 1637 occurred the touching drama of the "book of hours": the queen, under suspicion of treason, expected that she would be seized at any moment and accused of conniving with the Spaniards. Fearing the worst for herself, Anne arranged for a warning to be sent by Mme. de Hautefort to Mme. de Chevreuse, who was hiding at Tours. A red-bound prayer book was to be sent to her as a signal for flight over the border. A green one meant that all was well. The crisis passed and the queen was not apprehended. But Mme. de Hautefort mistook her instructions and sent the wrong book. Mme. de Chevreuse went racing off on horseback, disguised as a man, to needless safety in Spain.

She was assisted on her way out of France by her lover of the moment, the young Prince de Marsillac, whose head was as full of dreams of glory as her own. She gave him her jewelry for safekeeping (a favorite gesture of trust) and galloped off, reciting lines from *Le Cid*. What an explosion of freedom she must have felt, alone under the stars, with the wind in her hair and the poet's rhetoric clanging in her heart:

> Va, cours, vole et nous venge!

> (Go, run, fly, and avenge us!)

She arrived at the border, an exhausted young cavalier, her sex unknown even to her traveling companions, until she got off her horse and they saw the saddle covered with menstrual blood.

Young Marsillac, not to be outdone, was up to his neck in a plan to carry off Anne of Austria on horseback to Brussels. Both she and Mme. de Hautefort were to flee with him from Richelieu's terror. Many years later, when Marsillac had become the disillusioned Duc de La Rochefoucauld, he wrote wistfully of this marvelous escapade that never came off:

Despite all the obstacles and dangers of such a plan, it gave me more joy than I had ever felt before in my life. I was at the age when one loves to do extraordinary and dramatic deeds and I could imagine nothing more extraordinary than to snatch the queen away from her husband the king and from Richelieu who was jealous of her, and to take away Mme. de Hautefort from the king who was in love with her.[3]

Mme. de Chevreuse was a far more reckless plotter than Mme. de Hautefort or the queen, but she was just as ineffectual. There is an almost endearing quality to the incompetence of these ladies so perilously close to the center of power at the French court. Politics were hopelessly entangled in their sentimental attachments. They were no more perspicacious than schoolgirls. They played with fire heedlessly and enjoyed an innocent idealism which absolved them from guilt whenever the house burned down.

What sets Mme. de Chevreuse apart from the decorous ladies we will meet at the *chambre bleue* is perhaps largely a matter of temperament. Her shameless sex life and her aggressive politics were precisely the kind of thing Mme. de Rambouillet wanted to avoid. This passionate amazon was a woman of action whose energies were blocked and frustrated by the coherent Machiavellianism of the cardinal.

But Mme. de Chevreuse did also learn something of the niceties being elaborated at the *chambre bleue*, even though her frequent periods of exile put her out of touch. Her house in Paris was just next door to the hôtel de Rambouillet, and she brought Buckingham there at least once to hear Mlle. Paulet sing. It was unavoidable that some of the literary veneer should rub off on her. She saw herself as a virile heroine, always centerstage in the unfolding tragicomedy of French politics. And the poets in turn drew on her adventures—whitewashed, elevated, of course, but still recognizable. The Emilie of Corneille's *Cinna* comes to mind, that fiery Roman maiden who drove two lovers to plot against the emperor Augustus. Emilie is the kind of noble troublemaker that Mme. de Chevreuse liked to play.

She hardly noticed the vulgarity of the Louvre from which Mme. de Rambouillet turned away. But she was just as impatient of the dullness of this court, frozen as it was in protocol, sealed in ritualized boredom.

The court was dull because the king and queen were dull. It was not for any lack of pomp and glitter. A great deal of satin and pearls and ceremonial armor flashed in the light of thousands of candles at each of their court balls. The king never went forth into Paris without a small army of handsomely dressed heralds, bodyguards, ministers, footmen, doctors, confessors, and historians. The queen was always surrounded by at least half a dozen pretty ladies who stood (or sat if they were duchesses) in waiting upon her pleasure, enjoying the queen's company as an absolute value having nothing to do with entertainment. Royalty was a mystery wrapped in liturgy.

And yet the king lacked the gift of entertaining his courtiers. Neither he nor Anne was possessed of the verbal wit that challenges the mind and fills up the idleness of people who do no work. Louis was at his most comfortable when making things with his hands, frequenting servants whom he could bully, exercising himself physically. The only "courtly" amusement he enjoyed was hunting, but here again he was a lone and serious hunter. He would ride for days through mud and rain and bush, never getting off his horse but to fall into bed exhausted with his boots on. His courtiers despised him quietly for his lack of culture.

If the king and queen were not interested in culture, Richelieu was. He gladly relieved Louis of the kingly duty of being generous toward the arts. It is Richelieu's name, not that of Louis, which is associated with the monumental architecture of the twenties and thirties, with the theatrical entertainments at court, with pensions for needy poets.

The cardinal's munificence toward authors was prompted by a love of grandeur but also by policy. He did not trust intellectuals. They were capable of independent thought, which could lead to heresy or, worse, sedition. The best way to neutralize them was to turn the spotlight of public attention on their discussions, give them money only for works of orthodoxy, keep them in a state of economic dependency that turned them into conformists. It was in this spirit that the French Academy was born. This institution, which bound the minds of thinking men over to the state, was Richelieu's intellectual gift to posterity and the final guarantee of his immortality.

This did not endear him to Mme. de Chevreuse, but it certainly diminished somewhat the disaffection of Mme. de Rambouillet, who received the cardinal occasionally at the *chambre bleue*. She knew he sent his spies there too, but she blandly pretended not to notice. Even one or two of her closest friends were reporting to him regularly on the conversations at her home. Her only defense was to avoid doing or saying anything that could be considered controversial.

Richelieu may have been more cultivated than the royal couple, but there was one function he could not take over from them. And at last they did it themselves. Three years after the creation of the Academy, Louis and Anne gave to France what seemed a far more precious and miraculous gift. In 1638, after twenty-three years of childless marriage, they brought forth a dauphin. The most significant event that could possibly take place at the Louvre had taken place at last. Anne must have conceived the infant during one of the worst phases of Richelieu's persecution of her, perhaps even while she was planning her escape from the court. With the birth of a son all was forgiven. Or nearly all ...

The infant Louis XIV was nicknamed *"Dieudonné"* because such an unhoped-for blessing seemed to come direct from a Heavenly Father who believed in monarchy.

The extraordinariness of this event, and of the arrival two years later of another son, can be judged by the fact, known to everyone at the time, that relations between Louis and Anne had long ago gone completely sour. And yet a king was born, and lived. The monarchy would continue.

Richelieu and Louis passed away within a few months of each other (Richelieu in December 1642, Louis in May 1643), leaving Anne of Austria to govern as regent for her five-year-old son. After living most of her married life as an unwanted, suspicious alien, Anne suddenly came into her own, merely by surviving both the cardinal and her husband, and producing, almost at the last minute, two male offspring. The widowed queen now started a new life. She gave up the foreign intrigues of her youth and became more loyally French than anyone else at her court. She appointed a new cardinal-minister, Mazarin, to handle the political task. She was very fond of this handsome Italian prelate who did not exercise any priestly functions, and probably married him secretly.

The regency of Anne, *"la bonne régence,"* was quite different from the disheveled years of Marie de Medici's rule. But every regency is a dangerous vacuum which sucks in troublemakers. Louis warned her on his deathbed not to let the old gang of traitors come back. Richelieu had killed a great many of them, but there were always others marking time in exile, waiting for their chance. He thought particularly of Mme. de Chevreuse. *"Voilà le diable, voilà le diable!"* was his last impotent judgment on her, and he made Anne promise that she would not take this pernicious woman back when he was gone.

The queen promised, but then she forgot or relented. No sooner was Louis buried but Mme. de Chevreuse was back in Paris.

Yet things were not the same as before. Both she and Anne had grown middle-aged. They were no longer friends. Richelieu, the queen's old enemy, had been replaced by Mazarin, the queen's new friend. Mme. de Chevreuse, impatient as ever for the stimulation of intrigue, took a dislike to the new cardinal. It was not long before she joined the anti-Mazarin party of the *Importants*. A new round of sedition was set in motion. The Fronde was about to begin.

Mme. de Hautefort came back from exile, too, when Louis died. For her it was a triumph. She was still young and lovely. Anne welcomed her and favored her with the *"tabouret,"* a stool to sit upon in the royal presence.[4] But the welcome wore thin when this lady let herself get involved, like Mme. de Chevreuse, in the plots of the gathering Fronde. Before long she found herelf banished again, this time by her old friend Anne.

The queen must have felt she had more in common with another widow, Mme. de Motteville. This intelligent, mild, dull young lady was content to sit with the queen night after night for the rest of her life, at the center of their stiff, brocaded feminine throng, gossiping about courtly society and affairs of state. When the queen retired to bed, Mme. de Motteville wrote down in her diary all that she had heard, in a lucid, commonsense style. Naturally a partisan of Anne's interests, and seeing the world through chaste eyes, Mme. de Motteville described the stirring events of the regency and the Fronde, which filled the hearts of so many other romantic ladies, from the safe distance of an indignant onlooker. She was never tempted to plunge in and try to make history herself.[5]

The court of Louis XIII thus faded away in a murmur of placid feminine voices.

NOTES

1. For a few more years Marie schemed to get control again, and at last one day in 1630, in concert with the young queen, she extracted a promise from Louis that he would dismiss Richelieu. But this was the famous *Journée des Dupes* (Day of Dupes), the day of her last illusions. Richelieu surprised everyone by winning back the king's confidence and driving Marie into permanent exile.

2. On Mme. de Luynes/Chevreuse, see Tallemant, *Historiettes*, I, pp. 159–64. Mme.

de Chevreuse was discussed at length by Mme. de Motteville, the Cardinal de Retz, and other memorialists of her time and has also engendered much romantic biography in our time. A good serious work is Louis Batiffol, *La Duchesse de Chevreuse* (Hachette, 1913).

Somaize calls her "Candace" (*Dictionnaire*, I, p. 54).

3. La Rochefoucauld, *Oeuvres complètes*, ed. L. Martin-Chauffier and J. Marchand (Pléiade, 1957), p. 58.

4. The burlesque poet Scarron wrote an ode on "Mme. de Hautefort's ass," congratulating that "beautiful and cultured" part of her anatomy on now being allowed to repose on a stool. Whatever the merits of this poem, it shows how far a poet could go in addressing a lady of the court:

Stances pour Mme. de Hautefort

On ne vous verra plus en posture de pié
Dans le cercle accroupie,
Au grand plaisir de tous et de vostre jarret,
Vostre Cul, qui doit estre un des beaux Culs de France,
Comme un Cul d'importance,
A receu chez la Reyne enfin le Tabouret.

Comme on connoist souvent une chose par l'autre,
D'un Cul comme le vostre,
J'ay connû le destin, voyant vostre beau Nez:
Et sans estre Devin, j'ay predit que sans doute,
Ce Cul qui ne voit goutte,
Seroit veu dans le rang de nos Culs Couronnez.

Nostre Reyne, Princesse aussi juste que sage,
N'a pû voir davantage
Un Cul plein de mérite et trés-Homme de bien,
Tandis que d'autres Culs sont assis a leur aise
A costé de sa chaise,
Debout, ou mal assis, comme un Cul bon à rien.

Ce Cul de satin blanc, dont sans doute la face
Ne fit jamais grimace,
Devoit asseurément estre un Cul Duc et Pair;
Car qu'auroit-on pensé de ce qu'un Cul si sage,
Qui vaut bien un Visage,
N'eut pas eu chez la Reyne où reposer sa chair?

Que les hommes n'ont pas pareille Destinée!
Et que vous estes née
Sous un Astre puissant et favorable aux Culs!
Tandis que le vostre est prés de ceux des Princesses,
Assis sur ses deux Fesses,
Le nostre n'est assis que sur deux os pointus.

(We will not see you any more standing on your feet
among the sitting circle;
to everyone's delight, as well as your legs',
your ass, which is among the loveliest asses in France,
a most distinguished ass,
has been given a stool in the queen's presence.

As one often knows one thing by another,
I could have guessed the fate of an ass like yours
by looking at your lovely nose:
and without being a seer, I predicted that without a doubt
this ass, though it can't see a thing,
would be seen among the ranks of crowned asses.

Our queen, as just as she is kind,
could no longer bear to see
such a deserving and gentlemanly ass
standing, or badly seated, like a good-for-nothing ass,
while other asses sat at their ease
beside her chair.

This ass of white satin, whose face
has certainly never frowned,
was bound to become a peer of the realm,
for what would one have thought, to find so virtuous an ass
which is easily worth another's face,
with no place to lay its flesh at the queen's apartments?

But how different are the destinies of men!
And indeed you are born
under a powerful star, favorable to asses!
For while yours sits beside those of princesses
on its two buttocks,
ours sits on two sharp bones.)

(In *Poésies diverses,* ed. M. Cauchie (Didier 1947), I, pp. 342–43. Somaize calls Mme. de Hautefort "Hermione" (I, p. 113).

5. Mme. de Motteville's *Mémoires* were reedited in 1855 by M. F. Riaux (Charpentier). We refer to this edition hereafter.

Somaize calls this lady "Melise" (I, p. 161).

La Divine Arthénice

FRANÇOIS de Malherbe was the badly paid and badly chosen "official poet" of Henri IV. He was not Henri's kind of poet at all, this fussy grammarian whose consolations did not console and whose love lyrics did not unlock the heart. When Henri died Malherbe was handed on to Marie de Medici and then to Louis. He fared little better under their protection, although he exerted himself to sing of the queen's virtues and the king's prowess. Malherbe's real ambition, however, was to raise the quality of speech manners of the courtly people of his time, *"dégasconner la cour,"* as he put it, stamp out sloppy provincialisms, and get people to read poetry with more attention to what he considered the essentials, such as correct rhyme and euphony. He was an implacable critic of other men's poems, especially any that were soft, careless, spontaneous, or lacking in form.

A bitter, cynical man to whom fame came late, he began frequenting the *chambre bleue* in 1612, when he was already in his late fifties.

To Malherbe, poetry was a stylization of reality, a smart game, where form mattered more than content. There is a clear connection between his literary point of view and the social program of Mme. de Rambouillet. For the cachet of the *chambre bleue*, what made it different from the Louvre, was deliberate artificiality, a stylization of social intercourse, and ultimately a stylization of life itself.

It was Malherbe who coined the anagram "Arthénice" on the name of the marquise. Such Arcadian pseudonyms soon became extremely popular, often being taken from the endless cast of characters in the pastoral novel *L'Astrée*. No married lady was addressed in public by her Christian names, even by her equals or

Mme. de Rambouillet and her daughter Julie d'Angennes

members of her family, let alone underlings. The poetic pseudonym provided an illusory informality, while the poet still kept a respectful distance. The name of Catherine, an intimate part of the person of the marquise, gave way to Arthénice, her literary mask. Catherine could not be aspired to; Arthénice could. Malherbe made a flourish of being the faithful and hopeless admirer of Arthénice. This gave the lie to his real feelings toward women, cynical and demanding and contemptuous of their virtue. He was not called *"Papa Luxure"* (dirty old man) for nothing. But the marquise was his sentimental exception. He addressed poems to Arthénice as the "lovely shepherdess to whom the Fates seem to have devoted my last years," for he was thirty-three years older than she. Once he went to visit her and, not finding her at home, stayed to chat with a young lady he found in her drawing room. An accidental musket bullet suddenly whizzed through the window between him and the girl, narrowly missing him. The next day he came again to see Mme. de Rambouillet and she inquired about the incident. "I wish I had been killed by that bullet," he said. "I am old, I've lived long enough. I might have been honored by having people think that Monsieur de Rambouillet had ordered the shot fired." This rather rhetorical way of indicating that he wished her husband could be jealous of him was really a compliment to the gentle but resolute virtue of the marquise. But what about that musket shot? Tallemant recounts the incident as though bullets flying in at windows were a fairly normal occurrence, and we have to suppose that they were.

These early years of the *chambre bleue*, when Malherbe was the lion in the drawing room and *la divine Arthénice* was gathering her friends around her, are the period during which the new artificial style was set.

The marquise had a most interesting task in the schooling of the nobility. The graceless barons of the Louvre took off their muddy boots and put on their good behavior when they went to the *chambre bleue*. Mme. de Rambouillet imposed her decorum with an indefinable charm. She never told anybody what to do, but took it for granted that her own good taste was shared by everyone. Ladies were a major attraction here, virtuous ladies with delicate sensibilities and a fine sense of their own dignity. And poets were invited, to sing of the ladies' qualities. Every woman was a lady in this house, no matter what she chose to be elsewhere. It caught on like a fashion. Here was the notorious Mme. de Rohan, Sully's daughter, who had entertained a string of cavaliers both before and after her very early marriage, sitting demurely in the *chambre bleue* beside the aging Princesse de Conty, whose sexual career was so well known that only a half-witted deaf-mute would marry her. A number of ex-sweethearts of Henri IV graced the *chambre bleue* at this time. Mlle. Paulet and the Princess de Condé, whom we will study closer, were only the most celebrated of them. There was also Mme. de Moret, who had been sold to Henri for thirty thousand écus by her aunt. To save appearances the girl had been married to the Comte de Cézy, a poor man deep in debt who was willing to assume the awkward position of husband cuckolded on his wedding night by the king, for the sake of the price paid. Henri having insisted on getting his goods directly after the ceremony, Cézy wished to exercise his rights thereafter, but the girl refused, and the marriage was dissolved. When Henri tired of her, Jacqueline de Moret pretended to go blind and became very devout, hoping for a handout from Marie de Medici. Her newfound virtue was not easy to get used to, but she tried hard to make it look convincing. Malherbe wrote to his friend Peiresc in 1610:

Mme. la comtesse de Moret is submerged in piety, though she can't persuade many people that she means it. But you know how skeptical people are.

She came to the *chambre bleue* to practice. But she relapsed occasionally. Malherbe writes again to Peiresc in 1613:

They say Mme. de Moret has started buttoning up her neckline again. I don't know what this may mean. Perhaps you can guess. It may be the cold.

This remark surely tells us more about Malherbe's masculine insensitivity than about the countess's spiritual condition.

In any case, she was beautiful enough to be forgiven her former lapses at the hôtel de Rambouillet, and she came there for decades after, a gentle fading relic among the prudes and would-be prudes of her generation. She was a cousin of the poet Racan, Malherbe's disciple, who courted her among many other suitors. This shy, stuttering poet addressed his arcadian stanzas to the lady in the shadowed embrasures of the *chambre bleue* and was content with her passive, cow-eyed gaze acknowledging the gift.

Others came: that durable invalid, Mme. de Sablé and her friend the Princesse de Guimené, ladies whose private lives could not bear scrutiny but who displayed their modesty here, after the manner of their hostess, and received official homage from the poets for their pains. The sweetness and discretion of their hostess was universally venerated—to the point of monotony. Mlle. de Scudéry gives us a Catherine de Rambouillet so bland and woodenly perfect that we yearn for a few faults:

Cléomire [another nickname for Catherine] is tall and well-proportioned; ... the delicacy of her coloring defies description; and an indefinable light comes from her eyes, inspiring all who look at her with respect.... A peacefulness is visible on her face which makes clear what is in her soul ... But the wit and heart of this marvelous person are better than her beauty.... She knows several languages, and indeed all that is worth knowing, but without seeming to claim to know anything, and she is so modest that to hear her talk about everything so intelligently you would think she knew everything by simple common sense and experience of the world.... [etc.] [1]

She had the gift of constraining others with a very light touch. Her outstanding virtues were negative ones, in the spirit of her Italian upbringing. She was a talented listener and could bring out the best in people simply by paying attention to them.

There was also a positive organizer in Mme. de Rambouillet. She could think up entertainments ranging from mildly malicious practical jokes to carefully planned literary events:

The Comte de Guiche, having eaten too many mushrooms while staying at the château de Rambouillet in the country, goes to bed feeling bloated. While he sleeps, the ladies prevail on his valet to lend them all his doublets. They have them quickly sewn a few inches tighter. Next morning he cannot get into his clothes. Having tried on each of his garments and finding them all too small, he is forced to attend mass in his dressing gown. He imagines he has been "blown up" by the mushrooms. They must have been poisonous! He begins to feel really ill. "What a stupid way to die, in the flower of my manhood!" His terror grows until at last someone suggests the remedy to him: one pair of scissors applied to the seams of his doublets.

Another joke on the Comte de Guiche: he is served a complete dinner of specialties which he had expressly said he did not like. Trying to be polite while the ladies urge him to have a little more boiled turkey and milk soup, he smiles weakly, nervously crumbles his bread, searches his wits for a tactful escape, until they take pity on him at last and remove the offending dishes to bring on a magnificent banquet that was waiting for him in the kitchen.

The accent on the artificial and the refined was often quite expensive. Mme. de Rambouillet liked to treat her friends to elaborate surprises. Her mania for building contributed to the grandiose nature of some of these. She had an extra nook built on to the *chambre bleue*, jutting out into the garden, and kept the entire construction a secret. One evening a tapestry is drawn aside to reveal to her marveling guests the paneled alcove, completely furnished, with an elegant bay window. In this alcove stands a goddess—her daughter Julie d'Angennes in a toga. The poet-critic Chapelain was so enchanted that he was moved to compose a poem, "Stances de Zyrphée," in which he promises Arthénice that because of her exquisite generosity her beauty will never be attacked by the years. The new room was christened, after Chapelain's poem, *"la loge de Zyrphée."*

Again, she invites the Bishop of Lisieux, Cospeau, to go for a stroll with her in the formal gardens of her country home. Suddenly they come upon a rockery, among which living nymphs have been disposed in a tableau. Cospeau rubs his eyes in amazement. The nymphs turn out to be Julie d'Angennes, of course, with her sisters and girlfriends, clad diaphanously as Diana and her handmaidens, and placed there by the marquise to astonish and compliment the good bishop.

The theatrical nature of these displays is in keeping with the desire of the marquise to rearrange an unacceptable world. That other stage set so loved by the romantic poets, the wild green domain of forest and mountain, is completely absent from the poetry that emanates from her circle. The Marquise de Rambouillet saw nothing good in this exterior chaos. When she visited her country home she brought Paris with her: it had to be cultivated and filled up with nymphs.

Divine Arthénice chose her poets well. Besides Malherbe, there were foreign lions like the Italian cavalier Marino Marini, who read the florid verses of his *Adonis* [2] to the company. They found this confection too rich for their blood, but they liked feeling that they were participating in an international cultural event.

She received Malherbe's disciples, Racan and Maynard, who in their separate ways reinforced the master's views on prosody. Racan, a genuine aristocrat, carried on the pastoral tradition of D'Urfé in sweet *"bergeries."* Maynard, a man of the robe on indefinite leave from his provincial presidency, wrote conventional love lyrics for the ladies, but then, like Malherbe, licentious sonnets about them behind their backs.

Malherbe's rigid principles on the proper construction of verse, his notion of poetry as a game that must be played well and according to the rules, correspond exactly to Mme. de Rambouillet's decorum. Poetry becomes, under Malherbe's strictures, a mental gymnastic ("A good poet is no more use to the State than a good player of skittles" [3]). He avoids spontaneity. Moral content, except of the most conventional sort, is unnecessary. In fact, his pornographic poems follow the same artistic discipline as his prayers. Poetry, like the conduct of the guests at the hôtel de Rambouillet, is seemly rather than moral. This approach is the very opposite of the loose fervor of lyricism which had flourished in France with Ronsard and was still flourishing, more or less underground, in the odes of Théophile de Viau and Saint-Amant. Malherbe buried Ronsard by attacking his last mawkish imitator of the turn of the century, Desportes.[4] He was not interested in sentiment; it was usually false anyway. He focused on the values of euphony, clarity of meaning, common sense, rhythm, proportion. He enjoyed deflating unearned reputations, exposing the technical errors of second-raters.[5]

Much real poetry was shoveled away with the rubbish. We do not regret losing Desportes, but the genuine lyricism of Ronsard and Théophile were also relegated to the appreciation of unfashionable readers. Virtually everything Malherbe said about poetry has been found to be untrue since the French Revolution. The central idea, of a correct technique of poetry to be imposed not only on oneself but on all poets, is the most dated in our age of expressive freedom. But then, how is it that we can still enjoy Malherbe's poetry? He never forgets to be a good technician, even when he is angry or deeply moved. The conventional patriotism of his odes to the authorities, the unfelt "consolations" to bereaved friends, the sonnets of purely formal adoration for an inaccessible "Caliste" are interspersed with expressions of genuine fervor, the cry of pain in the sonnet against his son's murderers, the occasional line that sings out of his love lyrics:

... L'air est plein d'une haleine de roses.

(The air is replete with a breath of roses.)

But it is all neatly contained in the same cage. Such lines are little miracles. They seem to defy our belief in the uninhibited and even anarchic nature of poetry, which appeals to our yearning for freedom. Malherbe's poetry appeals to another innate need, a need for pattern and regularity, a need to make sense of the universe.

The Malherbian cage suited the hôtel de Rambouillet very well. Freedom of expression was going out of style, not only in poetry but in ideas, in manners, even in dress. Individuality was being replaced by modishness. Between 1610 and the middle of the century the movement is all in the direction of ever more elegant and fragile garments, ever more symbolic accessories. Clothes are just as unfunctional, unworkable, uncomfortable as ever, but they become more subtle, like the attitudes assumed by the women who have laid aside the brazen adventures of Henri's court and taken up the new modesty. The leather and iron that men wore in Henri's time are replaced by fussy ribbons and passementerie. The rough-and-ready saddlery, the boastful codpiece, the hobnailed footwear fit for walking in the muddy streets of Paris, the heavy sword belt of the military hero give way, in the salon, to the shoe, silk stockings, cosmetics, and that ultimate emasculator, the male wig. And this in spite of the fact that war had installed itself in France as the permanent seasonal occupation of the class that launched these styles. The ladies abandon the stiff ruffs and boned flat bodices of Henri's decade, which kept them warm and squared their shoulders. They begin to wear elaborate lace collars over balloonlike sleeves; their shoulders disappear altogether—by 1630 the neck slopes into the arms rather like a swan's—and they seem weighted down and helpless under intricate coiffures which emphasize their femininity. In the portraits of the '30s and '40s, the women flaunt a languid, heavy-lidded desirability, but their furbelows, mirrors, fans, pearl necklaces, reticules, and innumerable petticoats bar the way.

Malherbe and most of his literary colleagues were of a class distinctly lower than that of the princesses, cardinals, and ambassadors who circulated in the *chambre bleue*. But writers from the lower orders were beginning to be a necessity there. For having isolated themselves from politics and the court, the nobility had nothing much to do. Nothing to replace the struggle for precedence, the boot-licking and conspiracy which were the chief time consumers at the Louvre. Literature provided an alternative distraction. Already in the pallid *Bergeries* of Racan, as in the long-winded discussions of *L'Astrée*, Liancourts and Bassompierres on leave from the real world of war and diplomacy could pretend up to a point to be shepherds and dreamers, could act out charades of the land of Forez. Some still preferred the monsters and murders of tragicomedy, with its shifting scenery and spectacle. The odes of Théophile de Viau, more spicy and colorful than the measured psalms of Malherbe, were still read. But Théophile was twice an outlaw. His verse offended Malherbe; his atheism and bad moral reputation offended the marquise. Théophile, a freethinker and a sodomite, was to be thrown into prison for his sins in 1627 and emerge a year later to die, a broken man, a discarded genius, a reject of history.

Other writers, of modest nobility and means, less controversial, more docile, came to the *chambre bleue*.

The budding grammarian Vaugelas talked there every day of his wild schemes for making a fortune out of eel farms and his ideas on correct usage. Though a credulous businessman, he was a brilliant scholar. It was here at the *chambre bleue* that he listened for years to the polite conversation that later provided the authority for his *Remarques sur la langue française*,[6] a book which was to be the arbiter of usage for nearly two centuries. Malherbe had established an absolutism of taste in poetry; Vaugelas went further, making the French language an instrument of precision and clarity which, once fixed, must never be changed. But this purist of speech also had to make a living: he became the tutor of the children of the Princesse de Carignan, one a deaf-mute, the other a stutterer. "What a fate," said Mme. de Rambouillet, "for a man who is so articulate, and such a marvelous teacher, to be the tutor of the deaf and dumb!"

Guez de Balzac, a young man with literary and diplomatic ambitions, came to the *chambre bleue* when he could in the intervals of his travels in the entourage of the Duc d'Epernon. When he could not, he kept up his connections there by letter. He addressed well-wrought epistles to the Cardinal de La Valette, a regular guest at the hôtel. They were passed around among the ladies to be judged and admired. Balzac's long, measured periods expressed commonplaces in such harmonious style that his readers often believed he was being original and even pithy. He did for prose what Malherbe had done for poetry: he made of the sentence a thing of shape and proportion, rather than substance.

Many smaller talents came to pay homage to Arthénice and were welcomed by her. The *"poète hétéroclite"* (oddball) Neufgermain invented a kind of acrostic quatrain, in which the end words formed the syllables of his friends' names:

> Entre les Dieux doit tenir *ran*
> Proche Jupin au plus haut *bou*
> Plus belle que rose et qu'oe*illet*,
> La divine Rambouillet.[7]

> (Divine Rambouillet, lovelier than the roses
> and carnations, should be among the highest ranks
> in heaven, next to Jupiter himself.)

The novelist Gombauld, a stuffy, ceremonious writer, came to ask the marquise to rehearse him in a reading of his work before the queen. "You be the queen and I will be Gombauld." The marquise was amused by his simplicity, and patient enough to hear his work to the end. She said it was very well read indeed.

The ladies who came to these gatherings were not all refugees from the immorality and coarseness of life outside the *chambre bleue*, but they all shared with the marquise the insoluble womanly problems of their time: too-early marriage, too many children, an onerous double standard in sex, a frightening expectation of early death. Here in this blue-tinted island of safety they could forget those disagreeable facts.

"Arthénice" herself had seven children.[8] When she first opened her doors to the nobility of Paris she was already a young mother. A daughter, Julie, had been born in 1607, and the marquise was to have four other daughters and two sons over the next two decades, although her health became ever more delicate with the passing years. Not much is known about her relations with these children as children. The doings or feelings of the very young were rarely thought worth discussing, and Tallemant mentions the marquise's youngest boy at the age of seven only because he died in that year, 1631. No doubt she loved her children but, like everyone else, kept them at arm's length, leaving them to be brought up by servants and tutors. Julie was precocious and got special attention as the first-born and as future assistant hostess in her mother's drawing room. The elder boy, the Marquis de Pisany, presented an educational problem. He was to have been trained to glorify the family name by military exploits, but because of a childhood accident he grew up to be a misshapen hunchback and would have to be shifted into some other career, such as the church. We know nothing else about his childhood. The four younger girls were placed in convents at an early age.

Childbearing was not the marquise's talent. But she had to bear them anyway, at least until she got sick.

It is well to speak here of the Marquise de Rambouillet's illness, for it illuminates the whole "woman problem" of her time. She and the marquis were on the best of terms with each other; his respect and devotion to her were lifelong; her admiration for him lasted, though it may have dwindled a bit with their fortunes, and she was inconsolable when he died. But numerous pregnancies were a heavy burden for a lady of precarious health who had special talents as a hostess. A strange disorder began to afflict the marquise from about the age of thirty-five (c. 1623). She could not bear the heat of an open fire in winter or the direct heat from the sun in summer: something in her blood reacted painfully to heat. She fought against this disability, but was eventually reduced to entertaining in a cold room bundled up in fur rugs and woolen caps. Once on a trip to Saint-Cloud the heat was so severe that she fainted, and her blood seemed to be visibly boiling in her veins! (Her skin was delicate to the point of translucency.[9]) This malady, so seemingly inconvenient for a society leader, was the chief reason why she adopted the Spanish "alcove" arrangement, later to be so popular among the précieuses. The guests circulated in the main salon, then visited the hostess a few at a time in her colder alcove where she lay in bed swaddled in furs. She was lighthearted enough to joke about her condition, saying that she was always completely deaf by Saint Martin's Day (because of the number of head scarves) and only recovered her hearing at Easter.

How sick was Mme. de Rambouillet really? She lived to the great age of seventy-seven in this condition, and during several decades, especially the years 1620–1645, she found the strength to preside nightly over large numbers of articulate people, to receive every self-respecting poet and pedant of the half-century, and all with the equanimity of a queen granting audiences. Modern French doctors have tried to diagnose her illness, calling it in fancy medical Latin-Greek "peripheral vaso-dilation" and "thermo-anaphylaxia." [10] These names, worthy of Molière's doctors, do little more than describe her symptoms. My own excellent doctor offers the following interpretation: the symptoms of Mme. de Rambouillet resemble the menopausal condition of hot flushes, but occurred too early in her life, and lasted too long, to be attributable to mere change of life. Another purely somatic explanation is that Mme. de Rambouillet had a continual slight temperature, undetectable in an age without thermometers, which would indicate the presence of some toxic condition such as tuberculosis. But if this were so, Mme. de Rambouillet would have died much younger. In fact, her illness lasted forty years. The only medical explanation is therefore hysteria (or if the reader prefers, neurasthenia: imaginary illness). In pre-Freudian days, such physical disability caused by mental conflict was perhaps more prevalent than it is today. It was certainly more tolerable to others who had to adapt their lives to the sick person's incapacity. Especially upper-class women fed up with their womanly functions were inclined to take to their beds with some incurable ailment. They had real symptoms which gave real pain, but not as much as the pain of normal life. In the seventeenth century, when there were few cures for any disease, real or imagined, sickness was more socially acceptable than it is today, when it is our duty to be healthy. Mme. de Rambouillet, like Proust's Tante Léonie, could afford this benign hysteria because her social world could accommodate it. Her friends could even believe that in her case it was real and not "*une vision*" such as more foolish women nurtured.

Her illness had several practical uses: it was a form of unconscious birth control, for it put a distance between her and her loving husband. The premature menopausal nature of the symptoms give us the clue. She became accustomed to this illness, and the symptoms stayed. Despite all the discomfort the illness caused, it was more convenient to be sick, to stay indoors, to stay in bed, and have the world approach reverently, in small groups, as they would a sybil in her grotto, than to be well and have to move about and dress and visit—and go on breeding.

This interpretation of her illness in no way belittles Mme. de Rambouillet. Her cachet, throughout a long life, was gentleness of temper, a benign smile on the anxiety-driven, passionate people who surrounded her. She healed their wounds with her genial detachment. Her hysteria, if such it was, was a success.

It is nevertheless strange to imagine that this lady, of all ladies of her generation, this one who was so lucky in the husband she was given, so entirely free to pursue her hobbies, to read what she liked, to entertain and be admired by many men, may have been in a state of revolt, however gracious the disguise. Of her five daughters, four went into convents (it is true, we do not know how willingly), while the other, Julie d'Angennes, married late, at thirty-eight. The youngest convent-bred daughter left the religious life later and also married, at about thirty, but only after having spent several years as a précieuse in the public eye, conspicuously refusing all offers of marriage. Who but the marquise could have communicated to her daughters this negative kind of birth control, this refusal or postponement of the fate of all women? Much later, when her golden age was over, Mme. de Rambouillet confided to Tallemant that, had she remained single until the age of twenty, she probably never would have married at all. This remark, made by an old woman looking back on a perfectly successful marriage, illuminates her situation most marvelously. She regretted this marriage and, had she been given a choice, would have chosen otherwise. It is perhaps precisely because she was favored with more freedom in marriage than most of her female contemporaries that Mme. de Rambouillet was able to imagine and desire more freedom still, and to get it by the grace of her illness. It was as a relatively independent wife that she could counsel her daughters against the slavery of wedlock. Counsel? We have no proof. We only know that her daughters' admiration for her was boundless, and that the *précieux* refusal of love and marriage was more noticeable in these daughters than anywhere else.

By 1625 the pattern was set. Mme. de Rambouillet had gone to bed. She was nearly done with childbearing. Her daughter Julie was eighteen and already a poised and elegant assistant in the tasks of entertaining. She had social Paris in the palm of her hand.

NOTES

1. Scudéry, *Artamène, ou le grand Cyrus* (1650–54), VII, p. 257.

2. Marino lived in Paris and frequented the hôtel de Rambouillet between 1615 and 1623.

3. Quoted in Tallemant, *Historiettes*, I, p. 115.

4. His marginal notes on a copy of Desportes' verses are the chief expression of his poetic doctrine, for this theoretician of prosody never wrote a theoretical work about it. See Ferdinand Brunot, *La Doctrine de Malherbe d'après son commentaire sur Desportes* (G. Masson, 1891).

La Divine Arthénice

5. His own reputation grew to staggering size. At the height of the classical period Boileau put the ultimate seal on it by calling him the first truly great French poet:

> Enfin Malherbe vint, et le premier en France
> Fit sentir dans nos vers une juste cadence. . . .

> (At last came Malherbe, and was first in France
> to bring a proper cadence to our verses.)

6. This little work of enormous authority first appeared in 1647.

7. Neufgermain, poem cited in an article by J. Mathorez, "Le Poète hétéroclite, Louis de Neufgermain 1574–1662," *Bulletin du Bibliophile et du Bibliothécaire* (1918), p. 168.

8. They are: Julie d'Angennes, Leon-Pompée d'Angennes, Marquis de Pisani, Claire-Diane d'Angennes, Catherine-Charlotte d'Angennes, Louise-Isabelle d'Angennes, Angélique-Clarisse d'Angennes, and le Vidame du Mans. No other name is known for this last child.

9. Tallemant describes these symptoms in detail in vol. I, pp. 451–52.

10. Drs. Sardou and Crouzel, in *Chronique Médicale*, Feb. 1, 1930, and Dr. Trénel in *Bulletin de la Société Française d'Histoire de la Médecine* 23 (1929), nos. 7–8, cited by Adam in *Historiettes*, I, p. 1093.

The Poets

T HEN CAME Voiture. This was the entertainer that the hôtel de Rambouillet had been waiting for. Malherbe had achieved his victory over the undisciplined baroque poets. He was growing old and taciturn. Mme. de Rambouillet had achieved her hegemony of politeness. Now it was time to relax a little.

Voiture was twenty-eight when in 1625 he was "born again" to a new life upon being presented by his friend Chaudebonne to the marquise. An indoor type himself, subject to colds and disliking bodily discomfort, he responded enthusiastically to this atmosphere of warm, joyous artifice. They recognized him, too, as a kindred spirit, and he was welcomed at once. From that moment the hôtel rang with the witticisms of this very superior court fool. He played his role well for the next twenty years; they came to call him *l'âme du rond*, the soul of the inner circle of lighthearted young people.

He was a commoner, more common than Malherbe or Balzac, who had both laid claim to a modest, lower-echelon gentility. Voiture made no secret of his plebeian origins, though he wanted nothing to do with them. His father was a well-to-do vintner who had not tried to press him into the family business. Voiture had also been to law school and found this career even less to his liking than selling wine. He preferred the life of a gentleman of letters. His idleness was modeled on that of his betters, but he was much smarter at it than they. He knew how to fill up his time and theirs with ingenious productions which teased and disturbed but did not upset them. He was a master of the most conventional and hollow of compliments to ladies, and could also balance on the edge of the ludicrous or the improper without ever falling in:

The Poets

*Stances à une demoiselle qui avait les manches
de sa chemise retroussées et sales:*

Vous qui tenez incessamment
Cent amants dedans votre manche:
Tenez-les au moins proprement,
Et faites qu'elle soit plus blanche.

Vous pouvez avecque raison,
Usant des droits de la victoire,
Mettre vos galants en prison;
Mais qu'elle ne soit pas si noire.

Mon coeur qui vous est si dévot,
Et que vous réduisez en cendre,
Vous le tenez dans un cachot,
Comme un prisonnier qu'on va pendre.

Est-ce que brûlant nuit et jour
Je remplis ce lieu de fumée
Et que le feu de mon amour
En a fait une cheminée? [1]

*(Stanzas to a young lady whose shirt-sleeves
were rolled up and dirty:*

You with the hundred lovers up your sleeve,
you could at least keep them there more neatly
if your sleeves were cleaner.

You can, of course,
by right of victory,
put all your admirers in prison,
but please, not such a black one.

My heart is all yours:
you've reduced it to ashes;
you keep it in a gloomy cell,
like a prisoner about to be hanged.

Can it be that, burning for you night and day,
I fill the place with smoke,
and the fire of my ardor
turns it into a chimney?)

He could whip up a poem on any absurdity: he wrote a sonnet to a lady whose skirt flew up when she fell out of her carriage; another to the consonants which do not have the honor to appear in the name of Neufgermain. His decorum was punctuated by occasional lapses of taste (they were deliberate) as in the poem where he pleads with his lady not for total gratification but just a few liberties:

> Je n'attends pas tout le contentement
> Qu'on peut donner aux peines d'un amant,
> Et qui pourrait me tirer de martyre.
> A si grand bien mon courage n'aspire.
> Mais laissez-moi vous toucher seulement
>   Où vous savez.[2]

> (I don't expect all the relief
> that could be given to a lover's pains,
> to save him from misery.
> My heart doesn't aim so high.
> Just let me touch you—you know where.)

His family "trade" background could be turned from a liability to an advantage too. Once a cruel nobleman accused him of being a nondrinker through shame at his father's business. Voiture promptly replied with a rondeau explaining that a drinker of plain water is likely to be a more successful lover than a man in his cups.

He was a little man, agile and talkative. Though not handsome, his sharp little face was as volatile as his wit. He spent a lot of time on that face before the mirror in the bachelor quarters across the street from the marquise where he took up residence with a pet crow and two fierce dogs. He wore cosmetics and perfumes and curled his hair. His clothes were as coquettish as a woman's. He was a dandy. And he was prepared to devote all his time to the celebration of women.

When Voiture came to the hôtel de Rambouillet the marquise was thirty-seven. He found her at the center of her world, lying on her bed, in her prime, a goddess, the divine Arthénice, remote yet approachable. She seemed happy and fulfilled, assisted by her teenage daughter Julie d'Angennes and eldest son the Marquis de Pisany, attended by her devoted if bumbling husband, surrounded by adoring guests. Many libertines circled around her hopelessly. Voiture, as hopeless as all the others, wrote ruefully:

There never was a woman so good at recognizing flirtatiousness and so bad at recognizing flirts.[3]

Voiture became, of course, a favorite victim of the girlish pranks of the Rambouillet set. Julie d'Angennes once dumped a bucket of water on his head, knowing he hated to get wet. A gentler and cleverer trick was devised by the marquise: a poem he has composed and recited for her is secretly bound in an anthology of someone else's works. The book is left open on a table where he will see it, and when he does he is embarrassed to find he has been guilty of unconscious plagiarism. When he discovers the trick he pays the marquise back by bringing two large bears into the *chambre bleue*, frightening the ladies out of their wits.

After Voiture came other bourgeois men of wit and learning to the *chambre bleue:* Chapelain and Conrart, the four Haberts, future fathers of the Academy, commoners with no social pretensions but mental gifts of the highest order. The numerous intellectuals of the Arnauld family came, to reason with the marquise about love and friendship. They mingled almost at their ease with gentlemen and ladies of quality. Still other writers of modest but indisputable nobility, Georges de Scudéry, Malleville, Desmarets, were just as pleased to get a foothold in the *chambre bleue* because of their literary talents.

When we read through the poetry they turned out for the ladies we are struck by its emotional unadventurousness, but at the same time by a certain glittering virtuosity. Love is its principal theme, paradox its favorite device. The lover is a being of little enterprise. He no longer urges the lady to seize the day, as more robust sixteenth-century poets and even Malherbe had done. He is content to remain on his knees forever. Or if he does invite her to surrender, as in the case of Voiture, he is understood to be half-joking. The madrigals of 1630–1650 give voice to an amorous despair that is all wit and play. The poet's devotion is no longer acceptable on its own; mere stubborn adoration is a bore. The poet must be eternally faithful, but now he must be clever about it:

> En vain je tâche de sortir
> Des fers qui m'ont l'âme enchainée;
> Je ferais mieux d'y consentir.
> La raison a beau publier
> Que de l'amoureuse folie
> Le seul remède est d'oublier;
> Le remède est ce que j'oublie,
> Si bien que le malheur qui cause mon souci
> Vient de n'oublier point et d'oublier aussi.[4]

(I try in vain to escape
the irons that enchain my soul;
I'd be better off accepting them.
It's all very well for reason to argue
that the only cure for love's madness
is to forget:
it's the cure itself that I'm forgetting;
thus my sorrow comes from both forgetting
and not forgetting.)

We are not surprised that the poetic taste of the hôtel moved away from the emphatic protestations of Henri iv's time, written on behalf of vigorous warriors who wanted something for their pains, to the heartless badinage of a poet who enjoyed writing love poems to please a lady's image of herself, but took his business elsewhere.[5] This evolution in taste was shaped partly by a change in the needs of the ladies, and partly by the exigencies of the Thirty Years' War. While their men went off to the battlefronts during the summer, these ladies were flattered and preened by bourgeois poets who stayed behind. Ultimately it was class—the warrior class being occupied half the year in combat while the scrivening class provided entertainment at home in the drawing room—which determined the nature of this literature. Poetry was firmly declassed. A high-born gentleman might put his hand to a madrigal, might even enjoy doing so and be proud of the result. But he would not think of printing it. Such professionalism was for the sons of notaries. And these latter, the professionals, could not aspire to the ladies' favors.

Voiture was an anomaly. Although a commoner, he refused to be a professional. He would not publish his poems. He preferred to let it be thought that the glory of his success at the *chambre bleue* was enough for him. He also took up a semimilitary, semidiplomatic employment in the entourage of Gaston d'Orléans, in an effort to associate himself more closely with the aristocracy. Snobbery colored his whole career. Yet he was never considered more than a clever servant by the gentry with whom he hobnobbed. Once when an acquaintance of the marquise was leafing through the posthumous volume of his poems and letters, and made the remark that he had really been quite a delightful writer, the marquise replied, with unconscious disdain, "Well, what do you think we all liked him for, his nobility or his looks?"

The Poets

There were affinities of temperament which cut across the class barriers at the *chambre bleue*. An invisible tug-of-war was always being fought there by the lively clique, consisting of Voiture and his protectors, the marquise's son Pisany and the Comte de Guiche, and the serious clique consisting of Chapelain and Conrart and their protector the Marquis de Montausier. Nobody won this war of temperaments, but the personal disputes of the poets who rallied around one group or the other provided almost as much entertainment as their works. Chapelain started a vapid quarrel over the *Suppositi* of Ariosto, which Voiture disliked. Julie d'Angennes, the arbitrator, opted for Voiture's opinion, and Chapelain had to pay up: a pair of gloves. But then Georges de Scudéry got into the act by writing a puerile *"défi"* (challenge) to Julie's camp.

The little quarrels were frequently interrupted by tours of duty at various fronts, when the noble patrons were not on hand to support their protégés. For however bright or lively the poets were, they needed the "real people" to make the final decisions.

In the end, it was always class that won. Voiture's poems and letters had all the gaiety on their side, but the Marquis de Montausier—whose laborious screeds from the battlefield fell limply on the cold heart of Julie d'Angennes—finally married the girl.

One wonders how the marquise could tolerate the serious clique. They were pedantic and humorless. Chapelain had all the bourgeois vices: avarice, greed, meticulousness. He was even rather dirty. But she owed him money. And Montausier, despite his dour countenance, was to be the financial mainstay of the marquise's declining years. He married Julie with virtually no dowry.

There were also wars within the warring camps. Voiture and the abbé Godeau, both of the frivolous camp, vied constantly to attract attention by proposing new literary games. When Voiture had established a vogue for the *rondeau* or the *ballade*, Godeau hit back with the *gloss* (an expansion of an existing poem, by writing a quatrain for each line) and the *bout-rimé* (a sonnet composed on a set of given end-rhymes, chosen expressly for their unrelatedness, to make the exercise more difficult). Such word games alternated with silly pastimes: Voiture brought back from a trip to Savoie a talent for tying knots in string which he could unravel easily. Before long everyone at the *chambre bleue* was tying knots.

Voiture was relieved of a troublesome rival when Godeau retired to the South of France finally to become the Bishop of Grasse.

77

But it was not long before he was threatened by another nuisance, the abbé Cotin, bringing a new game: the enigma.

> Je suis une nymphe invisible
> Qui fait de l'Air mon élément,
> Et qui ne serais plus sensible
> Si je n'avais point eu d'Amant;
> Encor ce bel objet me touche,
> J'en parle et je n'ai pas de bouche;
> Cent fois je meurs et revis en un jour,
> Et ceux qui, comme moi, sont martyrs de l'Amour,
> Me viennent me consulter au fort de leur martyre.
> Mais je leur donne un conseil décevant,
> Autant en emporte le vent,
> Et je ne leur dis rien que ce qu'ils me font dire.[6]

> (I am an invisible nymph.
> The Air's my element.
> I would have no feelings now
> if I hadn't had a Lover.
> I still love him.
> I speak of him and have no mouth.
> A hundred times a day I die and live again.
> Love's martyrs come
> and ask me for advice
> but I give them disappointing counsel:
> The wind could have said as much.
> I tell them nothing but what they make me say.)

The solution to this enigma: Echo.

Finally Voiture launched the *Metamorphosis* and got on top again. There was a heavy rain of metamorphoses, of Julie into a Diamond, of Mlle. Paulet into a Pearl, etc.:

> In that part of the world where the sun rises and
> precious stones rain down from Heaven, a Naiad was
> born miraculously. She was the most accomplished
> maiden the Gods had ever made.
> The sea had never seen anything so lovely, not
> even the day Venus was born. Neptune fell in
> love with her and made Thetis and all the nymphs
> of the ocean jealous. But tiring of her scorn,
> he changed her into a stone, which the Greeks
> call unique, or Diamond.
> As she had been incomparably beautiful, divinely

wise, and insensible, haughty and obstinate, the
stone too has a beauty which effaces all others,
and a fire which seems divine. It cannot be
broken by any force. It resists iron and fire,
and rises to the very heads of kings. As she
had been loved by all who knew her, all men,
great and small, love her still, and she is
desired by everyone. Indeed, Heaven and Earth
have produced nothing so perfect, and men know
nothing more precious.[7]

Meanwhile, the pedants were hard at work counterattacking. Chapelain began to read the paralyzing stanzas of his epic-in-progress, *La Pucelle*, to the nodding company in the late 1630s. For twenty years he was to labor at this monumental poem about Joan of Arc, giving out judiciously spaced bulletins on its progress. When at last *La Pucelle* was unveiled in 1656 she proved to be a dried-up old maid. She sank mercifully into oblivion like a stone in a pool. Elsewhere she would have to bear the cruel tavern songs and satires of Lignières and Boileau. But the hôtel protected its failures by wrapping them in silence.

In the 1640s, by which time the poets had become completely domesticated, a literary quarrel exercised the judgment of the regulars of the hôtel. Voiture and Malleville had both written several sonnets on the theme of the *belle matineuse*. This conventional type of poem says that the poet's lady, Philis, is more bright and beautiful in the early morning than the rising sun, who is astonished and resentful at finding himself thrown into the shade by her. Voiture wrote this version:

Des portes du matin l'amante de Céphale
Ses roses épandait dans le milieu des airs,
Et jetait sur les cieux nouvellement ouverts
Ces traits d'or et d'azur qu'en naissant elle étale,

Quand la nymphe divine, à mon repos fatale,
Apparut, et brilla de tant d'attraits divers
Qu'il semblait qu'elle seule éclairait l'univers
Et remplissait de feux la rive orientale.

Le soleil se hâtant pour la gloire des Cieux,
Vint opposer sa flamme à l'éclat de ses yeux
Et prit tous les rayons dont l'Olympe se dore;

L'onde, la terre et l'air s'allumaient à l'entour,
Mais auprès de Philis on le prit pour l'Aurore,
Et l'on crut que Philis était l'astre du Jour.[8]

(From the doors of morning Cephalus' lover [Dawn]
was spreading her roses across the sky,
and throwing against the heavens newly opened
those streaks of gold which announce her coming,

When the divine nymph appeared, she who is fatal
to my composure, and shone so seductively
that it seemed she alone lit up the universe,
and filled the eastern shore with fire.

The sun, hurrying to support Heaven's reputation,
came and matched his fire against the glitter of her eyes,
and used all the rays that gild Olympus.

The waves, the land, the air lit up all around,
but next to Philis, they took him for the Dawn,
and thought that Philis was the star of Day.)

And this was the best of the offerings of Malleville:

Le silence régnait sur la terre et sur l'onde,
L'air devenait serein et l'Olympe vermeil,
Et l'amoureux Zéphyre, affranchi du sommeil,
Resuscitait les fleurs d'une haleine féconde;

L'Aurore déployait l'or de sa tresse blonde,
Et semait de rubis le chemin du soleil;
Enfin ce Dieu venait au plus grand appareil
Qu'il soit jamais venu pour éclairer le monde,

Quand la jeune Philis au visage riant,
Sortant de son palais plus clair que l'Orient,
Fit voir une lumière et plus vive et plus belle.

Sacré flambeau du jour, n'en soyez point jaloux:
Vous parûtes alors aussi peu devant elle
Que les feux de la nuit avaient fait devant vous.[9]

(Silence reigned on land and sea,
the air was peaceful and Olympus glowing,
and amorous Zephyr released from sleep,
was waking up the flowers with his fertile breath.

Dawn spread the gold of her blond tresses,
and sowed the path of the sun with rubies;

at last the God appeared with the greatest retinue ever,
to light the earth.

Then young Philis, of gay countenance,
coming out of her palace brighter than the East,
brought forth a light more dazzling and beautiful.

Holy torch of the day, do not be jealous of her:
compared to her you looked as insignificant
as the lights of night had seemed before you.)

The exaggeration renders the theme so remote and unreal that we want to protest, as Shakespeare had done against the euphuists: "My mistress' eyes are nothing like the sun!" But in these poems the conventional compliment to the lady is too trite to be the main point. She is flattered, of course, but not by the literal meaning of the poem, which is too farfetched to be taken at face value. The poet's real gift to the lady is his ingenuity in fitting a pretty set of phrases into a demanding literary mold for her sake. The cleverness of the effort to renew the used-up theme of the beautiful early-rising nymph is the obvious secret of these sonnets, in a world where intellectual ingenuity counts more than real feeling.

But they have a deeper secret. Hidden in the conventional theme, obscured by the hard crystalline images, is a great elementary truth: the love of woman is a blinding force stronger than the force of the sun, a compulsion stronger than rational Apollo, who is the god of light and art, of culture and of all civilization. This shining fact of nature affirmed by the poet was a tremendous source of reassurance to the ladies who received such homage. Trapped as they were in the painful plight of their feminine liabilities, knowing themselves to be the real prisoners of sex, the real playthings of nature, what a triumph it was to hear the poet confess that *they were nature*.

Did they believe it? They certainly accepted the homage as if they thought it might be true. They were willing to be regarded as goddesses of nature, triumphing over the poet's· reason. But they did not behave as forces of nature; they were anything but instinctual, untrammeled, physical beings; they could not afford to be. Their disputes over the relative merits of these two poems have nothing to say about this secret meaning. The ladies treated both poems as though they were pocket mirrors in which to examine their own beautiful faces. This is why the imagery is so sharp and unsentimental (rubies, Dawn, golden tresses) and ultimately only a reflection of a highly civilized Philis.

This is a very expensive kind of literature. It sacrifices all spontaneity of form or feeling for the sake of a limited originality in the arrangement of words. The price is surely too high. But this was the kind of poetry the hôtel de Rambouillet needed. Its hidden affirmation of nature is buried deep under its burnished wit. Poetry had to be for these ladies an instrument of civilization, and civilization was felt to be something imposed on reality, rather than interpreting it. Civilization was not the control but the denial of the brute world of physical force and mindless instinct. It was a man-made, artificial construction, not transforming but covering up the uneven powerful earth on which it rested. It was a stage set. Dawn was the curtain, the sun a villain reduced to impotence; Philis, having taken over all the powers of the sun, a new kind of heroine shining on her audience with the luminous unseeing eyes of a Nature encased in the jewel-box of art.

Throughout the years of its heydey this salon exercised an unconscious tyranny over the men of letters who went there regularly. No writer could escape, because nearly every writer depended for his livelihood on the generosity of the rich and powerful. But also because *taste*—that is, the right to judge and dispose of a work of art—was the property of the aristocratic society which paid the poet. The writer was immersed in society. Artistic independence was not regarded by anyone as a virtue.

Official sanctions gained ground everywhere in these years. Malherbe had established narrow laws of prosody. Balzac had invented a well-proportioned prose style. Other disciplinarians were setting up the laws of the drama. When Richelieu created the Academy in 1635, a number of middle-class men of learning rather than talent found themselves in a position to enforce those laws. No individual poet could any longer afford to flout the combined strictures of his colleagues and his betters.

The case of Corneille illustrates this. Here was a poet of enormous energy and independence, already established on the Paris stage with half a dozen comedies to his credit. He took the town by storm with his heroic tragicomedy *Le Cid* in 1636. But despite its popularity, or rather because of it, the play earned the disapproval of the Academy. Some of the theatrical norms recently set up by authors of smaller merit had been disregarded by Corneille: the action of the play took more than one day; Chimène remained in love with Rodrigue, the murderer of her father. The Academy —those same Chapelains, Scudérys, Haberts, and Conrarts who frequented the *chambre bleue*—decided to publish an official rebuke to the poet. This act of literary despotism was prompted by the jealousy of Scudéry, the pedantry of Chapelain, the obscure machinations of Richelieu who needed a public discussion, at anyone's expense, to launch his newly formed fraternity of immortals. But ultimately it was a collective desire for form and limit, in art as in life, that made them blame *Le Cid*.

Naturally the quarrel of the *Cid* was closely followed at the hôtel de Rambouillet. Everyone who went there knew and loved Corneille's play, thrilled to the intransigence of the heroine and the hero's perfect chivalry. But no one questioned the fact that the play had broken the rules and should be punished. Amateur theatricals were popular in this circle, and the ladies of Rambouillet knew a thing or two about Aristotelian correctness as interpreted by the theoreticians of their own century. In the summer of 1636, at the château de Rambouillet, the ladies of the inner circle put on an impromptu performance of Mairet's *Sophonisbe*, with the help of the Arnauld brothers, hearty young officers on a brief leave from the front. This was the first French play to observe the dramatic unities strictly. They preferred it to *Le Cid*. Elegance of form won out over passion.

Balzac wrote Scudéry a letter, intended, of course, to be circulated at the hôtel de Rambouillet.[10] In it, he ingeniously praises Corneille and raps Scudéry on the knuckles while seeming to do just the opposite ("You won in the study; he won in the theatre"). The contradictions of artistic freedom and conformity were thus resolved for the Rambouillet circle. Corneille was both great *and* wrong. They eagerly awaited his next production to see if he had learned his lesson. After a suitable delay, Corneille's capitulation to the Academic censure was sealed in 1640: *Horace* and *Cinna* broke no rules. Balzac wrote joyfully to the author: "Where Rome was made of brick you have rebuilt it of marble!" This unqualified praise could now be freely given. The great Corneille was to struggle painfully for the rest of his life to fit his heroic visions into the tight receptacle of the Academy's rules.

But the quarrel of *Le Cid* was only his first, not his last humiliation. Corneille had a chance, in 1641, to give a reading of his next play, *Polyeucte*, to the company at the *chambre bleue*. They did not like the play, and told him so. No doubt his stolid middle-class personality, his lawyer's black, his hesitant delivery were not equal to the rich eloquence of his verses. But worse than that, these worldly ladies and gentlemen considered the play's religious theme inappropriate to a profane art like the theatre. The stark moral confrontation of the play—a story of early Christian martyrs overthrowing the established gods—was not designed to make these latter-day establishment Christians comfortable.

NOTES

1. Voiture, *Oeuvres*, ed. Ubicini (Charpentier 1855), II, p. 303.
2. Ibid., II, pp. 319–20.
3. Ibid., I, p. 176, letter 57, dated October 1633.
4. Claude Malleville, *Poésies* (1649–1664). Cited by Mongrédien in his anthology of précieux poetry, *Les Précieux et les précieuses* (Mercure de France, 1939), p. 231.
5. Voiture had a "backstreet" girlfriend, Mme. de Saintot, herself a literate precieuse, who requited him physically for all the mental courtship he engaged in at the *chambre bleue*.
6. L'abbé Cotin, in *Recueil des énigmes de ce temps* (1646–1655). Cited by Mongrédien, p. 241.
7. Voiture, II, pp. 269–70.
8. Ibid., II, p. 312.
9. Malleville, "La Belle Matineuse," in Mongrédien, p. 226.
10. *Lettres de Monsieur Jean Louis Guez de Balzac*, (1652), Book 3, letter 20, August 27, 1637, p. 132. Also Book 3, letter 9, January 17, 1643, p. 354.

The Ladies

Over the decades several dozen great and little feminine personalities were formed at the *chambre bleue*, and some stood out in the crowd. For the most remarkable of these ladies the *chambre bleue* was a springboard for their own further careers as hostesses. Mme. de Sablé started here, as well as Mlle. de Scudéry. Mme. de Longueville would appear here too in her turn, as a very young girl. We will meet them later on their own ground.

All the ladies aimed for a distinction comparable to that of the marquise, a distinction composed of serenity, detachment, and of course desirability. For it is of no use to be irreproachably virtuous unless there is somebody who wants you.

They cultivated uniqueness of judgment: one sang or danced well; another knew languages or wrote wonderful letters. Naturally their talents must be kept within the limits of amateurism. No public existed for their achievements beyond the range of a social gathering.

The trouble with such distinction is, as I have already mentioned, that when all have acquired it, it is no longer distinct. This was the ultimate dilemma of *préciosité*. The logic of their need to be remarkable in this airless context of the drawing room was to lead many ladies to bizarre and even ridiculous conduct. But for the moment, in the *chambre bleue* at least, the search for perfection through both conformism and diversity did not seem like an impossible reconciliation of opposites.

The ladies were all assumed to be of very high degree. But in actual fact a more mixed crowd appeared there. Money had become more powerful and was beginning to replace blood as the ultimate secret arbiter of human value. Moneyed families brought with them into the nobility the enterprise and intelligence that had made them rich. They soon acquired all the visible symbols of the higher caste, so that it was scarcely possible to tell the difference. But there was no comparable evolution in the outlook of the marquise. She never showed any eagerness to welcome the wives of lawyers and financiers—unless they were very interesting, like Mlle. Paulet, and then their common breed was forgotten.

The daughters of the marquise—Julie, the oldest, and later Angélique-Clarisse, the youngest—helped set the tone for two generations of guests. These girls belong to two distinct age groups. The older group, born within about ten years of the turn of the century, are the earliest known friends of the marquise and of Julie. The younger generation, born around 1620 or later, have a different outlook, are more agitated and independent, less loyal to the moderate marquise and her social style. This chapter deals with the older group.

Julie d'Angennes

Julie (1607–1671) grew up in the inner circle of the *chambre bleue*. Inevitably she became the spoiled darling of its older guests. She was witty and gracious, but not as gracious as her mother. She lacked the warmth and generosity of the marquise and was vain, self-important, and aggressively virtuous. There is something restless, perhaps even desperate about her rectitude. Every man in the room went through the motions of desiring her without hope, and she seems to have enjoyed the little jealousies that blew up around her. Voiture and the abbé Godeau (nicknamed "Princess Julie's dwarf," for he was even smaller than Voiture) competed for her favor, and she played one against the other. Twice untouchable through her virtue and her class, she was nevertheless something of a tease. Once she provoked Voiture to go so far as to kiss her on her bare arm. He was banished temporarily from the *chambre bleue* for this.

Julie had her pick of a wide range of eligible gentlemen for a husband, but her parents did not press the issue, and she was in no rush to get settled. In her twenties she became sensible of the charms of a handsome soldier, Hector, Marquis de Montausier, and it was thought by everyone that she might marry him. But another lady, a certain Mme. Aubry, had got there first and was having an affair with him. Mme. Aubry was a good-looking commoner who sang almost as well as Mlle. Paulet. She never quite made the grade socially with the Rambouillet set, but it was she who introduced Montausier there. He was in a sense her property, her ticket of admission. Before showing her prize at the hôtel she made the dashing cavalier correct his provincial Saintonge accent and smarten up his manners. She was ashamed of her liaison with him, and explained their private meetings by letting it be known that she planned to marry him to her own daughter.

Hector went away annually to the war, and on the long winter leaves in Paris he would resume his intimate relations with Mme. Aubry and flirt with Julie at the hôtel de Rambouillet. This went on for four years, but then Mme. Aubry became domineering and possessive and began to complain of imaginary infidelities. Julie, on the other hand, was trying to detach him from his mistress without coming down from her own high perch of maidenly dignity. The triangle was a source of amusement to others. Even Mme. de Rambouillet called Hector's dilemma by the name of "hell of Anastarax," after a hero of the *Amadis de Gaule* who was torn between the attentions of two ladies. And the little abbé Godeau once drew Hector's sword and pointed it at him, in a mock-heroic gesture, to defend the honor of Julie against the "party of Mme. Aubry." When the hôtel de Rambouillet played a malicious practical joke on Mme. Aubry, sending her an anonymous uncomplimentary madrigal in the middle of the night, she took offense and forbade Hector to go there again. He went anyway behind her back.

There was a fatality hovering about this handsome young ladykiller. Once Mme. de Rambouillet read his palm and found that he was about to be responsible for the death of a woman. Indeed, Montausier had by now wearied of the *bizarreries* of Mme. Aubry and jilted her. This upset the lady so much that "after a general confession she went to bed and died." This was in 1634. Julie was now twenty-seven. The chief obstacle between her and Hector was gone. But their union was never to be. Before leaving for the summer campaign of 1635 Hector told Julie that he would die and she would marry his brother. This sad romantic prediction came to pass. Hector fell in battle that very year.

His younger brother Charles assumed the title of Marquis de Montausier when Hector died. He too had courted Julie, but silently, with reverence and inexhaustible patience, in the shadow of the more glamorous Hector. He lacked his brother's sparkle but made up for it in persistence. He had fallen in love with Julie at first sight in 1631, filled with admiration for her selfless devotion at the bedside of her plague-stricken little brother. He did not hope to replace Hector in the heart of the unattainable Julie, but accepted the ungrateful role of devoted servant and yearned glumly after her for many years.

The culmination of Julie's hegemony as reigning queen of hearts was that sweet, fragile little document, the *Guirlande de Julie*, a typical product of the *chambre bleue* and perhaps its highest literary expression. The faithful Charles de Montausier spent seven years writing the madrigals of this *florilège* and pressing his friends for contributions. It is a garland of praises addressed to Julie by the rose, the poppy, the pansy, the tulip, and a dozen other flowers, each of which acknowledges that she is more beautiful than any flower:

> *La Tulipe flamboyante*
>
> Permettez-moi, belle Julie
> De mêler mes vives couleurs
> A celle de ces rares fleurs
> Dont votre tête est embellie:
> Je porte le nom glorieux
> Qu'on doit donner à vos beaux yeux.[1]
>
> (Permit me, lovely Julie
> to mingle my bright colors
> with that of those rare flowers
> which enhance your crown:
> I bear the glorious name
> that should be given to your eyes.)

It was finally presented to her on her thirty-fourth birthday in 1641, hand-painted and hand-lettered by the calligrapher Jarry and bound in a pretty blue cover. It contained sixty-two poems by various hands: Chapelain, Conrart, Colletet, Corneille, Godeau, the Haberts, Malleville, Racan, Scudéry, and the abbé Tallemant, Academicans all, who added their madrigals to those of Montausier. The gloomy marquis hoped to win Julie's hand by this manifesto of devotion, but he had to wait another four years and renounce his Protestant faith before she relented. She kept him at bay for a total of fourteen years. Why? Perhaps because of a lingering sentiment for the dead Hector. But also, no doubt, because she

La Guirlande de Julie
COURTESY OF THE BIBLIOTHÈQUE NATIONALE

preferred to be free to receive the homage of many men. And surely also because she could see from her mother's example that marriage could ruin your health. She held out for perpetual postponement, living the sentimental idyll her mother had been denied at the age of twelve.

And really, the *"mourants"* (those who were "dying" for her) were delightful. Voiture wrote her his most charming letters from abroad—wheedling, bantering letters, which partly masked and partly exposed his feelings for her:

Mademoiselle,

I've been reading all day long the letter you wrote to me at Midnight, and though I don't normally enjoy gifts sent to me at that hour, I received this one with more pleasure than I can say. After studying it thoroughly, I do not believe it was written in your sleep. It confirms my former judgment of you, namely that this is the hour when you are most awake, most alive, most intelligent. In searching out the reason for this, I am far from suspecting anything evil in you, Mademoiselle, or observing that it is strange that the hour of goblins should be yours too.

I prefer to believe that there can be no night in your mind, but that, as it is a source of light, the darkness which obscures the minds of others cannot affect yours. When others are under its blanket, you shine more brightly, and the shadow of the earth cannot reach the stars of your wit.[2]

Charles de Montausier could not muster that kind of chatty homage. He brooded morosely on his love-inflicted wounds and was not witty or clever about them, precisely because they were real. In the thick of battle he wrote her long letters giving no news whatever about the interesting war he was fighting. His battlefield is a forsaken "desert" because she is not there.

And why, in the end, did Julie consent to marry Charles? Many of her friends encouraged her. Even Mazarin and the queen regent became interested in his suit and spoke to her on his behalf. At last the marquise, whose opinion she valued more than any other, advised her to accept him. Financial pressure was certainly a factor. Suddenly Julie made up her mind. She was getting old anyway, and would soon cease to hold sway among the new swarm of pretty girls twittering in the *chambre bleue*. She had a genuine *précieux* aversion to marriage and would have preferred to remain single if the role of Diana, untouchable virgin-goddess, could have gone on forever.

The Montausier wedding was a major society event in 1645. It took place at Ruel, the country estate of Richelieu's niece, and everybody who mattered socially was invited. The ceremony was performed by the little Bishop of Grasse, Godeau, who had for so long been "Julie's dwarf."

Tallemant tells us that the marriage was consummated with dispatch and the rest of the wedding night passed in verbal exchanges of poetic sentiments. This may be true, but the disenchantment set in soon after. After fourteen years on his knees before a beautiful and unattainable goddess, Montausier woke up to find himself married to a middle-aged witch. She was three years older than he and had never been remarkable for her sweetness. Now she became a sinister gossip, a puller of strings, having secrets with everybody. Montausier took her away to the province of Angoulême where he was governor, but could not keep her there for long. She came back to Paris when she liked, sometimes for a year at a time.

Despite these absences, and her age, she had children. Two boys died in infancy. A little girl was born at a cost of great suffering to Julie. A miraculous relic, the belt of Saint Catherine, had to be sent for to ease the agony of this long and difficult delivery. She had no more children after that.

In her fifties, Mme. de Montausier was appointed official governess of the legitimate children of Louis xiv. Her husband became the tutor of the dauphin. This appointment was the triumph of Julie's social life, for by this time the court of the handsome young Sun King had made great advances in elegance and splendor over the previous reign. Montausier was now made a duke. She sat in the presence of the queen.

But Saint-Simon tells us that she played an undignified part in the liaison of Louis xiv with Mme. de Montespan, supporting the lady against her husband and furthering the royal relationship.[3] Mme. de Montausier replaced the pious Mme. de Navailles as maid of honor of the young queen Marie-Thérèse, because her predecessor had refused to allow the king into the women's apartments at night. Mme. de Montausier was a more willing accomplice in the king's adventures. Street songs of the period confirm this:

> La Montausier passe pour maquerelle
> A notre grand roi Louis de Bourbon;
> Elle voudrait lui fournir une Pucelle
> Mais dans ce temps où diable en trouve-t-on?[4]

RAMBOUILLET

(They say La Montausier is the procuress
Of our great king Louis de Bourbon.
She'd like to find him a Virgin
But where the devil do you find one these days?)

A most inglorious end for a lady whose own youth had been one long refusal of love.

Angélique Paulet

A perennial fixture of the inner circle of beautiful prudes at the *chambre bleue* was Mlle. Paulet (1592–1651), *"la lionne,"* a lady famous for her mane of fiery red hair, like a lion's, her extremely white skin, her marvelous singing voice, and her iron respectability.[5]

It had not always been so. Many old-timers could remember the night in 1609 when she caused a sensation as a very young girl singing in the ballet of *Arion*. Everyone knew of her intimacies with Henri IV.

She was the daughter of an infamous administrator who had introduced the hated tax called after him *La Paulette*. This tax tithed the jobs of the upper bourgeoisie every time they changed hands, and resulted in the worsening of the practice of selling important financial and judiciary posts to the highest bidder, irrespective of merit. Paulet had made an enormous fortune out of this traffic and left it all to Angélique, his only daughter.

Angélique had begun a long series of love affairs quite early in life by sleeping with all three sons of the late Duc de Guise. At the Louvre one night the eldest Guise was said to have left a boot behind when departing from her chamber in a hurry by the window. She was also the mistress of Bellegarde and the Duc de Termes, his younger brother, and Montmorency. These were arrogant lovers, typical of Henri's Louvre, very noble and very uncouth. When a young provincial gentleman, Pontac, began courting Angélique with a view to marriage, Termes had him beaten up in the street. After this scandal Mlle. Paulet decided she had better have nothing more to do with Termes. Her reputation sank to a low ebb when the king's fool, Maître Guillaume, circulated a double-edged burlesque on the Pont-Neuf: *"La Paulette est-elle renversée?"* ("Has the Paulette [the tax *or* the daughter] been overthrown?")

Mlle. Paulet

Mme. de Rambouillet was drawn to Mlle. Paulet by her musical talent but refused to invite the girl until her name at least had been whitewashed. This was accomplished by the protection of an irreproachable matron, Mme. de Clermont, who took Angélique under her wing despite the objections of her husband. A conspicuous conversion, coinciding with the loss of most of Mlle. Paulet's fortune in the early 1620s, also helped. But not everyone was taken in by the elaborate piety displayed by this lovely hypocrite. Maynard, for example, tells her, in his *Priapées*, to stop pretending to be such a saint, for her provocative body movements give the lie to this pretense.[6] Of course, this poem was not written for the *chambre bleue*.

The pendulum had a long way to swing. Mlle. Paulet had several more lovers, even descending for a time to a dry-goods merchant; but there was no more loose talk about her, and Mme. de Rambouillet accepted her on that basis. She even welcomed her in a specially warm way the first time Mlle. Paulet came to visit at the château de Rambouillet. A bevy of flower-decked maidens of the village presented her with the key to the castle.

Once she decided to become a real prude, Mlle. Paulet grew extremely severe toward loose women, saying they ought to have their faces branded. She sent a pregnant servant girl to the Madelonnettes (a reform convent for wayward wenches), and replaced her with another maid uglier than the devil. She was without pity for any sort of feminine frailty.

Now safely on the path of virtue, Angélique took Godeau, the tiny Bishop of Grasse, into her home and thereafter began to be called "Mme. de Grasse." The Cardinal de La Valette was another swain, and she was laughingly called his mistress. But by now there was no breath of scandal attached to the arrangement.

When Voiture went on his travels in Spain and Africa in the service of his master Gaston d'Orléans, it was Mlle. Paulet who agreed to send him the news of the *chambre bleue* in a regular letter to which the other habitués added postscripts. From Africa he wrote to tell her he was greeting her "relatives," the lions of Lybia, and he sent her a present of several lions carved in red wax.

[I hope] you will receive [them] with more gentleness and pity than you usually show, and I think you will not find it unworthy of you to become the refuge of exiled lions.[7]

But during his absence Mlle. Paulet was courted by others, and when he returned he let his jealousy show in quarrelsome scenes which almost wrecked their friendship. Perhaps the fact that she was a commoner like himself, with a spotty past, made him entertain illusions about his chances with her which were out of the question with Julie d'Angennes. The absence of the class barriers probably made her inaccessibility more tantalizing to the fickle poet. Voiture went on trying, and with each new literary genre he made fashionable he would address himself to her:

Metamorphosis of Angélique into a Pearl

In the forest of Erimanthe lived Orcade, who was exposed from birth to savage beasts and brought up by them. She had a human face, a divine wit, and a savage heart. Love never served anyone as well as it served her, and never had a greater enemy. She killed all those she glanced at, and soon had done more murders than the bears and lions who raised her.

But the Gods, offended by her cruelties, wanted to save the men she would destroy and turned her into a pearl, which still has the purity and whiteness of her skin, throwing others in the shade. All the other precious stones are wedded to gold; only this one does without it and links herself only to her own kind. She is the most polished and pleasant work of heaven. For we see that pearls always clutch at the throats of those who wear them, and can only be dissolved by vinegar, as a memento of their former activities.[8]

Chapelain tried to cap this by writing a *Metamorphosis of Angélique into a Lion*:

Once there was a Nymph whose character was as savage as her body was beautiful. Her name was Angélique and among the perfections showered upon her by Nature were an invincible courage and an excellent singing voice. War was her passion and music her pastime. She dreamed only of blood and killing and her only regret was that she had not been born in the Age of the Amazons.[9]

Angélique was, to judge by these authors' laments, the cruel virgin par excellence. She exemplifies that curious dichotomy between bad women, who were very bad indeed, and good ones, who were good to the point of madness. If one had been a very bad woman, one had to behave in the *chambre bleue* as a particularly good one. Extremes call forth their opposites. When sexual chastity is the only index of a woman's value, she is driven to extremes of depravity or maniacal virtue. She cannot compromise. She must choose, either to be a beast or an angel.

But then, having chosen to be an angel, the woman is looked upon as another kind of beast, a ferocious dragon of virtue. *"La Lionne"* is reproached by the poets because her refusal makes men bleed. She is a pitiless vampire. This is of course meant to be an artful compliment to her strong character, but it still calls her a beast.

Mlle. Paulet, having already suffered the condemnation of society for her loose morals, was forced to make the choice of virtue. She made it with a vengeance. She saw to it that plenty of men were wounded by her claws.

She was the most prominent bourgeois personality among the women at the hôtel de Rambouillet, the only one who achieved any importance there without the advantage of birth. Her extraordinary life spans two worlds: she went from the brash court of Henri, where love was a quick cash deal and consummated on the most elemental level, to the rare world of Rambouillet, where intellectual pleasures replaced the rude sports of Henri, where love was a perpetual courtship and the elegant attitudes of unfulfilment were immortalized in the fragile verses of Voiture.

Mme. d'Aiguillon

Another formidable lady of this older generation is Mme. d'Aiguillon (1605–1675), Richelieu's niece.[10] She was born Marie de Vignerot, married against her will to the Marquis de Combalet at age fifteen, and widowed a year later. When Combalet died, she took Carmelite vows, fearing to be forced into another marriage of state. She dressed like a widow of fifty, although a very pretty girl, and never raised her eyes. Gossip went around that her marriage had never been consummated, and she herself promoted this belief by carrying a coat-of-arms of diamond shape—that is, a virgin's rather than a widow's symbol. The poet Dulot made an anagram on her name: *Marie de Vignerot: vierge de ton mari* (left a virgin by your husband).[11] However, Tallemant says that her husband was known to be extremely well-endowed sexually, *"un grand abatteur de bois"* ("a great feller of trees"), and rumor had it that Combalet had even once called in a valet to watch the act. In sum, everyone laughed at the idea of Mme. de Combalet being a

MADAME LA DVCHESSE DAIGVILLON.

L'ingenieux Graueur auec vn foible traict,   Ses hautes qualitez qu'vn chascun doit louer,
Ne peut bien mettre au jour dedans cette figure, Comme dons qu'a du Ciel tirent leur origine,
L'admirable Beauté dont tu vois le portrait,   Produisent des effets qui nous font aduoüer,
Qui'n nous representant la Vertu toute pure,   Que dans vn si beau Corps loge vne Ame diuine.

le Blond excud.   Auec Priuilege.

Mme. d'Aiguillon
COURTESY OF THE BIBLIOTHÈQUE NATIONALE

virgin. The sober Montglat says in his memoirs that Richelieu tried to "marry Monsieur to Combalet's widow, his niece, who has recently become a virgin again." [12] Richelieu did indeed favor this match between his niece and Gaston d'Orléans, at a time when Monsieur seemed the most likely successor to the crown. If Mme. de Combalet was going to be queen of France, she had better be a virgin.

Whatever the facts, when her uncle became all-powerful in 1630 she changed her style, threw off her widow's weeds, and began to paint her face. Some said outright that she was Richelieu's mistress, sharing him with Mme. de Chaulnes and the courtesan Marion de Lorme. There was the incident of the bottles of ink thrown at Mme. de Chaulnes in her carriage. The lady narrowly missed being scarred for life. It appears that this attack was a warning from Mme. de Combalet acting from jealousy.

And yet we must leave in doubt the existence of a carnal liaison between Richelieu and his niece. She certainly spied for him at the hôtel de Rambouillet; she furthered his literary efforts by finding ghost writers for his memoirs. She pacified him in his jealous rages against Anne of Austria. Her intimacy with the cardinal gave her political power, and this probably attracted her more than his diseased old body. Richelieu repaid her loyalty with the rich duchy of Aiguillon in 1638, after which she became known by this name.

Everyone at the hôtel de Rambouillet treated Mme. d'Aiguillon with kid gloves. Voiture addressed conventional love letters and poems to her not because he liked her, but because he thought Richelieu might yet succeed in pulling off a marriage between her and Gaston, who was Voiture's own master. One poem in praise of her shoe alludes clearly to this marriage project:

> Le pied qui cause ma peine
> Et qui me tient sous sa loi
> Ce n'est pas un pied de roi,
> Mais plutôt un pied de reine:
> Car je vois dans l'avenir
> Qu'il le pourra devenir.[13]

> (The foot that causes my distress,
> the foot beneath which I cringe,
> is not a king's foot,
> but rather that of a queen,
> for I can see that in the future
> it might become just that.)

Gaston never did succeed his brother, for Louis XIII finally produced not one but two sons. And Mme. d'Aiguillon never got married again. She did not like men anyway. The evidence is strong that her relationship with another lady, the Baroness du Vigean, was much more than a friendship. Passionate letters were exchanged and unmistakeable gestures noticed by their friends.[14] Evidently this lady's virginity, if any, was a mere technicality.

In later years she grew avaricious and excessively devout. "She gives to the church and doesn't pay her debts," says Tallemant sourly. "She has spent whole nights prostrated before the altar at Saint-Sulpice. They say that now, 1659, she scrapes the unused sugar off her dessert plates."

The abbé Boisrobert told Tallemant of his frequent requests to her for a parish, which she always put off. Suspecting deliberate ill-will, he asked her one day for the priory at Kermassonnet. "Oh my poor dear Monsieur de Boisrobert, I am so sorry! If only you had come two hours sooner you would have had it." He answered, "I wouldn't be any better off, Madame, because this priory is no more in your power to give than the moon . . . It doesn't exist. Thank you however for your kindness. I am more convinced than ever of your sincerity and good faith." This rejoinder is a bit too satisfying to ring perfectly true. But it is true that Mme. d'Aiguillon was influential at court, even after Richelieu died. She secured for Montausier the governorship of Saintonge and Angoumois, and also got the direction of the Abbaye d'Yerres for three of the Rambouillet daughters. She tried to get a post for Georges de Scudéry. She gave a part of her lucrative monopoly of the public transport of Paris as a wedding gift to Julie d'Angennes. This was a substantial part of Julie's meager dowry. Perhaps Mme. d'Aiguillon was not all that stingy.

Her piety was very real in later years. She was noted for the pompous remark, *"Ah, ma chère, ça donne dévotion!"* When Julie was contemplating marriage to Montausier, Mme. d'Aiguillon urged her on. "Dear child, dear child, there's nothing like it in the sight of God; it will make you pious."

This rich and influential lady strikes us as having been born old, though she was only two years older than Julie. She must have been a sinister presence at the hôtel de Rambouillet, with her political ambitions and her secret reports to her uncle. Perhaps the family were glad to include her in their circle of intimates as a kind of insurance against the cardinal's attention.

Her extant letters show that she was literate and intelligent. Corneille dedicated *Le Cid* to her. But she did not defend the author against the persecutions of her uncle and the Academy. And she let Richelieu's wonderful library run down out of neglect. She never bothered to finish his tomb.

Mme. du Vigean

The Baroness du Vigean, who was Mme. d'Aiguillon's closest friend (and perhaps more), also became well known at the hôtel de Rambouillet as a lady of taste and merit. She was very rich, and the poets flattered her carefully, Voiture above all:

> La belle baronne darde
> De ses yeux mille trépas;
> Mais dites, n'a-t-elle pas
> La mine un peu gaillarde?
> Je pense que sa vertu
> A bien souvent combattu.[15]

> (The beautiful baroness's eyes cause
> a thousand deaths.
> But say, don't you think
> she has a rather provocative glance?
> I bet her virtue has often
> been put to the test.)

Mme. du Vigean became famous at the *chambre bleue* for her modesty. She went against the décolleté fashion, wearing instead covered-up necklines. Once Mlle. Paulet plucked the "*mouchoir*" off her bosom, revealing to the whole company that she had hidden charms as appealing as anyone else's. It is interesting that this lady was teased for being more proper than was really necessary. For what, then, are we to make of the whispered talk about her peculiar relations with Mme. d'Aiguillon? Her public image and private secrets do not seem to match at all. Notwithstanding, she was included in the excursions to the château de Rambouillet, and often returned the compliment by inviting the Rambouillet family to her own lavish country estate at La Barre. Voiture, no doubt eager to be invited too, caressed her vanity by drawing an age-old comparison:

Baronne, pleine de douceur,
Etes-vous mère, êtes-vous soeur
De ces deux belles si gentilles
　　Qu'on dit vos filles?

Vous avez l'humeur, ce dit-on,
D'un doux et paisible mouton;
Mais votre peau blanche et très fine
　　Est d'une ermine.[16]

(Sweet baroness,
are you the mother or the sister
of those pretty girls
　　they call your daughters?

They say you have the temperament
of a soft and gentle lamb,
but your skin is white as an ermine's.)

La Princesse de Condé

But perhaps the most dazzling of the older ladies at the *chambre bleue* was Charlotte, Princesse de Condé (1593–1651) [17]—the same Charlotte de Montmorency who as a girl of sixteen had driven Henri IV mad for love in his old age. She grew even more beautiful with the years, despite a severe case of smallpox which left her temporarily disfigured, and a perfectly miserable married life. (She had married the Prince de Condé in 1609.) She became the famous one by whose standard other girls were measured. At the *chambre bleue*, they said, "So-and-so is almost as beautiful as (or more beautiful than) the princesse."

Her husband, having carried her off to Flanders out of Henri's reach, returned with her to Paris right after the assassination, with his honor intact. But new troubles were in store for her. This haughty prince remembered that he had once been heir to the throne, when Henri had no legitimate children. It was a bitter pill for him to swallow when the crown passed into the hands of the dauphin Louis, his nine-year-old cousin. Condé inevitably plotted against the regent, bungled the job, and by 1616 was locked up in Vincennes prison. There were as yet no Condé children and no one expected there would be any, for the prince was a notorious sodomite. Charlotte, however, demanded permission to go to prison with her husband, pointing out to the queen-regent that her chances of continuing the name of Condé were being thwarted by the separation. Permission was granted. She then lived with her husband in the Bastille for a little over two years, during which time—such are the pleasures of seclusion—she was almost continually pregnant. One premature child did not live; a pair of twins also died; and finally a daughter was born, Anne-Geneviève de Bourbon-Condé, who survived. Another child was conceived in prison and born in 1621, shortly after the prince's release. This was the Duc d'Enghien, later to become the glory of France in war as the Grand Condé. Another son, the Prince de Conty, was to be born in 1629 to this inauspicious marriage. Thereafter relations between the Prince de Condé and his wife cooled to below the point of indifference. They actively disliked each other. But Charlotte remained submissive to his decisions, as in fact she had to. Naturally, Condé did not go to the hôtel de Rambouillet. He had no time for genteel patterns of respect for womanhood; he was busy with his pages. He treated Charlotte and his children with distant authority, a cold, proud man absorbed in his dynasty.

Charlotte's life had been full, but it was not over. She now became the object of the long-term devotion of a soldier-prelate, the Cardinal de La Valette, who came daily to feast himself on her presence at the *chambre bleue*. La Valette's speech was sometimes too free for the ears of the Rambouillet ladies, but the marquise was very fond of him and he belonged to the inner circle, an intelligent enfant terrible like Voiture, though far above the poet in rank. La Valette was a very ugly man, swarthy of skin and with thick lips hardly hidden by his beard. His weather-beaten complexion earned him the nickname of *"Scipion l'Africain."* But Charlotte de Condé was fascinated by him and found him infinitely more amusing than the prince. He even liked to get down on the floor and play with Charlotte's children, and once spent two thousand écus on a doll house, fully furnished with beds and chairs, right down to the underclothes of the dolls, for the little daughter of the princess. He gaily squandered nearly all his fortune on Charlotte.

This libertine cardinal was curiously also a link to power. La Valette had performed a service for Richelieu which earned him the protection of the cardinal-minister for his lifetime. It was in 1630 at the time of the *Journée des Dupes* (see note 1, p. 55). Richelieu had abandoned all hope of regaining the upper hand in the government and had his bags packed and his boat ready to sail up the Seine to a quiet retreat at Le Havre-de-grace. All his friends had left him. He was alone in his house at Pontoise. La Valette came to see him and argued vehemently against this withdrawal. Richelieu was convinced by his reasoning, and decided to go back to the king's hunting lodge at Versailles instead of up the river to oblivion. This decision tipped the scales. Louis was won over again, Richelieu's enemies were the "dupes," and the cardinal continued on as first minister of France.

La Valette had saved his career. Nevertheless, there is a cloud over the friendship of the two cardinals. Richelieu spied on La Valette. He sent his *éminence grise,* the père Joseph, on a special visit to the hôtel to ask the marquise to report on the liaison between the Cardinal de La Valette and the Princess de Condé. Mme. de Rambouillet replied with supreme tact, "Father, I do not believe the princess and the cardinal are having an affair, but even if they were, I would not make a very good spy." [18]

The relations between the princess and the cardinal were, however, honorable only on the surface. They went out of their way to leave doors open so that their private conversations could be seen by everyone to be innocent. But after a long courtship La Valette finally overcame the princess's resistance—by a ruse which amounted to sentimental blackmail. Finding himself refused by the princess again and again, he went to a pesthouse to expose himself to death. He sent her a farewell letter from this place, and she was so upset by this histrionic gesture that she felt compelled to save his life by acquiescing in his suit.

The ladies of the *chambre bleue* whispered this story discreetly behind their fans, while resolutely denying it in a louder voice. But out in the street, in the hurly-burly of the Pont-Neuf and the taverns, more malicious tongues were shouting their resentment of the *chambre bleue* and all it stood for:

> La Combalet et la Princesse
> Ne pensent point faire du mal,
> Et n'en iront point à la confesse,
> D'avoir chacune un cardinal.
> Car laisser lever leur chemise
> Et mettre ainsi leur corps à l'abandon
> N'est rien que se soumettre à l'église
> Qui, en tout cas, leur peut donner pardon.[19]

(Mme. de Combalet and the Princesse [de Condé]
don't think they're doing anything wrong
and will not have to go to confession
just because they are each having affairs
    with cardinals.
For letting such men lift their skirts,
and offering them their bodies,
is simply submitting to the church,
which in any case will give them absolution.)

Mme. de Clermont-d'Entragues

The hôtel de Rambouillet harbored more than its share of eccentrics and nitwits among the ladies who came there to be amused. When we look under the blanket of decorum we see a splendid array of personal quirks. Nobody was allowed to commit bad manners, but anybody could be crazy. Mild and serious forms of delusion and mania were tolerated, as well as the most shocking ignorance. Many of the ladies could scarcely read; many were unaware of the elementary facts of life, and seem to have thought, like Molière's Agnès, that babies came out of your ears. They were sheltered in their foolishness, and only very gently chaffed by the more sophisticated.

The Comtesse de Clermont-d'Entragues, that unattractive, charitable lady who had taken Mlle. Paulet under her roof and restored the girl's good name, was always, according to Tallemant, "running to church and always falling asleep there; then she could not sleep all night. They say she has been to more sermons and heard less of them than anyone else in the world." This pious lady had her first child without realizing what was happening to her. She felt slightly ill one day, sent for an apothecary who discovered she was pregnant, sent for a midwife, and immediately the baby was born, healthy and whole, to her husband's astonishment.

These few elder *habituées* of the *chambre bleue* are not the only noteworthy ones, but they demonstrate in a special way how Mme. de Rambouillet organized her society and even created a new feminine type. Literature was the most useful tool in this creation; but it had to be literature of a certain kind. A giant such as Corneille was not really suitable, although his plays did provide model heroines to feed the fantasies of women. Serious lesser authors like Malherbe and Balzac were better. They gave shape to language and elevated the tone of conversation in the salon. But Malherbe was too crusty, Balzac too far away in Angoulême, to be the real heroes of the *chambre bleue*. That hero was Voiture, the master of the light touch, the inexhaustible flatterer, the devoted clown. Voiture helped the women towards self-definition by constantly telling them, in ways that were always fresh and new, how wonderful they were. Even when he did it with tongue in cheek, they loved him for it. His very refusal of seriousness was a kind of extra bonus of clever complicity: if he did not mean all he said, neither were they taken in. They were above flattery anyway, and did not need to believe his hyperboles.

And yet they did believe him. They believed all the poets who had consecrated their pens to the service of women. These poets helped them create an essence they could not have created by themselves, an essence more significant to them than the embarrassing facts of their actual lives as observed by realists like Tallemant. Thus, Mlle. Paulet was not a former call girl of Henri IV, she was "*La Lionne*," the essence of pride. And Julie d'Angennes was not a selfish aging flapper, she was metamorphosed into a diamond or a pearl, everlasting, inorganic, perfect.

These first précieuses were the first women to identify themselves, as a society, in terms of an idealizing literature which turned them to stone and made them immortal and priceless.

Mme. de Rambouillet, the guiding spirit in this notion of reality, achieved a remarkable feat in forcing her society to accept it. The world out in the street was cold and violent; poetry readings in the *chambre bleue* were peaceful and enlightened. She kept out the dark night, the passions, the yearning for the infinite. She put in their places the rituals of order, the conventional expression of unfelt sentiments, the flexing of wits in a strict framework of house rules.

The futility of the pastimes of her salon can be quite irritating. It is shocking to think that Voiture's little feathery *rondeaux* were generally preferred by her guests to the plays of Corneille. These people had good taste, but their vanity interfered with their appreciation of depth. The idea of civilization proposed by the hôtel de Rambouillet and its stable of poets made for self-indulgence on the part of the participants, rather than any sort of energetic assault on their environment. They wanted insulation. Their poetry closed them into themselves.

Yet real life (that is, death) was just outside the door, and occasionally sneaked in. The marquise suffered her share of calamities, no matter how many poets told her she was safe. Of her seven children, two were males. The first was the Marquis de Pisany, who suffered in childhood a dislocation of the spine that crippled him for life. Although his birthright as the first-born son was the family name and fortune, his disability canceled all that. He had become a hunchback, small, twisted, and ugly. He was fit only for the church. A gaily sociable and lusty young man, he considered the clerical life a prospect worse than death, and so, although he could barely sit on a horse, he went off to the wars with all the other brave young sons of the sword. He tried to compensate for his deformity by reckless prowess on the battlefield, and died at the battle of Nordlingen in 1645, in his mid-thirties.

Mme. de Rambouillet's only other son, the little Vidame du Mans, had been stricken long before, in 1631, at the age of eight, with a disease they called the plague (though it may have been cholera) and died. He had caught the disease from a nursemaid who had visited a pest house, brought the infection back to the hôtel with her, and died of it also. Is it hard for us to understand the need for an illusory order, symmetry, a ritualized synthetic art in a world where even the beloved son of the most elegant woman in Paris could die of a disease associated with ignorance and dirt? Civilization was a very thin crust at best. Outside the twinkling drawing room where chandeliers flickered on stiff satin sleeves and heads and hands moved in solemn obedience to orders from the mind, outside in the slimy, malodorous alleys of the night, thieves lurked, babies were abandoned, knives slipped into hapless hearts, and nameless illnesses worked in the entrails of men.

Perhaps the worst feature of the Rambouillet atmosphere was not the domestication of the poets but the snobbery shared by all who had any pretensions to social position, and accepted by all who had none. The marquise herself encouraged this. She kept a deep sense of her tribal superiority to the end of her days. Tallemant des Réaux, that distant cousin of her husband who listened sympathetically to the reminiscences of her old age, tells us that "she is a little too much persuaded, to say no worse, that the house of

Savelli was the best in the world." It was this conviction about her-self that made it possible for Mme. de Rambouillet to entertain not only high-caste nobility in her home, but also interesting members of the bourgeoisie. Her own rank was so far beyond theirs that it could not be compromised by association with ordinary people. The belief in one's innate superiority was always unspoken here; perhaps it was therefore more insidious. Voiture could chat with the Duc d'Enghien, the future Grand Condé, on terms of apparent insolent familiarity, as in the much-cited "lettre de la carpe au brochet":

Well if it isn't my old pal the Pike! I always suspected that the waters of the Rhine wouldn't stop you. And knowing your strength and how you like to swim in hot water, I knew you wouldn't be frightened and would glide through them as gloriously as you've gone through so many other adventures. . . . Though you've been excellent in all sauces so far, I must say that Sauce Allemande gives you a special flavor and the laurel will make you tastier still. . . . However, now that your fame has gone about as far as it can, why don't you come back to the waters of the Seine and refresh yourself joyously here with all the pretty minnows, perches, and gentle trout that are waiting for you so impatiently? [20]

And he could get away with it. The young prince merely shrugged off such overfriendly advances, saying, "If Voiture were of our class he would be insufferable." Maynard or Malleville might be Julie d'Angennes' "*soupirants*" (sighing suitors) just as well as the Marquis de Montausier, provided their poems of praise were couched in terms of utter self-abasement and no real passion was ever hinted at. But the invisible line between art and real feeling must never be crossed. It is not surprising that Voiture and Godeau, the favorites among the merry literary clowns, were physically small: they were playthings, toy poodles, teddy bears; unsexed and unthreatening. Once, toward the end of his life, Voiture made the mistake of challenging Chavaroche, the steward of Mme. de Rambouillet's household, to a duel in the garden, because he was jealous of the other man's attentions to Angélique-Clarisse, the youngest Rambouillet daughter. For his presumptuousness, and be-cause of the scandal he might have caused, Voiture was banished from the house. The Rambouillets had been entertained by Voiture for twenty years; they listened with delight to his lover's moans; they passed around his letters full of cleverly worded adoration.

But they could not tolerate that he should really desire their daughter. And so they turned him out.

This rupture occurred in 1646–47. Julie d'Angennes had already married Charles de Montausier in 1645 and gone away to Angoulême with him. In that same year the Marquis de Pisany was killed. This was the end of the most brilliant period of the hôtel de Rambouillet.

The world outside was changing, too. Louis and Richelieu had passed away. A new regency, a new cardinal, had taken over. Relief at the disappearance of Richelieu gave way to dissatisfaction and resentment of Mazarin, and this resentment began to spread to all classes. A terrible civil war, the Fronde, was just around the corner, about to burst on the city of Paris, suspending the free circulation of society for five years. But the Marquise de Rambouillet did not close her doors altogether. Throughout the late forties and early fifties the thinning ranks of old faithfuls kept on coming to the *chambre bleue.*

After the Fronde, the 1650s would bring a new wave of middle-class salons which sprang up all over town. The *"bonne régence"* of Anne and the handsome young Louis XIV (he was fifteen when the Fronde came to an end) brought a new genteel gaiety to the court, attracting the fresh crop of highborn young girls to the Palais-Royal. Other hostesses, such as Mmes. Fouquet and Du Plessis-Guénégaud, learned to entertain magnificently. But the hôtel de Rambouillet was still glorious enough to attract a young matron, Mme. de La Fayette and her girlfriend, the widowed Mme. de Sévigné. These ladies were later to move on to other circles, but in the fifties and even early sixties, right up to the death of the divine Arthénice in 1665, they were glad to be seen at the hôtel, silhouetted against the faded and shabby, but still elegant, blue tapestries.

The hôtel de Rambouillet was a cultural landmark in the history of France. What made it so? When we look at it more closely, the entertainments offered by the marquise resemble nothing so much as the parlor games we would today associate with a Victorian girls' school. It is true that their very innocence and benignity were in contrast to the vulgar and violent behavior of men and women elsewhere. It is true that the marquise had dignity and poise and raised the status of women, at least within her own walls. And yet when we assemble all the facts and clues, we find that she did very little after all that we can put our finger on and characterize as plainly significant or useful. We are left with the feeling that Voiture bringing a couple of bears into the *chambre bleue,* or Julie d'Angennes posing with her bow and arrow as the goddess of the moon, are isolated happenings, interesting in themselves but not enough to make this house the very embodiment of culture for nearly four decades. There are so many things wrong with this environment that we may well ask, not only how the marquise tamed all those bloodthirsty dukes and lubricious countesses, or why it was so successful, but whether it was worth doing.

We dimly guess that the real game was being played behind the visible parlor games. Something was happening at the *chambre bleue* that was never recorded in the gossip and letters and memoirs of the time because it was not really meant to be understood by outsiders. A fund of shared attitudes was composed, a subtle universally understood secret, never published because everyone who was there took it for granted: for the first time there was a social group that recognized itself as separate and special, as a positive force, because it had applied standards to its own conduct and therefore could impose its excellence on the world. This society invented a new value— the value of collective self-possession. Self-possession had existed before, but it had never been raised to such a high level as a general, shared social virtue. The hôtel de Rambouillet had its own private language for confirming that new value among its members, a language of wordless complicity, a language composed of apparently foolish and frivolous gestures, but a language nevertheless which conveyed precisely and without any doubt the *precious* nature of that shared self-possession. The overwhelming human need for personal distinction found a home, an audience, a community of kindred spirits in the hôtel de Rambouillet.

It is true that snobbery and class consciousness, a formalization of sentiment and a refusal of depth, were the price paid. But a language of personal distinction, as practiced by a group with exacting standards, is in the long run a language of self-surpassing and can bring its users to push out further the frontiers of human possibility.

Mme. de Rambouillet's great contribution to the art of social intercourse, and ultimately even to civilization as we understand it, was to provide the atmosphere in which that language could be invented, to set it going, and then to sit back and listen to it, with her enigmatic Italian smile, giving nothing more than her gentle, unruffled attention to the way her friends and admirers used it.

NOTES

1. Montausier, madrigal for the *Guirlande de Julie.*
2. Voiture, *Oeuvres*, I, pp. 237–39, Lettre no. 78.
3. Saint-Simon, *Mémoires*, ed. Gonzague Truc (Pléiade, 1947–61), II, pp. 255, 371.
4. Bibliothèque Nationale, mss. fonds français, 12676, 7, 8 (1665), II, p. 240.
5. See Tallemant, *Historiettes*, I, pp. 473–78 et passim. See also Mongrédien, *Libertins et amoureuses* (Perrin, 1929), pp. 1–52.
Somaize calls her "Parthénie" (*Dictionnaire*, I, pp. 193–94).
6. Maynard, *Priapées*, privately printed (1864); mss in the Arsenal Library, Paris, and in the library of Toulouse.
7. Voiture, I, pp. 167–68, Lettre à Mlle. Paulet, October 22, 1634.
8. Ibid., II, p. 270.
9. Chapelain, in Mongrédien, pp. 33–34.
10. See Tallemant, I, pp. 304–11 et passim.
Somaize calls her "Damoxede" (I, p. 210).
11. Cited by Tallemant, I, p. 306.
12. Montglat, *Mémoires*, in *Nouvelle collection des Mémoires pour servir à l'histoire de France*, ed. Michaud and Poujoulat (Lyon: Guyot, 1851) 3rd series, vol. V, p. 125.
13. Voiture, II, p. 301.
14. Mlle. de Montpensier, for example, alludes to such in her *Mémoires* (1637), ed. Chéruel (Charpentier, 1857), I, p. 27.
15. Voiture, II, p. 346.
16. Ibid., II, p. 355.
17. Her history is part of the history of France and her public life is much documented. For her private life at the *chambre bleue*, see Tallemant, I, pp. 67–74 et passim.
18. Quoted in Tallemant, I, pp. 443–44.
19. Cited by A. Adam in Tallemant, I, p. 982n.
20. Voiture, I, pp. 401–4, letter of November 1643.

Rivals and Outsiders

W<small>E ADD</small> a few notes on Mme. de Rambouillet's nearest rivals in hospitality in these early years—Marie Bruneau, Dame des Loges, and Charlotte des Ursins, Vicomtesse d'Auchy. Their failures illuminate her success.

Mme. des Loges

Mme. des Loges (c. 1585–1641) [1] was three years older than the divine Arthénice. She was born a Protestant during the wars of religion and shared the sufferings of her people at an early age, when her father, a rich merchant of Troyes, seeking to avoid persecution, had to flee with his two little daughters to the fortified Protestant city of La Rochelle, hiding them all the way in two baskets on a donkey.

Marie was the younger daughter. Her sister was pretty; but she was the smart one. When she became engaged to des Loges, her father wished her to delay the marriage until her sister could also find a husband. But unfortunately Marie became pregnant and had to marry her fiancé in a hurry. She was fourteen. Years later she amused her friends by speculating openly about this mishap. "How did I ever get into such an awkward situation? We were both so young and innocent, we didn't know what we were doing."

Her youth and innocence were brief. She had nine children and several love affairs, and eventually had to leave Paris under a political cloud.

Mme. des Loges was friendly with Malherbe, Conrart, Chapelain, all the pedants of the early decades. They liked to come to her house in the rue des Tournons to discuss questions of religion with her.

She also entertained a number of foreign royal Protestants such as the King of Sweden and the Duke of Weimar.

She became a distinguished letter writer. Tallemant says she was the first woman ever to write intelligent ones. All the writers praised her: they called her *la Céleste*, *la Divine*, and *la Dixième Muse*.

This "tenth muse" was a generous and hospitable woman, but not as authoritative or as placid a hostess as Mme. de Rambouillet. She did her own writing surrounded by visitors who came and went at will, chattering at her elbow while she whipped up impromptu poems. Her life style is faintly bohemian. Among her "galanteries" was one with a man named Hautefontaine, a Huguenot like herself. Voiture was the go-between. She said to the poet afterward, *"Celui-là n'est pas bon, percez-nous-en d'un autre"* ("That one wasn't very good; open up another keg"—an unkind allusion to Voiture's wine-selling background).

A certain Chenailles, a president of the treasury, wrote to her, "Ah! how happy one is when one can slake one's thirst in the waters that flow from you, Madame!" This gentleman had already spoken with bourgeois overemphasis of her "torrents of eloquence."

An example of that "eloquence" reported by Balzac: Mme. des Loges called the Archbishop of Rouen "a beast of burden who has been laden with all the luggage of Antiquity"—that is, an indiscriminately learned man, rather than a wise one. Balzac capped this by calling the archbishop "an overturned bookcase."

Balzac addressed to her a long artful letter in which he thunders against the "Amazons" and *femmes savantes* who dare to assume the functions of the opposite sex. His letter suggests that he is warning her not to be too clever herself:

There are limits which separate the sexes and demarcate our duties and functions. . . . Brave women are as blameworthy as cowardly men, and a woman who wears a sword is as wrong as a man who would carry a mirror on his belt. . . . As for the lady-lecturer you complained about to me, I know her . . . and I can no more approve a learned female than a woman on a horse. She ought to look to you and learn from the good example you give to intelligent and clever women. You know an infinite number of remarkable things but you do not display your learning as she does, and you have not learned them in order to preach them to others. You speak plainly to her, Madam, while she lectures you. You answer familiarly her enigmas, and reply to her confusion with clarity.

It is an achievement, Madam, to have acquired a most honorable fund of knowledge, but it is an even greater one to hide that knowledge like a theft. We see your embroidery-canvas, your silks and your needles, but your papers and books are out of sight. You need not therefore, Madam, have any esteem for that person who is so different from you, however cordial you are to her, nor should you ever think of changing your own clear speech for the learned nonsense she speaks.[2]

A revealing document, for it shows what a learned man expected of an intelligent woman in 1628. Balzac admired Mme. des Loges not for her positive intellectual gifts but because she could shut up and listen to him.

This letter was written when Mme. des Loges was at her social apogee. Her troubles began soon after, when Gaston d'Orléans gave her a pension of four thousand livres. The king's brother was then a very young and foolish man, but already a focal point of sedition. She had been listening to his grievances against Richelieu. Gaston's association with this charming, older Protestant woman was frowned upon by the court, and gossips were beginning to call him *"la linotte de Mme. des Loges"* (*linotte* = linnet, or a foolish person).

Richelieu, smelling a political rat, cut her pension in half. Her friendship with Gaston was dangerous, more of course to herself than to him. She felt the pressure of Richelieu's sinister hint and withdrew from Paris in 1629. It was not exactly a forced exile, but a prudent one. She knew that she would be left unprotected in any political shake-up in which Monsieur was involved. Her Protestantism did her no good with the cardinal either. She was now forty-four anyway, and it was time for a "conversion." She spent the rest of her days doing good works and writing exemplary pious letters. One last visit to Paris in 1636 was a social triumph. Everyone at court received her warmly. She had become old, devout, ailing, and was no longer a threat to that foolish young man's morals. In fact, she was the only intelligent woman who had ever taken Gaston seriously.

This lady, who must have been delightful in a more positive way than Mme. de Rambouillet, could have become as great a success had she not fallen into the snake pit of court politics. Her retreat cut short a promising career as a society hostess. She had all the talent, amiability, and tact needed for the role, and lacked only the luck to be ignored by Richelieu.

Mme. d'Auchy

Madame d'Auchy (c. 1570–1646)[3] is another matter altogether. This lady was a fool throughout her long life and is in much more conspicuous contrast with Mme. de Rambouillet.

To begin with, she became Malherbe's mistress. This was a shameful descent for a lady whose Italian extraction was almost as good as that of Mme. de Rambouillet. Malherbe was a rude and even brutal lover. Although he wrote her poems, about a dozen of them, under the name of Caliste in 1606–7, when she was in her late thirties, he also took to beating her when he suspected that she was entertaining another author. Finding his mistress alone in bed one day, he grabbed her two hands and slapped her in the face so hard that she cried out for help. When help came, he was sitting back in his chair calmly as if nothing had happened.

She tried to launch herself as a court beauty, but had little to recommend her. Her complexion was grey, her eyes dull and perpetually running water. Malherbe's line, *"Amour est dans ses yeux, il y trempe ses dards"* ("Love is in her eyes, he dips his arrows in them") made Mme. de Rambouillet say that this was a true observation indeed, for her eyes ran tears constantly and Love would find there enough water to plunge and dampen his arrows. Maynard refused to accept that Love resided in the eyes of Mme. d'Auchy,

> Sinon qu'il s'y logea, ainsi qu'un président
> Prononçant ses arrêts en robe d'écarlate.[4]
>
> (Unless he lived there like a magistrate,
> pronouncing his judgments in a scarlet robe.)

Mme. d'Auchy tried to cover up her poor vision, saying, "I called in Thevenin [an eye specialist], who said there was nothing to be done to my eyes," which the doctor confirmed, saying they were beyond repair. The whole court made rather savage sport of this poor lady. Yet her husband was jealous and took her away to the country for ten years.

So much for the lady's youth. Age did not bring wisdom. Having been "sung" by Malherbe and a few others, she now wished to have a reputation for literary talent herself, and persuaded a theologian named Maucors to ghost-write for her some *Homilies on the Epistle of Saint Paul to the Hebrews*. This ponderous work appeared under her name, with a frontispiece portrait of the lady kneeling before the Virgin Mary, in 1634. But she had neglected to read the Epistles herself, and when someone at court asked her to interpret a passage from Saint Paul, she replied, "Oh, is that by him?"

Her dream was to operate a sort of Academy, in competition with the official one recently formed by Richelieu. At her home each learned guest would read his works in turn, just as at the real Academy. Heavy sermons and philosophical disputes were on the agenda. At first many people came to her meetings—so many, in fact, that Chapelain, after one visit, called them a "mob" and did not go back. If a pedant like Chapelain disdained Mme. d'Auchy's circle, it must have been boring indeed. A typical meeting: A soldier named Pagan reads a learned paper on fortifications, excusing himself for its military style. Someone in the audience calls out that it is a fine translation of the *Miles Gloriosus* of Plautus. The testy abbé d'Aubignac speaks up to say that boastful people ought to look around them with both eyes before they speak (Pagan happens to be one-eyed). A fight starts.

Another day a certain Boutard has fun at the expense of Mme. d'Auchy's Academy. Having come to read a speech, he begins his lecture as soon as he comes in the door. He continues to speak all the way up the stairs and into the salon, and takes his seat still talking. His speech is a discussion of the different ways of spitting. He describes fifty-two spitting techniques, demonstrating each of them on Mme. d'Auchy's rug!

Among the long-forgotten men of learning who flourished their talents at the Academy of Mme. d'Auchy was L'Esclache, a well-known public speaker who gave popular lectures on philosophy, especially for ladies. He was not a great thinker, but rather one of those unsung heroes of popular culture, the type that Molière's *femmes savantes* would have fussed and cooed over and that geniuses cannot stand. He was an important source of higher education for women throughout this period, when it was still a debatable question whether women should be educated at all.

Another look at that boastful soldier Pagan and we find that he, too, was a man of some scientific substance, having written books on geometry and astronomy as well as fortifications. Perhaps, after all, something worthwhile was going on at Mme. d'Auchy's meetings, heavy though the style, something that the Rambouillet set failed to appreciate.

But however earnest and perhaps useful the circle of Mme.

d'Auchy, she committed the unpardonable error of showing off her knowledge. She fits perfectly the description of the lady ridiculed by Balzac in his letter to Mme. des Loges, reproduced above. She lacks the finesse to hide her books and papers behind her embroidery. She is an easy target of male prejudice against feminine encroachment on his monopoly of learning.

And of course she is no match for the elegant insouciance of Rambouillet. Mme. d'Auchy did everything wrong. She had herself served at table ("like a duchess!" exclaims Tallemant) by her maître d'hôtel in cloak and sword, a form of ceremoniousness used only at the most kingly of feasts elsewhere. She was always overdressed and obsequious in manner. She yearned to be appreciated by the Rambouillet circle, but was only a figure of fun there.

She often took extreme unction, whether very ill or not, in her later years. Once when she had done so, she asked if Mme. de Rambouillet had sent for news of her health. A wistful, worldly thought, even at death's door.

Mlle. de Gournay

One last lady we must mention in connection with this older generation is Marie de Jars, Demoiselle de Gournay (1565–1645).[5] The *"fille d'alliance"* (adopted daughter) of Montaigne is a still more complete outsider, who may appear at first very oddly in the company of such precious women. She was a literary crank, a stranger even in the seventeenth century, who had outlived her real period and had no social connections in the glittering feminine world we have described. She had spent her whole life in dedication to the sixteenth-century ideas and outlook of Montaigne. As his "adopted daughter," she edited and reedited the famous essays lovingly and, for her time, scrupulously. She also had a set of unfashionable ideas on language and style, expressed mainly in her book *L'Ombre de Mlle. de Gournay.*[6]

To her contemporaries Mlle. de Gournay looked like a crazy old fanatic, a shabby die-hard fighter in a lost cause, the cause of Renaissance lyricism against the relentless advance of Malherbian discipline. Yet although she did launch a one-woman crusade against Malherbe's rigid doctrines, she was not blindly defending the past. She was a vigorous partisan of the evolution of language then taking place. Her own writing style reflects this trend toward greater clarity and sobriety.

But where she is irreconcilable is in her definition of poetry, in flat contradiction to Malherbe's. For her, poetry is a creation of genius; its soul is emotional and spiritual; technique and form must be subordinate to matter. Poetry is different from prose, not by its form but by its function. The poet's language is not that of other men. It is *"surhumain."* Freedom is the mainspring of creation. Diversity is needed, and not, as the modernists of her day were advocating, impoverishment of language in the name of simplicity and purity.

Mlle. de Gournay's viewpoint seems to us today a far more "modern" one than that of Malherbe, with his passion for fixity and proportion. But she was a very bad poet. Her prose is better, rich in images though heavy and convoluted. Yet the trouble with Mlle. de Gournay was not that her ideas or style were bad, but that she was invited nowhere. She lacked the social gift of adaptation to her public.

Unlike the Rambouillet set, she had a professional approach to language and was a convinced partisan of her archaisms. The worldly attitude of Rambouillet was nonprofessional, antidogmatic. At Rambouillet you did not speak French in a particular way from conviction; you spoke French in a particular way as a means of conforming to a social mood.

Mlle. de Gournay lived on and on (eighty years) in severe poverty. By the time she reached sixty she had become an institution. The romantic girl who had vowed at sixteen eternal devotion to the intellectual discipline of her father-figure Montaigne became a disgruntled old maid living among her cats in a third-floor apartment in Paris on a tiny pension from Richelieu. She was credited by some with the "founding" of the Academy—that is, with rallying together the literary lights, poets, and pedants who were to become the nucleus of that official body. It is true that she knew all the writers, from Colletet to Cotin. Every future Academician at one time or another climbed the stairs to her den and braved the scolding of this "Alceste in petticoats." But she did not share many of their views. And of course, being a woman, she could never join their club.

She was an ardent feminist. Two books, *L'Egalité des hommes et des femmes* and *Les Griefs des dames,* show that she was a crusader by temperament; but her feminism is more than a demand for equality. She was, for an old maid, amazingly tolerant and sincere in her approach to sexual morals. She wanted freedom and honesty in the relations between the sexes. An early work, *Le Proumenoir de M. de Montaigne,* written when she was twenty-three, concerns an unmarried girl who risks reputation and life and goes into exile to escape a marriage of convenience and follow the man of her choice. But then he abandons her for someone else. The point of this psychological novel is that the girl accepts an irregular marital situation for love. The novel is turgid with quotations from Latin and Greek. But it is honest. And it was successful: three editions and five reprints. This was Mlle. de Gournay's real legacy to the world: her generous and humane view of women's rights. Her own life, a life of celibate indigence, was sacrificed to such advanced ideas.

The abbé Boisrobert collected Gournay anecdotes. Once he took her to see Richelieu, who laughed at her archaic speech. She said, "Laugh, your Eminence, since we must all contribute to your amusement." Richelieu, chastened by this sensible answer, told Boisrobert he would give her a pension. Yes, but what about her old servant? says Boisrobert. All right, two hundred livres for the servant. But what about her cat? Very well, another fifty livres a year for the cat. But the cat is about to have kittens! Richelieu threw in another pistole for the kittens.

Everyone knew the story of the "three Racans." Racan had made an appointment to go and see Mlle. de Gournay. The Comte de Moret got there first and announced himself as Racan. This first imposter received a copy of her latest book and thanked her warmly. Next the Comte d'Yvrande presented himself and was received, less cordially, as the real Racan. By the time Racan himself arrived, all unawares, puffing asthmatically up the stairs and stuttering, she was out of all patience with the joke and ordered him out of her apartment.

Mlle. de Gournay had many virtues and many masculine literary connections, but her social position in feminine circles was nil. Her linguistic crusade, stemming from a desire to save the rich, savory language of the sixteenth century, was very different from the later *précieux* game of coining new words. The précieuses were looking for "smart" words and phrases; she had been looking for greater freedom of expression. Theirs was an act of snobbery;

hers was a desperate effort to save a scrap of culture that she under-stood. Her cry of independence, the modest but honest feminism which pervades her writings, went unheard in the *chambre bleue*.

Somaize remembers her dimly, in 1660, as a "famous and learned précieuse" of yesteryear.

NOTES

1. See Tallemant, *Historiettes*, I, pp. 606–7 et passim, and Conrart mss. in the Arsenal library in Paris, where several of her letters are preserved.

2. Balzac, Letter to Mme. des Loges, September 20, 1628. First printed 1665.

3. See Tallemant, I, pp. 132–37; II, p. 290.

4. Cited by Adam, in Tallemant, I, p. 816n.

5. Ibid., I, pp. 379–84. See also M. H. Ilsley, *A Daughter of the Renaissance* (The Hague: Mouton, 1963).

Somaize calls this lady "Gadarie" (*Dictionnaire*, I, p. 106).

6. From the 1634 edition onward, this work is called *Les Advis ou les présents de la demoiselle de Gournay*.

The Children

WHAT WAS it like to be a child in the seventeenth century when the whole of French society was much younger than it is today, when grandparents were scarce and the race was barely reproducing itself? Were not their children more precious than ours, the darlings of their doting parents, the hope of the future?

The memorialists are strangely silent. They are interested in family but rarely in children as such. Of course, they say nothing at all about the children of the poor. The patient demographers of our own day tell us more. From studies based on parish records in small towns we get a picture of a seventeenth century wherein the lower classes, living in a state of total insecurity, close to famine and destitution, had fewer children than their betters, because of worse living conditions, later marriage, earlier death. Upper-class families, though more secure, had sometimes more children than they could provide for in a manner suitable to their class, and surplus offspring were likely to be disposed of on the battlefield or in the clergy. Primogeniture was a cruel but effective way of conserving property and titles in one line.[1]

In genteel circles parents seem to have kept a remarkable distance from their young children. Fraternizing with one's own on the child's level was bourgeois.[2] The higher the social position, the less the parents had to do with them in any direct physical or emotional way. Children of kings and queens were the most alienated of all from their parents. The peer of the realm, pledged to the king's service, must be ready to offer his sons to the defense of the realm, and therefore did not own them in the same sense that a commoner owned his children. Fathers could be brutally authoritarian, but not, in the upper classes, from simple possessiveness. Children were a special kind of property; they represented the clan's future identity. They had to pass a blood test and prove their nobility by submitting to principles that stood in the way of simple family pleasures. The value of nobility dehumanized ordinary family relationships, and in the seventeenth century the formalization of parent-child contacts had gone rather far. But we should not look at the evident coldness of ladies in the *chambre bleue* toward their children from the perspective of our own time. Something important has changed that perspective forever. We have learned to sentimentalize our children. Since Rousseau, Blake, and Wordsworth we have learned the nobility of the savage, the holiness of ignorance, the sincerity of spontaneous gestures. The idea of a child being wiser than a man was unheard of in the seventeenth century, the value of innocence trailing clouds of glory unimaginable. Perhaps we may consider this sentimentalization of innocence as a luxury those people simply could not afford. Their children were as savage, ignorant, and impulsive as children everywhere and at all times. But they were punished, rather than congratulated, for being what they were. Childhood was not a happy, carefree time which the child has a right to enjoy. A child was an unfinished adult, defective, inadequate, a little less than human. If he belonged to the master class, he must be made ready as soon as possible.

The seventeenth-century child has few toys or games appropriate to his age.[3] He must begin his arduous education as early as he can be made to sit still. He learns to read from obscure texts from scripture, to be learned by rote. This education is meted out by clerics or soldiers or men-of-letters who do not especially like children. The clothes of the seventeenth-century child are cut-down versions of adult ones. They are tight and stiff and painful to wear. The only regular physical caresses this child gets are from servants. Fortunately, there are a great many of them, devoted to the children in elementary ways, and the child is enveloped in the unsanitary warmth and noise of the inferiors who look after him. He learns their superstitions, curse words, and sexual games before he is handed over to the austere tutors who are to beat Latin and strategy into him. He may possibly have had a richer and more interesting, if less comfortable, physical life than the average middle-class urban child in Europe today. But his future was cut out for him. A girl child in that world knew as well as her brothers what to expect: submission to her father, followed by submission to her husband, frequent pregnancies and extremely bloody deliveries; a narrow range of pleasures on which chastity, her highest virtue, would press down like a lid; hell and damnation if she overstepped the rules. The best resource of a girl child in this world was patience.

Another feature of the condition of the children in the seventeenth century—as in all centuries before the enormous population explosion which followed the Industrial Revolution—was mortality. The children simply died. Upper-class children, almost as mortal as poor ones—for the doctors their parents could afford to consult did more harm than good—were hurried into the adult state lest they die before having lived a whole life, and especially before having passed the blood test. Kings crowned at thirteen, girls married before puberty reflected the anxiety about their survival. Childhood was not only worthless, it was a positive threat to the continuity of the species.

If it seems hard and unfeeling to regard children as unfinished adults, we must realize that the terrible mortality of children must have made parents steel themselves to the likelihood that they would not see their children grow up. They had to have as many children as they could, in the hope that a few would survive. The constant presence of death produces an apparent indifference to it.

Nowadays, when the death of a child in comfortable Western culture is a relative rarity, we can afford to invest emotionally in our children and in the concept of childhood. We can celebrate the goodness of ignorance, of undifferentiated energy, regarding it as perhaps more valuable than reason, self-control, or sublimation. Does this mean that the seventeenth-century upper-class mother, who saw her child only on formal occasions, felt the loss of her children less than we do because she had less emotionally invested in them, and the loss came as less of a surprise?

We must suppose that the elemental love of parents, the visceral, instinctual love which precedes cultural adaptations, was there in the same measure as it is in us, despite the appearances to the contrary. They surely loved their children as automatically as we do, regardless of their rules. We have a few examples of the breaking of the rules: Henri IV getting down on the floor and carrying his children around on his back; mothers deeply attached, in the highest emotional and physical degree, to their offspring (what better example than Mme. de Sévigné?). Such love may well have enjoyed the same scope of physical expression that we take for granted today. But it was not common. And it was not romanticized. It is we who have enlarged the sentiments we have for our children—built up the instinctual parent love by studying it passionately and portraying it infinitely. We devise freedom-oriented childhood artifacts, toys, clothes, educational systems; and our heartstrings are constantly wrenched by our children's responses to them. Is it because we love them more?

The pain of loss of a child, which reduces everything to zero, is probably the same whether the attachment has been enlarged and sensitized or not. The seventeenth-century child was not appreciated *as a child* to the same degree as we appreciate ours, but he was certainly just as much cherished as a possible continuing future self. The loss of a child was, then as now, one's own death. And it must have been unspeakably cruel when it was the last child who died. This sorrow is too intimate to measure.

Yet we are confronted with the apparently hard-hearted detachment of seventeenth-century upper-class parents from their children, especially the superfluous ones. They dumped them in the army, or in convents, without a twinge. The effect of this emotional distance, this "abstraction" of parenthood, on their children can only be speculated about. Can we presume that, just as only the robust child would survive the attacks of smallpox and cholera, so also those who survived the harshness of their parents' authority and the psychological wounds of childhood must be possessed of special armor, inner resources, "moral qualities"? This is not likely. The physical diseases killed the child or rendered him immune. The emotional wounds did not kill but surely crippled him in ways for which there was no clinical name or description, and these wounds were then inflicted in turn on his own children.

But we cannot judge the mistakes of yesterday until we can judge the mistakes of today. We are still in the dark about our children. We love them. The seventeenth century loved theirs, too. They expressed it in ways that have grown so strange to us that we are humbly conscious of their irretrievable distance from us. We search in vain for their children, for we find only dwarflike adults.

When we come to the younger generation at the *chambre bleue*, they are already grown up. Even eleven-year-old girls are addressed by the poets as young ladies. No one has seen fit to record with benevolence their childish laughter. They had, as it were, no childhood.

NOTES

1. For a sociological study of family life in this period, see Pierre Goubert, *Le Beauvais et le Beauvaisis de 1600 à 1730* (1960), reprinted as *Cent mille provinciaux au XVIIe siècle* (Flammarion, 1968).

2. Cf. Molière's aristocratic Dom Juan inquiring ironically after Monsieur Dimanche's little boy: "And is he still beating on his little drum?" Dom Juan, acte IV, scene 3, in *Oeuvres,* ed. Maurice Rat (Pléiade, 1956).

3. At thirteen, Richelieu's niece Claire-Clémence is given a doll and told to play mother. But it is *after* her marriage to the Duc d'Enghien. An heir is required, and she is a little retarded.

The Girls

THE PRETTY young ladies at the *chambre bleue* looked out in 1640 on a world very different from the one Mme. de Rambouillet had looked upon in 1610. It was still a world of courtly relations, limited to a few dozen interlocking families, revolving around the vacuum of a royal household. All these girls, Condés, Montmorencys, Colignys, La Trimouilles, Gonzagues, had entrée to the Louvre. But none could remember the blatant sexuality, the roaring banquets, the mud and spittle and straw of Henri's court. Nor did they remember the incoherent regency of Marie. Louis and Richelieu had introduced a semblance of rational planning into government, while committing France to war and expansion. They had silenced the laughter along with the curses.

Mme. de Rambouillet had gone further. She had invented private society. Thanks to her, there was a place to go.

The girls took all this for granted. Their privileged position as women, which their mothers had built up so gradually, seemed a natural right. Alas, it only seemed: their destiny still consisted of the husband each would get.

One thing had changed for the better: very early marriage was going out of style. Granted, it could still happen. As late as 1641 Richelieu's thirteen-year-old niece Claire-Clémence de Maillé-Brézé was shoved into wedlock before she could read, her puny little body wobbling on high heels at the wedding ceremony, so that she would not look too ludicrously elfin as the wife of the Grand Condé.

But there was now widespread criticism of the auctioning off of young girls before puberty. Courtship, the dream of all pastoral romances, was at last possible. There was time for a girl to get hold of a copy of *L'Astrée*, to learn to write a sentimental letter, before being disposed of forever by her father. The poets invited these girls to expect an intensity of satisfaction in the realm of love beyond the imagination of their mothers.

Mlle. de Clermont,[1] daughter of that good and pious lady who did not know where babies came from, dreamed in her teens that a handsome knight such as Hector de Montausier was going to carry her off. Instead she was given to the terrible Marquis d'Avaugour, an impotent ogre obsessed with cuckoldry. He had caused the death of his first wife by exposing her to smallpox in his keep in Brittany. Jealousy made him an excellent locksmith. After his marriage to Mlle. de Clermont he barricaded her into his manor at Clisson, one of the most forbidding fortresses in France. She was too meek to rebel, and when her friends suggested taking this tyrant to court to get an annulment based on his impotency, she replied, "An honest wife does not complain of such things." This virtuous girl sat within her moated prison for the rest of her life, remembering the bright badinage of the rue Saint-Thomas-du-Louvre.

Other girls seemed to come a little closer to their dreams. The sisters Anne and Marthe du Vigean (those lovely daughters mentioned in Voiture's poem, cited on p. 101) belonged to the young Condé set, Louis, Duc d'Enghien, and his sister Anne-Geneviève de Bourbon, who played the parlor games organized by Voiture, Godeau, and Cotin. They had thrown off the studied prudery of their elders. The girls were chaste, but they wanted to have fun. D'Enghien was their hero. Not yet twenty, he already had a full measure of Condé pride, and his eagle-beaked profile proclaimed him a commander of men. But for a season in 1640 the young prince was composing madrigals in the *chambre bleue* to the demure loveliness of Marthe du Vigean.

Every day they met there and even talked of marrying. A foolish idea. D'Enghien would one day bear his father's name of Prince de Condé and so could not marry whom he pleased.

We have met the older Condé before. After spending his own youth corrupting boys and plotting against the throne, he had grown old in avarice and sanctimonious pride, and his only thought now was of securing the privileges of his dynasty. He made a deal with Richelieu for the marriage of d'Enghien to Richelieu's niece. "Take my son and do with him what you will. He is your creature."

The wedding was briskly dispatched in 1641 over the desperate objections of the bridegroom. As for the bride, fresh from the country and only half-grown, she was so dazzled by her good fortune that she submitted willingly to her uncle's orders.

But wedded is not bedded. D'Enghien boycotted his little wife and began seeing Marthe du Vigean again. He even thought of demanding annulment. Marthe was consoled by her lover's loyalty. She bloomed under his respectful attentions and was the envy of all the other girls at the *chambre bleue.*

We cannot say that it was all for love of Marthe that this marriage was so odious to the Duc d'Enghien. Richelieu had beheaded d'Enghien's maternal uncle, Henri II de Montmorency. Besides, a Richelieu niece was beneath the rank of a Condé. If he must make a marriage of state, they ought to have given him a princess, like Mlle. de Montpensier.

These considerations did not figure in the thoughts of Marthe, who went on hoping that somehow the obstacles would be removed and she would be united with her prince.

However, marriage was now a fact of his life. D'Enghien might spend his evenings chatting in an embrasure with Mlle. du Vigean, but he had to go home and sleep beside Claire-Clémence. After two years his wife became pregnant. The news came as a rude shock to Marthe. D'Enghien was immediately sent off to war and covered himself with glory in the first great victory of his career at Rocroi. This was in May 1643. Three months later he had a son.

The hopeless attachment of Marthe du Vigean did not end there. D'Enghien continued to see her and surround her with loving attentions while publicly scorning his wife. Other young men came forward to ask for her hand. D'Enghien ordered them away. Her parents were furious at this compromising prolongation of an idyll that had no future. They wanted their daughter married and off their hands.

By May 1645 the sentiments of this pair of lovers had reached fever pitch. One day, as d'Enghien was taking leave of Marthe at the *chambre bleue* before the battle of Nordlinghen, an extraordinary thing happened. The girl began to cry and the young man, overcome with romantic despair, actually fainted at her feet. After this emotional display, he left for the front and won another great victory, exposing himself heedlessly to the flying bullets of the enemy. Of such stuff are *précieux* novels compounded throughout their endless pages, and we know that d'Enghien had a penchant for those of La Calprenède, which he read even in the trenches.

But such a state of tension could not go on forever. In 1647 Marthe du Vigean burned her lover's portrait and letters and stole away to the Carmelite convent of the rue Saint-Jacques. She took permanent vows and became Sister Marthe de Jésus. Her mother and father were beside themselves. The baron wanted to "kill every Carmelite in the world." But their daughter was now forever beyond their reach.

When this occurred d'Enghien had just succeeded to the title of Prince de Condé. He never saw Marthe du Vigean again. The rest of his life resembles that of his father. Profligate, seditious, and then aggressively loyalist, he became a cold-hearted person, the tyrant of his family, whose only remaining sentiments were dynastic. He sternly, distantly loved his weakling son, the new Duc d'Enghien, and saw to it that the boy married a princess.[2]

Not all the girls at the *chambre bleue* were as passive as Marthe. Her sister Anne had the courage to elope with Armand, Duc de Richelieu, over the threats and cries of "theft" of the boy's powerful aunt, Mme. d'Aiguillon. And an even more flamboyant case was that of Isabelle-Angélique de Montmorency-Bouteville, Duchesse de Châtillon (1627–1695).[3]

Isabelle was an infant in arms when her father went to the block for dueling (see p. 49). She grew up to be an impatient, selfish beauty. The symbolism of her coat-of-arms told her she was great by birth; the poets told her she was irresistible. Like her father, she decided early that she was beyond the law and could take her destiny into her own hands.

One of the big scandals of the regency was her elopement at eighteen in 1645 with Gaspard IV de Coligny, future Duc de Châtillon. This elopement was staged as a kidnapping.

Abduction was an extreme option for star-crossed lovers in this age of authoritarian parents. If the girl was returned to her family before being ravished by her abductor, she could still be disposed of elsewhere. But if she was no longer a maiden, the families usually just accepted the fait accompli, with much grumbling, and allowed her to marry her seducer. Of course, many abductions were cases of genuine rape, but the girl had to marry her ravisher anyway.

In the case of Isabelle, it was the only way to overcome the objections of the boy's family. Gaspard was the son and heir of the very prominent Protestant Châtillons. Although Isabelle had impeccable antecedents and a large fortune, his mother would not let him marry a Catholic, not even a Montmorency. Gaspard therefore snatched Isabelle at her doorway one evening as she was returning home from a party with her sister. A Swiss Guard came forward to protect the screaming maiden and was stabbed to death for his pains. Nobody gave him another thought in the ensuing commotion. The girl's relatives pretended to be greatly upset and went sobbing to the queen for redress. But it all blew over, amid the jeers of the songwriters of the Pont-Neuf, for everyone knew the girl was an accomplice in the crime.

And then? No sooner married but Gaspard lost interest in this beautiful bride. He suffered a fearful depression immediately after consummation of the marriage and remained that way. Gossips said he had an unnatural relationship with the Duc d'Enghien, and indeed most of the young comrades-in-arms of the Grand Condé were stigmatized in the same way. But Gaspard had proved his prowess with women by having affairs with the courtesan Marion de Lorme and Ninon de Lenclos.

What happened to Gaspard when he woke up married to Isabelle? Perhaps the very legitimacy of this love was enough to kill it. Young libertines like the Marquis de Bussy-Rabutin and the Prince de Marsillac considered love and marriage to be mutually exclusive, and Bussy wrote many *questions d'amour* like this:

Q. Should a man marry his mistress publicly, clandestinely, or not at all?
A. He who insists on marrying his mistress wants to be able to hate her some day. Living in sin keeps love alive, and marriage is the death of tenderness. But if you're afraid of sin, at least get married in secret.[4]

Now Isabelle, finding herself deserted by her husband so soon after the nuptials, did not wait long to be revenged. She flirted with various prominent courtiers, and on the eve of the Fronde was even ogling the ten-year-old Louis XIV. When Benserade wrote a madrigal about this,[5] her husband threatened the poet with a thrashing. He was defending his own name, of course, not Isabelle's reputation.

This lady became a famous manipulator of men through graceful flattery and artful sex. Among her conspicuous conquests, the most brilliant was the fickle and handsome Duc de Nemours. He was a prize that convinced everyone of her power. She seemed to have enticed him by a kind of black magic. He said that it was not choice but "his stars" that drove him to love her.

Other ladies, more pretentiously virtuous, were jealous of Isabelle's successes and watched her for a false step. When the civil war of the Fronde erupted, these jealousies erupted with it. Historians speak of a *Fronde des ruelles*, a war waged in drawing-rooms and, more especially, in boudoirs, where matters of state were settled on the basis of which lady could exert the most charm on the combatants. Isabelle was a champion on this battlefield. We will meet her again as we unravel the threads of that complicated war.

NOTES

1. See Tallemant, *Historiettes*, I, pp. 476–78 et passim; Voiture, *Oeuvres* (scattered references); Sarrasin, "Stanzas," in *Poésies*, ed. Uzanne (1877), p. 213.

Somaize refers to her mother, her sister, and herself as "Cassandre et ses deux filles," (*Dictionnaire*, I, p. 55).

2. References to the Condé-du Vigean affair are dispersed throughout the memoirs of Lenet, Mme. de Motteville, Mlle. de Montpensier, the annals of the Condé family, and many other sources.

3. See Motteville, *Mémoires*, ed. M. F. Riaux, 4 vols (Charpentier, 1855), IV, pp. 49–50; Bussy-Rabutin, "Histoire d'Angélie et de Ginolic," in *Histoire amoureuse des Gaules*, ed. G. Mongrédien, 2 vols (Garnier, 1930), I, pp. 67 ff; and scattered references in Tallemant. See also E. Magne, *Femmes galantes: Mme. de Châtillon* (Mercure de France, 1910).

4. Bussy-Rabutin, "Maximes d'amour," in *Histoire*, I, p. 176.

5.   Châtillon gardez vos appas
        Pour quelque autre conqueste;
        Si vous estes preste
        Le Roy ne l'est pas;
        Avecques vous il cause;
        Mais en vérité,
        Il faut quelque autre chose
        Pour vostre beauté
        Qu'une minorité.

        (Châtillon, keep your charms
        for some other conquest;
        you may be ready
        but the King isn't;
        he may chat with you,
        but in truth
        your beauty needs something other
        than a minority.)

Cited by Tallemant, II, p. 495.

Anne-Geneviève

A NUMBER of girls went forth from the *chambre bleue* determined to do something positive with their lives. Unfortunately, the only job suggested to them by the poetry they read was that of passionately influencing men of action. Everything depended on the man.

Princesse Anne-Geneviève de Bourbon-Condé (1619–1679) [1] was a girl with such active dreams of glory. Born in Vincennes prison, of another legendary princess, she was so favored with wealth, looks, and intelligence that she, if anyone, would surely marry a handsome knight and live happily ever after.

But she learned early that her life was not her own to live. It would belong to the great events of her time.

Voiture exerted his talents for the little princess as she was growing up. In one of his most delightful letters he tells her how he was tossed in a blanket as punishment for having failed to make her laugh. At each fling, he was cast miles aloft and saw below him all the surrounding countryside. But the finest sight of all was a radiant light "framing the most beautiful face in the world," [2] that of the little princess herself, of course.

She was eleven, already a young woman, dazzling everyone in a pastoral tableau composed by the ladies at the du Vigean château. The precocious nymph sang and flitted among the statues and topiary, striking the poet dumb with her grace.

But the Carmelite nuns of the rue Saint-Jacques were her teachers, and their influence was strong in counteracting this fluffy paganism. For a while the young girl thought she had a vocation.

Her father dashed these pious plans when he ordered her to attend a society ball at the Louvre in 1635. The princess was now sixteen. She wore a hair shirt to the ball concealed under her worldly finery. She had promised the good nuns to tighten it around her shoulders if the pleasures of the evening began to overwhelm her. But the world won that night. She danced in a ballet with the foremost beauties of the court. Next day she laid aside the hair shirt and forgot about it for a very long time.

Anne-Geneviève had her father's aquiline nose and her mother's blond hair. And she had something else: a dreamy, languid look, apparently passive, that made men eager to protect her. Underneath the blue-eyed gaze she was a Condé.

Separated from her brother d'Enghien in childhood by her convent school, she found him again, in adolescence, to be more than a brother. He was a friend and accomplice in the adventures of their lively circle. But he was more than a friend, too. This brother and sister felt an obscure mutual attachment that overstepped the limits of family affection. It made them ingrown and snobbish, domineering and meddlesome in each other's lives and loves.

Naturally, for a girl so highly placed the big question was: who would be good enough to marry her? Her father began working on the problem almost at her birth, but there were many postponements. Finally, when she was all of twenty-three, Condé made his choice: the Duc de Longueville, a widower of forty-seven. A far cry from Prince Charming, but the noblest catch in France for a Condé daughter. Anne-Geneviève resigned herself and married Longueville in 1642. It was a sad conclusion to her charmed girlhood.

Now a painful thorn in Mme. de Longueville's new married life was a certain Mme. de Montbazon. This voluptuous woman was her husband's mistress—and practically everyone else's. Longueville did not have the delicacy to end the liaison when he got married. His young wife decided to look elsewhere for solace, and found it in the devotion of Maurice de Coligny. Her swain was the younger brother of her cousin Isabelle's husband, Gaspard de Châtillon.

It was in the first months of the regency of Anne, when malcontents of every stripe were pouring back into Paris out of exile. On the surface there was relaxation and freedom, a renewal of joy at the disappearance of Richelieu and Louis. No one yet guessed at Mazarin's power over the queen. The queen had moved out of the gloomy Louvre into Richelieu's vacant Palais-Royal, and this newer edifice became a place for feasting, dancing, and flirting. Tongues wagged. The young people did as they pleased.

Mme. de Longueville

But a dreadful scandal cut short the budding romance between Anne-Geneviève and Coligny. Mme. de Montbazon happened to pick up a couple of stray love letters which she thought had fallen from Coligny's pocket. She showed these compromising letters to all her friends, claiming that they were by the hand of Mme. de Longueville. The Condé family was horrified and rose to defend their daughter and sister.

In the event, another gentleman confessed to the Prince de Marsillac that he had received the fatal letters from his own lady. Marsillac tactfully solved the problem: by comparing the handwritings he demonstrated the falseness of Mme. de Montbazon's accusation. He forced her to admit her error and then burned the letters in the presence of the Princesse de Condé, Mme. de Rambouillet, and the queen. This would have ended the affair, but was not enough for the Condés. They demanded a formal public apology. Mme. de Montbazon had to go to the hôtel de Condé and present her apology in person. She pinned it to her fan and laid it before the old Princesse de Condé on a hot day in August 1643. The princess had invited as many friends and onlookers as she could squeeze into her drawing room to witness this humiliation, and she received the apology seated on a dais. For the Condés, it was a triumph of scorn.

Coligny was a casualty of this affair. Wishing to avenge Anne-Geneviève personally for the calumny of Mme. de Montbazon, he fought a duel with one of that lady's admirers, the Duc de Guise. A fine gesture, but he was no match for Guise, who cut him down in the Place Royale in December 1643. When Coligny begged for mercy Guise struck him with the flat of his sword to conclude the encounter. But then Coligny bounded up and tried to wound his adversary. This cowardly act was, they say, witnessed by Mme. de Longueville from behind a curtained window.

She turned away from this episode to resume her round of social encounters and cultural hobbies. Coligny died a lingering death from gangrene a few months later.

Behind the personal vendetta of Mme. de Longueville and Mme. de Montbazon, two camps had begun to form.

The Duchesse de Montbazon had married, in her teens, a doddering old rake, Hercule de Rohan, Duc de Montbazon and father of the infamous Mme. de Chevreuse. His young wife took up with her middle-aged step-daughter, trading lovers and political schemes. A clique was developing around these ladies, which began to be called the *Cabale des Importants* because of their overweening hatred for Mazarin. The "important ones" disliked the Condés, too, for their loyalty and began to grumble against them. The affair of the letters accentuated their animosity. The queen tried to suppress the *Importants* by having them imprisoned or exiled. This was the prologue to the Fronde, though it took five more years of ominous cold war before the shooting began.

Anne-Geneviève de Longueville was to be at the center of nearly every chapter of this civil war. Somewhat in the manner of Mme. de Chevreuse before her (whom she considered her enemy, however, and morally and culturally beneath her), she saw herself as a "well-born soul," a Cornelian heroine in need only of a stage on which to act. The Fronde would be her stage.

The well-born soul is a moral as well as a racial aristocrat. Such a person owes nothing to the laws which govern ordinary men. The well-born soul cannot, however, in principle, do as he likes any more than a common one, for his private wishes have to be identified with his heroic destiny.

This self-image allows for any amount of innocent cheating. Anne-Geneviève was capable of great self-sacrifice when the higher purpose demanded it, and also of rationalizing her most capricious desires by pressing them into the service of the grand design. Her need for personal distinction was fulfilled in the Fronde—but at the cost of the war itself.

Along with a sense of political destiny, poetry and ideas filled the mind and entertained the vanity of Mme. de Longueville. She liberally supported the poets she met at the *chambre bleue*, both the frivolous (Sarrasin) and the ponderous (Chapelain). Chapelain's lengthy epic about Joan of Arc was dedicated to her and her husband, who paid the shrewd old pedant handsomely for his calculated praises of the Longueville family.

The hobby of the next few seasons (1644–45) was Jansenism. Mme. de Longueville was intelligent enough to join in the complicated theological dispute, and grappled courageously with Arnauld's *La Fréquente Communion*. But although she passionately espoused the Jansenist cause, it was an intellectual commitment only. She was far from ready to put on the hair shirt of her adolescence.

She needed an emotional commitment to match her sense of dramatic destiny. A man more worthy of her than Coligny, by birth and culture, and by a romantic belief in his own future, was already in her circle of friends. He had recently served her in the affair of the love letters as he had once served Mme. de Chevreuse and Anne of Austria in the days of Richelieu. He had beautiful manners and absolute devotion to the ideals of chivalry, within the terms of which, at thirty-two, he still expected to be launched on a glorious career. He was Marsillac.

It was 1645. Mme. de Longueville was pregnant. Her husband had been called away to Münster to negotiate a treaty to end the Thirty Years' War, and she had leisure to fall in love.

This new liaison was less troubled by her pregnancy than we might suppose. It lived on exalted sentiments as much as on physical communion. Neither of these lovers was of the sensual type to be driven into each other's arms without the stimulation of intellectual and spiritual attractions. And marriage had deflected at least some of their sexual energy—Marsillac had been married at fifteen and was the father of six children!

Years later, when the Fronde was all over and Marsillac had become the Duc de La Rochefoucauld, he claimed to have seduced her cynically for political reasons. But these vindictive memoirs do not tell the truth about his first feelings for Anne-Geneviève. Nor do the world-weary *Maximes*, written by a middle-aged moralist who has insulated himself from the shocks of love, reflect the state of mind of the younger man, the person he had been when his hopes were high and his illusions intact. The love-affair of Marsillac and Mme. de Longueville was consecrated, elevated, by their sense of righteous mission.

For in 1645 the political picture was becoming clear to many a noble eye, and this was how it looked: Mazarin had simply replaced Richelieu in power. Master of the queen's heart, he was usurping the rights which the nobility had expected to get back when Richelieu died. Mazarin must go.

An enforced visit to Münster by Mme. de Longueville to be with her husband suspended the affair for another whole year-and-a-half, but on her return in 1647 for her father's funeral—pregnant again! —she found Marsillac waiting for her, and a whole host of heroic possibilities.

She also felt a cold blast of scorn from her brother, d'Enghien, the new Prince de Condé. Condé was jealous of Marsillac and annoyed by the discovery that his sister had tried to drive a wedge between him and his own sweetheart, Marthe du Vigean, by finding other suitors for that unhappy girl. Brother and sister were equally meddlesome in one another's affairs. Marsillac and Mlle. du Vigean were to some extent both intruders on a possessive sibling attachment that went deeper.

But the coolness of one of Anne-Geneviève's brothers was partially compensated by the enthrallment of her other one: the Prince de Conty, just turned eighteen, fell passionately in love with his sister at this point. Conty was a poor prince, misshapen and stupid, but easy to manipulate.

Politics and literature are interwoven in Mme. de Longueville's romantic thoughts. She found time, while the mood of the Fronde was growing within her, to spend the winter season (1647–48) having a friendly quarrel with her brother Conty over the relative merits of two sonnets, Voiture's *Uranie* and Benserade's *Job*.[3]

This *cause célèbre*, perhaps the most futile of all literary disputes, provided an infinity of small talk and amorous dalliance of a purely verbal nature and occupied the leisure of brother and sister for another two years. Mme. de Longueville chose to champion Voiture, who was now fading from the scene at the *chambre bleue* and dying of gout. Conty favored Benserade, a young poet who aimed to take Voiture's place.

Both poems take for granted the usual conventions about the heartless and irresistible woman. In *Uranie* the poet's reason, far from releasing him from her thrall, joins his senses in binding him to her. He *must* love her by the inescapable Platonic logic: the mind aspires to perfection and therefore confirms the inclination of the senses. In *Job* the lady causes more suffering than that biblical personage ever had to endure because the poet is not allowed, as Job was, to make loud moan of his sorrow. He must suffer in silence.

The brittle texture, the very heartlessness of the hyperbole in these poems was a chief source of delight to society readers like Mme. de Longueville and her brother. Everybody interested in literature at that moment felt that a stand had to be taken on them. All the notables of the *chambre bleue* spoke up. And Mme. de Longueville was the queen of the young critics. Such literary quarrels, while giving the gentry something to talk about, could blind the eye of any poet to the true meaning of his craft. Almost any poet. To the women he wrote for there was no problem. Poetry was their jewelry.

Somaize, in his *Dictionnaire des Pretieuses*, devotes two pages to Mme. de Longueville's patronage of the poets, and says:

It is certain that, whatever men do to achieve glory, it is women who give value to their works, and launch them.

... For women shape men's lives.... It is women that authors wish to please, and it is to earn the glory of which the Précieuses are the arbiters that men work.[4]

This, it seems to us, is a perfectly accurate statement of poetry's purpose in the *précieux* aesthetic. Poetry is an instrument in the sentimental relations between the sexes. Its object is the greater glory of woman.

For underneath the hard brilliance of these stones is a gleam of real commitment: an affirmation of love's slavery, the power of the weaker sex, imperious and impervious, absorbing all the energy of the lover. Like Philis, the beautiful goddess of the morning light in the *Belles Matineuses* of an earlier quarrel, Uranie is going to stand there forever, letting the poet die and die for her. More detached than Job's masters, God and the devil, she refuses even to let him speak up. The Prince de Conty dared not declare his passion for the beautiful blue-eyed sister with whom he discussed these poems. But the poems spoke for him, in shallow clichés, of his underground desire.

The Duchesse de Longueville and her brother Conty kept up this sentimental charade through several seasons. But behind the public parade of elegant dilettantism her love affair with Marsillac had reached a pinnacle of reality: in the spring of 1648 she became pregnant again, with Marsillac's child. Fortunately, Longueville had come home from Münster just in time to cover the situation.

NOTES

1. On Anne-Geneviève de Bourbon-Condé, later Duchesse de Longueville, see almost everyone who lived through the Fronde and wrote memoirs. Gourville, Retz, La Rochefoucauld, Motteville, Montpensier, Lenet, Mme. de Nemours (the jealous stepdaughter of the princess who followed her movements, always on the lookout for a false step), and many others have left information, gossip, harsh criticism, and

praise for the famous princess; there are also a number of biographies, beginning in the eighteenth century with Villeflore, *La Vie de Mme. de Longueville*, 1738, followed by Victor Cousin's *Madame de Longueville: I, La Jeunesse de Mme. de Longueville; III, Mme. de Longueville pendant le Fronde*. (Volume II was never published), (Didier, 1867–72). Sainte-Beuve treats of her in *Portraits de Femmes* and in *Port-Royal*.

In our own century there are two excellent works on her, Jacques Debû-Bridel's *Anne-Geneviève de Bourbon, Duchesse de Longueville* (Gallimard, 1938) and Jeanine Delpech, *L'Ame de la Fronde* (A. Fayard, 1957).

She is also discussed by the numerous biographers of her brother, the prince who is known to history as Le Grand Condé.

2. Voiture, *Oeuvres*, I, pp. 40–44, Lettre à Mlle. de Bourbon, April-October 1630.

3. Benserade's sonnet:

> Job, de mille tourments atteint
> Vous rendra sa douleur connue,
> Et raisonnablement il craint
> Que vous n'en soyez point émue.
>
> Vous verrez sa misère nue;
> Il s'est lui-même ici dépeint;
> Accoutumez-vous à la vue
> D'un homme qui souffre et se plaint.
>
> Bien qu'il eut d'extrêmes souffrances,
> On voit aller des patiences
> Plus loin que la sienne n'alla.
>
> Il souffrit des maux incroyables,
> Il s'en plaignit, il en parla:
> J'en connais de plus misérables.
>
> (Job, with his thousand sorrows,
> will let you know about them,
> and may reasonably fear
> that you will not be moved.
>
> You can see his naked misery;
> He has painted his own portrait here
> Accustom yourself to the sight
> Of a man who suffers and complains.
>
> But though his sufferings were extreme,
> there are some forms of patience
> that go even farther than his.
>
> He suffered incredible ills,
> but could speak of them and complain.
> I know even greater miseries.)

Voiture's sonnet:
> Il faut finir mes jours en l'amour d'Uranie!
> L'absence ni le temps ne m'en sauraient guérir,
> Et je ne vois plus rien qui me pût secourir
> Ni qui sût rappeler ma liberté bannie.

RAMBOUILLET

Dès longtemps je connais sa rigueur infinie!
Mais, pensant aux beautés pour qui je dois périr,
Je bénis mon martyre et, content de mourir,
Je n'ose murmurer contre sa tyrannie.

Quelquefois ma raison, par de faibles discours,
M'incite à la révolte et me promet secours.
Mais lorsqu'à mon besoin je me veux servir d'elle,

Après beaucoup de peine et d'efforts impuissants,
Elle dit qu'Uranie est seule aimable et belle
Et m'y rengage plus que ne font tous mes sens.

(I must end my days loving Uranie!
Neither time nor absence can cure me,
and I can see nothing else to help me,
or bring back my banished freedom.

Long have I known her infinite rigors!
But when I think of the charms for which I perish,
I bless my martyrdom and, glad to die,
I dare not murmur against her tyranny.

Sometimes my reason, with feeble arguments,
incites me to revolt, and promises help.
But when I try, in my need, to use it,

after much pain and weakling efforts,
reason tells me Uranie alone is lovely and beautiful,
and engages me even more than all my senses did.)

Both poems appear in the Mongrédien anthology, *Les Précieux et les précieuses*, pp. 31–32, 78.
    4. Somaize, I, p. 242.

Queen of the Fronde

T HE "PETTICOAT FRONDE" was a garment woven of the romantic vanities of women. The Fronde of Mme. de Longueville, Mme. de Châtillon, and the Grande Mademoiselle de Montpensier was an adventure in boudoir politics and vain heroics generated by the novels and poetry they read at the *chambre bleue*. For them the Fronde was an effort to translate the delicate private sentiments, which seemed so important in their leisured indoor lives, into public action of universal value.

But the Fronde was more than a petticoat war. Thousands of foot soldiers and peasants fought and starved in it, all over France, and not for the beautiful eyes of Isabelle de Châtillon. None of the ladies fighting this war had any inkling of its larger meanings. They were passionately living events which revolved around them.

The Fronde is a little understood war,[1] almost unknown to the general English-speaking reader, and this book is concerned with it only as it relates to our women. But it is well to note that there was a Fronde of princes and a Fronde of citizens, which made of this conflict, in a dramatic way, at once the last gasp of feudalism and the first cry of the French Revolution. As such it was a turning point in French history. Princes and citizens made uneasy bedfellows against monarchy. They were aiming in opposite directions, historically, and so they had to fail. Absolute despotism was the dismal conclusion. But who could know that in advance? It took another century-and-a-half of absolutism, and of passionate underground discourse in France, before any of the questions of parliamentary freedom posed by the Fronde could be answered. But what of the Fronde of princes? Can we believe that the nobility lost this war when they came out of it with royal blessings and a welcome at court? We can, because their aim in fighting the Fronde was power

141

for their class. What they got instead was individual forgiveness and private places in the Sun King's pageant. Never again would they reach for the irretrievable past as they were now doing.

Parliament lost the Fronde, too, but lost less. The Fronde was a first small step toward 1789.

In the summer of 1648, when Condé won a final victory over the Spaniards at Lens, the noble defenders of France came home from the Thirty Years' War to find a wily interloper, Mazarin, fawning on the returning heroes but dictating to the queen the terms of her largesse. Surely Condé, who had won the war, ought to be handing out the presents!

Marsillac, typical of the disgruntled warriors, had expected from the queen a courtly appointment that would solve all his financial difficulties. The queen thanked him warmly, told him he was too good for any appointment, and gave him—nothing. He lowered his sights, curtailed his demands, but one last claim he would not withdraw: the *tabouret* for his wife. This honor was his due and he must have it; not for the comfort of Mme. de Marsillac, but as a symbol of his own rank and worth.

As for Mme. de Longueville, she wanted to do something extraordinary: to be the instrument by which her lover would get his *tabouret*, and her brother a hand in the regency.

Enter the Archbishop of Paris, Paul de Gondi, known to history as the Cardinal de Retz. This ugly little man also wanted something: a cardinal's hat and Mazarin's job. He began coming to see Mme. de Longueville at her house in Paris. A great womanizer, and remarkably fortunate in his conquests, Gondi sat by her bedside and measured his chances. He says in his memoirs that he decided not to try to seduce her, since "the living was not vacant" (he knew about her attachment to Marsillac).[2] He did, however, entertain her with seditious conversation.

The Parliament of Paris was resentful of Mazarin for its own reasons. These grave, long-gowned city fathers had been in session for some months, trying to effect fiscal reforms. They sent the queen-regent complaint after complaint, always couched in the most humble and reverent terms. They pressed her for lower taxes, for an end to the traffic in public offices, for the suppression of the "partisans"—bailiffs, financiers, bloodsuckers on the community who were devoted only to their own enrichment. This rat pack of partisans had no traditions; they had risen from nowhere, in one generation, by ruthlessness and greed, to become millionaires. They had been introduced by Richelieu. Now they were proliferating. It was easy to see in Mazarin just another of these rootless, selfseeking parasites who seemed to begin as lackeys and become rulers overnight.

The queen demanded that Parliament dissolve and go back to its purely judicial functions. They refused. Seeing Mazarin as the chief link between the crown and the financiers, they asked for his dismissal.

The trouble began on the occasion of a thanksgiving *Te Deum* mass in August 1648, to which all the notables of Paris were invited to celebrate the victory of Condé at Lens. A procession of dignitaries in full regalia of black and red—church fathers, aldermen, and magistrates—walked through Paris to hear mass at the cathedral. But one of them was absent: the leader of the most radical "republican" faction in Parliament, the Counselor Broussel. He stayed at home that day "taking physic" because he was afraid the queen's patience with Parliament had come to an end and his arrest by Mazarin's forces was imminent. He was right. Broussel was that day dragged from his home in broad daylight, thrust into a carriage, and carried off to a jail outside Paris. His wife screamed the news from her windows. There was an immediate outcry upon this rather inept arrest. The people of Paris, a rabble of small shopkeepers and idlers, were quickly inflamed. They erected barricades in front of the Palais-Royal and threw stones at the windows of Mazarin's henchmen. The queen, suddenly a prisoner in her own palace, turned to Gondi to placate the mob. The archbishop went out into the night, made a flourish of calming a few tempers, and withdrew. But Mazarin had to hand back the prisoner.

Now Gondi made proposals to Mme. de Longueville. And the lady listened. He said: Let us take advantage of these civil disorders and make common cause with the city fathers in a revolt against Mazarin. You will engage Marsillac, your husband, and above all your brother Condé in it. The glory will all be yours.[3]

Mme. de Longueville was thrilled and said yes. Marsillac, having been refused his *tabouret*, decided to join the rebels too. The coalition of Parliament and nobility was a fact. The royal family fled to Fontainebleau. Paris belonged to the Fronde.

A triumphant moment: On January 11, 1649, Mme. de Longueville displayed herself, with child in arms, to the people of Paris on the steps of the city hall. Gondi, in his exhilaration, threw hundreds of coins out of the windows to the mob.[4] *"Vive le roi et point de Mazarin!"* ("Up the king and down with Mazarin.") By concentrating their resentment on the cardinal, nobles and citizens alike could conceal, even from themselves, their latent hostility to the prerogatives of the monarchy. The battlecry of the Fronde covered all the obscure longings for a bygone feudal "king among his peers" or for a dimly seen constitutional monarch of the future.

Toward the end of the month Anne-Geneviève gave birth to Marsillac's baby. He was called Charles-Paris in honor of the city. All Paris was in revolt and the spirit of the Fronde was spreading around France. Mme. de Longueville was fulfilled.

But Condé disconcerted the rebels by remaining loyal to the crown, despite his dislike for Mazarin. He openly broke with his sister. He went further. When the queen asked him to rout the insurrectionists, Condé accepted. He found himself battling his sister's friends, and even his own brother Conty, for this incompetent boy had been placed at the head of the rebel forces. Condé made short work of them in one battle at the gates of Paris.

He lost his best friend Gaspard de Châtillon in this engagement. Gaspard died in the arms of his wife, commending her to the protection of Condé. Mme. de Châtillon, the fiery Isabelle who had eloped with him four years before with the assistance of the Duc d'Enghien, now looked up from her husband's broken body to smile into the eyes of the Grand Condé.

Condé's loyalty went unrewarded. His contempt for Mazarin and his irritation at being locked out of the government brought on a spectacular change of heart. He decided to join the insurgents.

But the queen acted swiftly. Before he could go into action against her, she had Condé, his brother Conty, and the Duc de Longueville apprehended and locked up in Vincennes prison, the prison where Condé had been conceived and where Anne-Geneviève had been born.

The shock of the jailing of the princes rallied a number of noblemen to their cause, and Anne-Geneviève found herself in a position of great prestige. She decided to carry on the war herself, incite the people of Normandy to revolt, and force the queen to free her brothers and husband. *"Je n'aime pas les plaisirs innocents,"* she said, as she galloped off to Rouen.

But the phlegmatic Normans did not respond to this kind of heroism. Forced out of Rouen by their stolid refusals of help, Mme. de Longueville fled back to Stenay, her brother's fortified keep. Here she settled down to the hard task of summoning friends to the rebel cause. The comrades-in-arms of Condé heeded the call of this literate princess. At Stenay the councils of war with the general Turenne alternated with the delights of poetry. Sarrasin was on hand to write madrigals and turn the fortress into an island of culture. Turenne fell in love with the princess. Neither he nor Marsillac thought any more than she of the treasonable nature of the pact they now made with the Spaniards. But the queen publicly declared them traitors. They responded with a rain of anti-Mazarin pamphlets.

The Fronde had more than one heroine. Following Anne-Geneviève's abortive revolt in the north, the Princesse de Condé went to Bordeaux to stir up the citizens in favor of her imprisoned husband. Yes, the Princesse de Condé, the young one, the little Richelieu niece, who had never been regarded with much respect by her husband or any of his family, suddenly took it into her head to contribute a gesture to their cause. Condé himself was touched when he heard this in his prison garden: "Who would have thought I would be watering my rose trees while my wife waged war?"

The gesture did not work. The Bordeaux citizenry watched respectfully while her barge sailed up the Garonne into the city. But they were anxious to harvest their grapes. Mme. de Condé was turned over to the authorities and placed in exile at Montrond. Here she received from her husband in prison the only affectionate letter he ever wrote to her, a letter of thanks and tenderness. She sewed it into her dress like an amulet.

The Duchesse de Longueville's love affair with Marsillac was enmeshed in the war. But so was her feeling for her brother. Politics, literature, and love had come together to nourish her heart in one unique experience. It was during the Fronde that a *précieux* novel in many volumes began to appear. Dedicated to the Condés, it was, in stylized fashion, all about them. *Le Grand Cyrus* by Madeleine de Scudéry, an endless tale of adventure and love, describes the exploits of a perfect knight (whom her readers identified as Condé) and the love of this knight for a perfect lady (who could only be Anne-Geneviève). It is curious that this brother and sister are cast as lovers in a book deliberately designed as a roman à clef. No one could fail to see the correspondence between the passionate affection of Cyrus for Mandane, on the one hand, and the unusual closeness of Condé and his sister on the other.

Meanwhile, Condé was still in jail and Anne-Geneviève's idyll with Marsillac–La Rochefoucauld [5] was constantly being interrupted by the shocks and displacements of the war. He had to sue for peace and accept exile in Poitou. She was isolated at Stenay. Embattled and alone, she learned of the death of her mother, condemning her for her revolt, and assisted in her last hours by cousin Isabelle. In the old princesse's feeble state, Isabelle had wheedled the family pearls out of her. This was intolerable news. Anne-Geneviève vowed to get even. She would have been delighted to know of Isabelle's pregnancy by the Duc de Nemours, an embarrassment which she escaped only by undergoing a frightful abortion that nearly took her life.

The Fronde dragged on, a war of skirmishes and haphazard planning. Until it took an unexpected turn:

A new and totally unlikely alliance was formed. The Chevreuse-Montbazon clique, the old *Importants*, now regrouped their forces and made an incredible pact with their worst enemies, the Condé faction. This was achieved during the imprisonment of the princes, by secret treaties engineered by yet another flamboyant alumna of the *chambre bleue*, Marie de Gonzague, Princesse Palatine. It was agreed that the Prince de Conty, when he got out of prison, would marry the daughter of Mme. de Chevreuse as a guarantee of good faith. Unfortunately, this girl was not a great bargain for any honorable husband, for she was carrying on the traditions of her mother by having a fairly public liaison with the Archbishop Gondi. The secret treaty also provided that Gondi would get his cardinal's hat in exchange for his mistress.

Anne of Austria, hearing of these extraordinary underground

formations, felt the cold chill of a takeover of her regency and she shrewdly decided to liberate the princes. For the secret pacts of Condés and *Importants* had been formed in adversity, by a universal hatred of Mazarin. As soon as the princes were free again to elaborate the details, their coalition began to fall apart, as Mazarin guessed it would. If it had worked, the princes would have easily toppled the regency and driven out Mazarin.

But this nobility could not work together. A conflict of vanities destroyed it. Mme. de Longueville could not tolerate the marriage of her brother Conty to a Chevreuse. The girl's reputation had been compromised beyond repair. Her mother, Mme. de Chevreuse, had once been the mistress of La Rochefoucauld. But above all, there was lurking in the background the unforgiveable Mme. de Montbazon, that brazen creature who had poisoned the Longueville marriage and then compounded the insult by spreading scandal about Anne-Geneviève. How could the Condés ally themselves with their bitterest personal enemies?

It was July 1651. Mme. de Châtillon now came on the scene, more dazzling than ever after her successful abortion and wearing the Condé pearls. Safe in the adoration of Nemours, she began to flirt with Condé. Mme. de Longueville, always sensitive to the emotional claims of other women on her brother, turned to Nemours to even the score.

The comings and goings of these amorous beauties, from lover to lover, from castle to castle around France, are not easy to follow and even harder to excuse. While the people starved and died in the trammels of a conflict without plan or direction, Mme. de Longueville slipped into a liaison with Nemours—partly from boredom, for La Rochefoucauld was far away in exile, and partly from a desire to show the superiority of her charms over those of Mme. de Châtillon. By this willful caprice she alienated the services of the general Turenne, who switched sides in disgust.

But worse than that, she lost La Rochefoucauld. When he learned of her infidelity he vowed to get even and did. By January 1652, through his intervention, Nemours was firmly back in the chains of Isabelle. Anne-Geneviève suddenly found herself abandoned by all her former admirers: Turenne, Nemours, La Rochefoucauld, and even her brother Condé, who was now sharing Isabelle's favors with Nemours! This relationship was masterminded by La Rochefoucauld to induce Condé to capitulate to the crown. Isabelle de

Châtillon was acting as go-between for the court and the rebels. She was the new queen of the Fronde, the irresistible little peacemaker.

But peace did not come yet. In July 1652 the last major battle of the war was fought at the gates of Paris. The citizens were weary of this frivolous conflict and had locked Condé's army out of the town. Forced to the wall by Turenne's loyalist troops, Condé appeared to be hopelessly trapped. He was saved by yet another young *frondeuse*, who stepped into action and tipped the scales in his favor. This time it was Mlle. de Montpensier, the Grande Mademoiselle, Gaston d'Orléans' daughter and a first cousin of Louis XIV. This princess, on an obscure impulse, gave the order for the Bastille cannon to fire on Turenne's troops. A horrified Louis XIV was watching the action from a nearby hill. This crucial act resulted in the storming of Paris by Condé. A new insurrectionist government was set up. And Mazarin had to flee the country.

During this last occupation of Paris the quality of the behavior in the camp of the princes can be judged by the Beaufort-Nemours duel. The Duc de Beaufort had recently been added to the list of Isabelle's lovers, and this caused friction between him and Nemours. Also, Nemours' abandoned wife was Beaufort's sister. The only solution to the insults which both men felt they had sustained was a duel. An elaborate one was arranged, during which Beaufort killed Nemours. Four of the eight seconds were also killed or wounded. Not a very edifying spectacle for the citizenry of Paris which had placed its destiny in the hands of these gallants.

Isabelle, dressed coquettishly in black, went to visit the widow of Nemours and cry with her over the corpse of her lover. But when Condé arrived, she lifted her veil and flashed him an amorous signal. There were no tears on her carefully painted face.

The uneasy coalition of princes and Parliament within the city lasted three more months. But the princes found they could not replace the king in the hearts of the people of Paris. The city finally repudiated them. Condé had to withdraw, and the king was invited back from his semi-exile in October 1652. Mazarin avoided showing himself until the following February. He then came back unopposed and quietly took up the task of government where he had left it.

This was the end of the Fronde. Nothing whatever had been achieved save the destruction of large areas of France. It was the end of the pretensions to political supremacy of France's vainglorious nobility. As for the citizens, they discovered that they did not yet want the burden of self-government. Their fear of confusion proved to be greater than their desire for power. They had too many privileges to lose.

Exile and even a few presents were meted out to the worst offenders. Gondi got his red hat. The Prince de Conty got a wife: instead of the tarnished Mlle. de Chevreuse—a Mazarin niece.

Mme. de Longueville returned at last to the hair shirt she had laid away at sixteen. Tired of rebellion, bitter about love, but still feeling heroic, she withdrew into herself, became a fervent Jansenist, and made peace with her enemies. The king forgave her. Her husband took her back. She even exerted herself to be charitable to cousin Isabelle. The distinction she had sought in the Fronde she now looked for in repentance.

She never saw La Rochefoucauld again. But years later, meditating on her spiritual state, she wrote, "More than anything I like to think about myself, and to have others think about me too; self-love makes us rather speak ill of ourselves than say nothing at all." Was she secretly reading her old lover's *Maximes?*

Only Condé did not quit at once with the others. He allied himself with Spain and was pursued all over northern France and Flanders by his former ally Turenne, until 1660, when Louis xiv, to end this "Spanish Fronde," took to wife an infanta of Spain, as his father had done. During the royal journey to the Spanish border, Condé presented himself on his knees to Louis, and the young king, on the threshold of his long absolute rule, granted forgiveness easily.

Longueville, Châtillon, Condé, Montpensier, Nemours, La Rochefoucauld—the noblest names of France, the flower of chivalry. The Fronde was the glorious daydream of their sentimental education. When they awoke from it, they found themselves reduced to life-size; weary and disabused of heroism. They would never dream this dream again.

RAMBOUILLET

NOTES

1. A good book about the Fronde is Pierre-Georges Lorris, *La Fronde* (A. Michel, 1961).
2. Cardinal de Retz, *Mémoires*, ed. Edith Thomas (Pléiade, 1956), p. 132.
3. Ibid., p. 131.
4. Ibid., p. 150.
5. It was at this moment that he acceded to his new and final title of Duc de La Rochefoucauld.

II

The Precious Decade

After the Fronde

F RANCE WAS weary and poor again, but quiet. The explosions and burnings had ceased. The bread was white and plentiful in Paris, and the streets were safer than they had been for years. There was a luxury of hours, in which the slow-flowering hothouse plant of civilized intercourse could be nurtured from first encounter to final resolution or heartbreak. The précieuses had seven years they could call their own.

These years (1653–1660) can be seen as a kind of hiatus in the history of France, a moment of suspension between the wild and wilful heroics of the Fronde and the final relieved descent into absolutism. Bourgeoisie and nobility, drawing away from violence, were beginning to feel the fascination of safety under a firm hand. A divinely invested monarch, if he had the will to take over their wills, could put everyone back into his rightful place and hold the state together.

They watched the young king. Louis was wearing the crown but taking his time about growing up. He was fifteen in 1653 and nearly twenty-three when the cardinal died. What was he doing in that seven-year interval but enjoying himself—dancing in royal ballets, flirting with Mazarin's nieces? Few of his courtiers guessed he might also be learning the craft of government.

That infinitesimal segment of society which enjoyed the means to think about such complex matters was holding passionate discussions of the varieties of divine grace, and this intricate Jansenist controversy transposed into the theological realm an uneasiness about freedom and responsibility that had its counterpart in civil life. How much of the future was theirs to create? How much choice did anyone actually have?

The nobleman who had hated Mazarin in 1648 and was now

153

almost ready to trust in the young king's eventual protection could not see that the Fronde had been, for his class, a hopeless rear-guard action. Nor did the citizen know that Louis xiv would be a mercantile monarch, would drive his nobility to bankruptcy with ribbons and lace while enriching and ennobling his bourgeoisie with jobs. Time was on the side of the middle class, but a very long time. Parliament would not win the Fronde until 1789—and they did not dream in 1654 that they would ever want to win it.

This seven-year interval was the pivot of the century, a moment of indecision between the heroic assertion of Cartesian free will (I choose to think, therefore I am; I am not God's slave but a willing believer in His Being) and the equally heroic Jansenist submission to destiny (Here we are shipwrecked in the void and only God's grace can pluck us from our misery). This was the momentary pause between the towering self-possession of Corneille's women and the helpless groveling surrender of Racine's. Between diversity and unity. Between baroque art, enormous and overflowing, full of optimism and guile, and the stately, lucid pessimism of the classical world view.

By 1661, after the cardinal's funeral, when Louis stepped into Mazarin's shoes and the Sun King declared himself to be the state personified, the long pause was over. Absolutism, the ultimate unity, was what everybody discovered they really wanted. France arrived at her final form, that of a social monolith where conformity and certitude were the highest virtues. It would last, they thought, forever.

The year 1653: the bloom of peace. There were handsome ladies everywhere. They seemed to have taken possession of Paris, some very conspicuously riding in their new open carriages in the Cours-la-Reine along the Seine or strolling in the Galerie du Palais where they went to buy the new novels. Or fingering the elaborate lace collars that were coming in again from Venice and Flanders. Or running to the théâtre de l'Hôtel de Bourgogne, with their masks secured by a button in the mouth. All these ladies seemed to be so busy. They were going somewhere. They had something to do. Who were they?

At the *chambre bleue* the Marquise de Rambouillet, now in her middle sixties, had taken to wearing heavy rouge on her withered

Louis XIV as the sun, in a ballet

cheeks. Most of her old friends were dead. Her health more fragile than ever, she had nevertheless reopened her doors to another generation of young ladies to replace the *belles frondeuses* who had scattered to the fortresses and country houses of exile. These new girls, the recently widowed Mme. de Sévigné and her girlfriend Mlle. de La Vergne, provided company for the youngest Rambouillet daughter Angélique-Clarisse, who had opted out of her convent to join the world at the *chambre bleue*. Another wave of amusements had started up around these ladies; they were better educated, more intellectually self-assured than ever.

But something was different in the air of Paris: before the Fronde there had been only a few interesting places to go; now there were dozens. At Mme. de Sablé's house in the Faubourg Saint-Jacques the habitués were still murmuring about Sufficient and Actual Grace while she sat up to sip her medicinal tea. But out of town at Vaux-le-Vicomte the minister Fouquet's chic new mistress, Mme. du Plessis-Bellière, could be seen—by those fortunate enough to be invited—presiding over magnificent dinner parties where her friends composed *bouts-rimés* on the death of her parrot. And at Mlle. de Scudéry's Saturdays in the rue de Beauce, the happenings were a much darker enigma. It was worth all the scheming it took to gain admittance into her dim sanctum, for Mlle. de Scudéry made, they said, excellent conversation and one never knew what sort of people one would find there. That whole neighborhood, the Marais, a new development of town houses in what had lately been a swamp, was now the last word in stylishness, because of her and friends of hers who lived there.

Even ladies who had never been to the *chambre bleue* were launching their own intimate gatherings, vying for the presence of some Academician or gentleman-poet. The richest ones could afford to "protect" any number of authors who became secretaries in their service. More modestly placed ladies caught whomever they could.

With the sudden multiplication of loci of society came a new publicity. Publicity presupposes an interested public, and until now there had not been, properly speaking, any such thing, at least not for the social doings of the *chambre bleue*. The guests had simply observed each other. The larger world had been the court, which was looking into its own mirror. But now there was a sizeable reservoir of outsiders on hand to watch and judge the new hostesses,

La Galerie du Palais by Abraham Bosse

COURTESY OF THE METROPOLITAN MUSEUM OF ART, ROGERS FUND, 1922

a literate populace of citizens and visitors which shifted and flowed in and around Paris. It was composed of newly leisured rich and less-rich bourgeoisie, provincial small nobility, fortune hunters, title hunters, hangers-on of the theatre and the tavern, the substance of postwar anonymous Paris. Many women were eager to learn quickly the style and manners of the Marais and take them back with them to Aix or the Place Maubert.[1] And many idle men were looking for something to laugh at.

A curious paradox: Privacy was the essence of social life; a selective, restrictive grouping of persons in their own frame, with their own rules. But most of the new hostesses, while they made a point of fleeing the prying eyes of those whom they "did not know," also wished to be known to do so. They therefore cautiously welcomed the attention of anyone who could be depended on to acknowledge their excellence. One result of the exposure of these new circles of refined ladies to the public stare is that they had begun to be called *précieuses*. In 1655 a fascinated observer, the abbé de Pure, wrote a long rich study in novel form, full of details on this new woman. He takes his time about it:

Perhaps you have not heard in your neighborhood about the précieuse. You think perhaps that it is some rare object from the Orient or some miracle of the Indies and faraway lands. Well, I will not leave you long in error or in a state of guessing. I'll tell you in few words what I have learned from informed people who know and are intelligent. She is not simply a work of Nature or of Art, but an effort of both; a précis of the mind, an extract of the human intelligence. The first lovely days of peace gave us this happy production, adorned their serenity and enriched our conversations with her.

These stars which shine on the earth have two kinds of heaven, which the new philosophy calls *Alcove* and *Ruelle*. The one and the other comprise but one sphere, and are in one circle called conversation. We can distinguish torrid, temperate, and frigid zones, but a wind blows there which is called Disguise, which makes them all look so like one another that the cleverest Astrologer can barely distinguish them and avoid confusion.[2]

The New Women were so talked about that it soon became apparent that the species *Précieuse* had several variations and wore many masks, however similar to one another observers said they were. Some said that the précieuse was a lady in the vanguard of fashion, a launcher of hair styles and flounces. She wore shoes to match her costume. She smothered her sleeves in ribbons. Her linen was snowy. She wore three petticoats, the outer one called *la modeste*, and under that *la friponne* (saucy or wicked), because it caught the eye and troubled the thoughts of the passer-by; while the innermost of all, *la fidèle*, bore the colors of the lady's lover, and "so to speak, touches with its fingertips the point of perfect love."

But no, this highly visible fashion-plate was not the real thing. Or at least this was not the truly precious element in her character. It was only when she came home from her outings, closed her gates to all but the faithful, drew her curtains, muffled her door-knocker to assure the essential peace and quiet—only then, in small, select secret meetings did the précieuse truly blossom. Her discussions were long and passionate. They turned on the four different varieties of love: *l'amour de oui, l'amour de non, l'amour de mais . . .*, and *l'amour d'eh! bien.*

But who could be sure, unless he had been present, what the précieuse and her intimate friends did talk about? The only thing that everyone agreed on was their variety:

We see in a *ruelle*, the movement of the whole earth, and three or four Précieuses will mention in one afternoon all that the Sun has seen in its various turnings over several seasons. Nothing is obscure to their eyes and their mind. They are so enlightened as to pierce through to the thoughts and secrets of hearts, and nothing can escape their curiosity or avoid their notice.[3]

There were self-styled précieuses now in the most unlikely places, in town, at court, in the country, lying on satin beds in elegant palaces, and dreaming on windowsills in tiny shops.

It is not easy to catch the tone in which the précieuses were finally named. When the abbé de Pure calls them "baroque pearls" he is complimenting them on their absence of uniformity. But though he lists their many different kinds of beauty (there are, in his catalog, proud and severe beauties, daily beauties, changeable beauties, beauties of *yet* and beauties of *more or less*, ageing beauties, consolation beauties, beauties of hope [4]), he seems to be gently chaffing them on their preoccupation with their looks rather than admiring their loveliness.

There were also downright cynics—the abbé d'Aubignac, for example, who wrote a churlish *Royaume de coquetterie* [5] insinuating that what went on behind those drawn velvet curtains was not all it should be.

The name *précieuse* certainly had very ambiguous overtones. Its history, to tell the truth, belonged more to the scoffers than to the flatterers. It had appeared in French as early as the fourteenth century, in a poem by Eustache Deschamps, in which he rails at a lady who considers herself too good to be wooed. *Elle fait la précieuse.* Her virtue is more precious to her than any delights he has to offer, and the poet implies that she has donned this virtue like a suit of armor; it is not a natural part of her person. A century later Charles d'Orléans confirms the masculine irritation with women who "*contrefont . . . les précieuses,*" that is, put on a touch-me-not act. Traditionally, then, the précieuse was not only an exasperating prude but a false one.

But by 1655 the modishness of the Rambouillet style of prudery had spread all over Paris. And now many a lady was advertising herself as a précieuse not merely because she was virtuous but because she was interesting. The flatterers all named the précieuses in this sense, and brochures and catalogues were now being compiled to list their attractions and talents, as well as their virtues.

The scoffers, the composers of street songs and rowdy lyrics in men's clubs, who saw that women were entertaining themselves independently, poured ridicule on them. They were now not only false prudes; their refinement and talent were also false, insidious ruses to promote their social advancement. Some précieuses, however, were too convincingly virtuous, or too highly placed, to be criticized in this way. They must be weeded out and spared. They were the handful of "true précieuses" of which all the others were to be considered bad imitations. The burlesque poet Scarron made this distinction as early as 1652:

> Mais revenons aux facheux et facheuses,
> Au rang de qui je mets les précieuses,
> Fausses, s'entend, et de qui tout le bon
> Est seulement un langage ou jargon,
> Un parler gras, plusieurs sottes manières,
> Et qui ne sont enfin que façonnières,
> Et ne sont pas précieuses de prix,
> Comme il en est deux ou trois dans Paris,
> Que l'on respecte autant que des princesses.[6]

(But let's come back to those annoying people,
among whom I place the précieuses,
the false ones that is, whose whole pleasure
is in highfalutin jargon,
and silly mannerisms,
who are just ceremonious fakes,
and not genuinely precious
like the two or three real ones to be found in Paris,
who are respected as much as princesses.)

But what was the difference between these true and false précieuses? What was the scale by which they could be measured? Class? Virtue? A princess was obviously "precious" by birth. Anyone below her was bound to be less so. Did that make her a genuine "précieuse"? It is difficult to see who in particular the poet could have had in mind in separating the true from the false précieuses, unless he was merely covering himself against attack by the rich and powerful. This vague distinction came to be repeated by others. Somaize wrote a play, *Les Véritables Précieuses*, to show that he could tell the difference, although his "true précieuses," at least in this play, prove to be only a pair of silly fools modeled more or less on Molière's.[7] Molière himself, when he came to write the preface to the printed edition of his *Précieuses ridicules* in 1660, was careful to announce that he had no intention of ridiculing the real ones.

But no one had the courage to name names in print. Who, then, were the true and false précieuses? Any lady could regard herself as a person of genuine distinction as long as she had even one friend to agree with her about it, and could perhaps look down on just one other lady as a poor imitation of herself. The whole idea of true and false précieuses implies that there is an objective quality, *préciosité*, which can be measured by some sort of exterior standards. But *préciosité* was subjective, residing largely in the minds of the ladies who chose to assume this identity. You cannot tell a lady her very identity is false when it is all in her head anyway, and of her own making. You can only tell her that she has not made the grade as a précieuse in the opinion of someone else.

True or false, successful or unsuccessful, all of the ladies now being called précieuses had one thing in common: they claimed the right to do as they pleased. Freedom was the crux and aim of their lives. Freedom to visit and receive company. To trot around the city, see and be seen, and then return to a comfortable retreat to read and think. Above all, freedom to talk. Hundreds of ladies were learning to converse politely in well-shaped sentences, and they were busy at it with a delirium of enthusiasm that could lead anywhere. Those who were mere beginners talked about curling irons, "virginal water," pomades and patches. Such vanities, a perennial scandal to the devout, were castigated by gruff bourgeois fathers as a terrible waste of money and scorned by aristocrats (who used them all the same) as a trivial topic of conversation. But to the ladies who had just discovered them they were educative and amusing, far more so than the dowries, marriages, babies their grandmothers chatted about.

For the more sophisticated there were more sophisticated subjects. As reading was a great effort for a woman, and writing even harder, they talked about their faulty training—and discovered solutions, such as spelling reform, "so that women can write as correctly as men." [8] They would suppress superfluous letters, they said, take the *s* out of *teste* and the *h* out of *autheur*, and generally shorten all words. We are not to assume that these changes, some of which became permanent in the language, were accomplished by the précieuses. The printers were the real arbiters of orthography in the seventeenth century and were in the process of fixing most variant spellings for all time. The précieuses were really only observers of this trend. But they took a passionate interest in it because they sensed that language was the magic tool that would liberate them.

There were now public lectures they could attend, where learned men laid aside their Latin to expound philosophy and rhetoric in simple French for the tender ears of ladies. The ladies came home from these excursions full of the excitement of new knowledge and eager to try it out on their friends.

They had discovered the practical power of social intercourse. The trapped wife, by associating with a free précieuse, found ways to escape the watchful eyes of her "Argus" husband. The jolly girl discovered she could tell stories, or propose questions for debate, such as this daring one: "Is it better for a man to marry a woman who would bring him a dowry of horns but after marriage would never make them grow, or a woman who would present him with this gift only after marriage?" This topic was a success in the *ruelle* of one Mme. de la Parisière, who found that all the husbands and spinsters in the gathering chose the first alternative, while the wives and young lads preferred the second! [9]

The melancholy girl found that she, too, could generate a mood in a whole company. Mlle. Dumont sits quietly dreaming throughout an evening party. M. Alméra approaches her and tries to draw her out, but without success. Later he writes her a letter to find out if the cause of her silence is perhaps just stupidity. Her reply is an elegant, well-turned self-analysis. She is not stupid, only shy. She is sensitive, suspicious, sad, and naturally reserved, as a result of having lived for years with a mean stepmother.[10]

These unknown précieuses delight as much as the most celebrated ones in the welter of new poetry that had materialized. It was the same old sharp-edged jewelry, but short and neat:

> Je mourrai de trop de désir
> Si je la trouve inexorable;
> Je mourrai de trop de plaisir,
> Si je la trouve favorable.
> Ainsi je ne saurais guérir
> De la douleur qui me possède;
> Je suis assuré de périr
> Par le mal ou par le remède.[11]

> ("I'll die of desire
> if she refuses.
> I'll die of pleasure
> if she accepts.
> Thus I cannot be cured
> of the pain that possesses me.
> I'm certain to perish,
> if not by the sickness, then by the remedy.)

The most refined ladies of all spent hours splitting hairs over the twenty kinds of sighs (the sigh of love, the sigh of friendship, the sigh of ambition, . . .) and the forty kinds of smiles (the smile of the inviting eye, the toothy smile, the disdainful smile, . . .). They talked for talk's own sake, because words were magic. They endlessly classified their sentiments and thought up ever more delicate ways of avoiding or postponing the ugly realities beyond words. *Pregnancy* became a word too dreadful to utter. It was for them "the ill effects of lawful love." An enema (taken frequently by nearly eveybody) was "the broth of the two sisters" who administered it.[12]

Did they really ban all common words, like *shirt, louse, headcold, to soil, to be in labor?* If we are to believe all we read in the notes of their friends and enemies, water was "the liquid element," a broom "the instrument of cleanliness," a fan "a zephyr," jealousy "the mother of suspicions." The language of the précieuses got stuck in a morass of periphrase and euphemism often quite impenetrable. Add to this the pedantic references, which they may have picked up from their public lectures (a doctor: a bastard of Hippocrates; to swim: visit the naiads; andirons: the arms of Vulcan; fish: citizens of the kingdom of Neptune), and the cuteness (the page on which a love letter is written "blushes for shame"), and we are ready to agree that they abused their freedom.

But it is also true that the language that the précieuses were so playfully twisting into knots was a narrow idiom from which many of the plain words descriptive of tangible common things had already been excised. Malherbe, the *chambre bleue*, and the Academy had done their work by the mid-century. The French language, as used by the better sort of people, had grown colorless, euphemistic, its vocabulary boiled down, its syntax ironed out, in the interests of clarity and "good usage," by Balzac and Vaugelas. Little was left of the rich gauloiserie of Rabelais' time, the natural lyricism of Ronsard, the free association of Montaigne. The functions of words had become precise and orderly. Words had grown heavier, more burdened with general abstract reference than with concrete meanings. Poetry already took this for granted. A *flamme* or a *chaine* were not a flame or a chain in the ordinary sense, but shorthand symbols for amorous passion and emotional constraint. Real flames and chains were the concern of bellows menders and locksmiths; such people did not make conversation. For those who did, the leisured minority of a few thousand to whom the précieuses belonged, or wished to belong, there was little interest in material objects. Everybody was talking about psychology. The assumption of such language was that human beings exist in a prepared, smooth world, a world emptied of ordinary day-to-day things such as clean mattresses and hot soup.

The dull, immaculate language composed by purists of the Academy out of the speech of the *honnêtes gens* at the *chambre bleue* had been fixed as a timeless and permanent tool for the clear expression of rational thought. But it was also a trap, a decorous, bland naming of essences. It excluded too much. The précieuses, suddenly using words for the first time to discover and defend themselves, might have been better served with some other language. It seems to us, in our age of techniques and objects, that they needed to be able to call a spade a spade. But they could only study themselves in the terms and style they trusted. No doubt they would have called a spade "the sword of Hesiod."

Many of the cynics and libertines who sang and laughed at them in the taverns did use a more rich and interesting vocabulary that would one day figure in the *Dictionary* of Furetière (1690).[13] If we compare this lexicon with that which the Academy finally published in 1694, we can see how much was lost of the French language by the century's effort to polish it until it became a focusing lens for the expression of elegant ideas. Furetière's French is more materialistic and practical, reflecting a bourgeois interest in techniques.

But *bourgeois* was a bad word to the précieuses. Everything bourgeois was "plunged in matter." They chose instead to use the language of leisure and elegance, the impoverished language of the official intellectual elite. To relieve the monotony of normal speech they embroidered it with playful paraphrase, turned it into a vehicle of wit. An insensitive man was one with a "paralytic soul"; ears were the "doors of understanding," dreams the "fathers of metamorphosis."

It was not utterly useless to them, this verbal game they played. For language, even before it becomes literature, can rename the things of the universe, rearrange the order of reality, transform life. The précieuses had discovered in their own way the magical power of words. Language could make a lady beautiful, interesting, perhaps immortal.

The *précieux* speech mannerisms have lingered on in French only as superficial vices. The excessive use of abstraction as a means of turning away from ugly particulars, the hyperbolic adverbs ending in *-ment* (*"elle est* furieusement *belle"*—"she's *terribly* pretty"): these are the bad habits of *préciosité*. But the *précieux* metaphor could be quaintly amusing. A lady says of her mirror that it is to her "a sort of counselor of graces."[14] The effect is of a simple and charming simile. If then she calls for her "counselor of graces," substituting a metaphor for the simile, something more subtle is being communicated. To the alcovist attending on her *levée* who has heard her invent the phrase, the metaphor is now a bond of private reference. A rash of such quotations went the rounds of certain *ruelles*, and a test of a lady's belonging was the recognition of these arcane turns of phrase. *"Hélas! mes chers souffrants!"* says the lady to her alcovist when she is tired of dancing. He heard her say yesterday while trying on her new shoes that her feet were her "poor suffering dears." The metaphor has now become a password for her circle. There is nothing bizarre about this intimate style, and it befits the exclusive nature of the coterie, to have a fund of private expressions which constantly changes, like the slang of twentieth-century teenagers or the argot of gangland. Naturally, if wrenched out of its appropriate setting and placed in the mouth of a fool, the expression becomes ridiculous. Molière's *précieuse ridicule* Magdelon speaks in this way to her servant, but neither she nor the servant belongs to *précieux* society. This is why she makes the mistake of thinking that the jargon ought to be intelligible to everybody. *"Voiturez-nous, les commodités de la conversation,"* she commands majestically, and the poor gaping valet does not comprehend that he is being asked to bring chairs.

It is in the nature of such speech to be useful only to a private group. When the phrase becomes too common, it is discarded. *"Le fidèle gardien"* (i.e., a door) is an expendable phrase of transient value to the adept who knows how and when to use it. Its fancifulness partakes of the inventive freedom of *préciosité* at its best.

But such fancies were too ephemeral for the exponents of a purer, timeless, "classical" form of expression. The great writers of the age of Louis xiv would soon begin to appear, refusing to be so easily original or to strain for effect as the *précieux* writers and public enjoyed doing. One of the glories of the French classical age is the deliberate banality of its speech, the mediocrity of ideas, the grand simplicity of form which clothed the image of Nature they saw. To match the absolutism of Louis xiv the classical authors were also to become absolutists of taste. With their eyes fixed on the sublime, they rejected the short-term delights of *préciosité*, the values of cleverness and allusion. To them the *précieux* expression was simply obscure and farfetched. La Bruyère pleaded honestly: "Speak plainly! I can't understand you!"

The précieuses, believing in the magical naming of states of mind and heart, busily trying to unlock the mysteries of their inmost

Un couple amoureux by Abraham Bosse

psyche with riddles and puns, flourished a spate of conversational talents that no one had ever dreamed women had. They felt the breeze and it was a "lover of flowers"; they looked in their mirrors and these treacherous instruments were "chameleons"; they caught their flesh on a pin and it became a "bloodsucker"; they put on their hats ("affronters of the elements ") to go out into the Cours-la-Reine ("the empire of coquettish glances"); they sat down to the table to "give Nature its due"; and they looked out of their casements at the "torch of night" before retiring to dream the "interpreters of the Gods."

Another curious detail of the *précieux* tableau which the busy gossips who knew them seem to have taken quite for granted and which no modern historian has seen fit to pick up and examine afresh: these ladies, these paragons of refinement and exquisite unavailability, these linguists who would faint at the sound of a suggestive syllable—entertained while in bed.

It is true that the reclining posture was fairly widespread in the seventeenth century; not *only* the précieuses entertained in bed. Ever since its invention the bed had been a feature of public life and a symbol of power to those in authority. The *lit de parade* on which royalty would receive was already a standard piece of furniture, full of political value. It was a throne, only the more symbolic because not entirely dissociated from the intimacies of the boudoir or the vulnerability of sleep. A king lying down is saying to his courtiers, "Here I am, more powerful than you, even on my back." Richelieu was never stronger than in his last months when his rotting body was carried up the Rhône to a final fateful meeting with the king at which he crushed the favorite Cinq-Mars.

A *queen* in bed was also a public figure, a symbol of royal fertility. Marie de Medici gave birth to Louis xiii in full view of a large roomful of people: men and women of the court were milling around her bed for hours while she sweated out her labor pains. Ministers and in-laws crowded up close at the moment of parturition, to make sure that the child was indeed a boy and indeed the issue of the queen. For blood, the blood royal, must be pure, and there must be no remote possibility of a substitution. The little seven-year-old Duc de Vendôme, Henri iv's illegitimate son by Gabrielle d'Estrées, was brought forward to see: he knew what it meant for him that the baby coming out of the queen was a boy. It meant he would never be King of France.

But the précieuse in her bed is quite another matter. Her position had no political value. She was a *private* person. Mme. de Rambouillet and Mme. de Sablé took to their beds not as to a public stage from which to pronounce laws or shape history, but to narrow down their social life to a more manageable size. Power was replaced by politeness.

The *réduits* of the later précieuses who copied them expressed a more classless privacy. These ladies found a whole new environment of expressive artifice in the little intimate alcove, screened from the public, hard to get into unless you played the lady's game. It was the last word in towny chic.

And in the *ruelle*, the stuffy corridor on the other side of her bed, knelt the lady's admirer, the *soupirant*, the man who sighed for her in vain. This ultimate confined space gave its name to the room, the locus of the précieuse. Her whole milieu came to be called a *ruelle*.

This tableau suggests a number of obvious things. To the lady herself it is pleasant to be the focal point of the conversation, and her situation in bed gives her confidence to speak up. All the loveliness and wit she can muster will flash with greater concentration there. The lady is saying: "I am the center of this small, well-defined universe. You must behave as I say."

The précieuses did not compose this tableau out of thin air. Obviously it came from the previous generation who had cultivated ironclad illnesses. But the hostesses of the 1650s are often blooming with vitality. Flimsier excuses must be found. One ready-made pretext was the lying-in period after a pregnancy. Getting pregnant may not seem like a very good form of birth control, but where women were pregnant much of the time anyway, it paid to make the most of the postnatal weeks. Women of means, regardless of class, spent a month or two in bed and were treated with great consideration after childbirth. A woman deserved to be fussed over when she had accomplished her duty and provided a child.[15]

The recently delivered mother had a special kind of beauty. Mme. de Longueville received the Archbishop Gondi in the apparently not compromising position of the bed on which she had just given birth to a daughter. Sitting beside this overwhelmingly enticing woman, all flushed with the excitement of her personal mission in the Fronde, it is no wonder that Gondi's fingers itched.

By the 1650s a lady need not be actually ill or recovering from childbirth to lie in bed. She might only be suffering from fatigue. So many life-and-death crises of a woman's life were associated with the bed that the précieuses, who liked to flaunt their grievances, went to bed even when well as a dramatization of their plight: "I am by nature weak and vulnerable. I could die. You must protect me."

There was hidden strength in their weakness. The whole apparatus of chivalry and the poetic attitudes that derived from it were based on the assumption that women were defenseless. This might be remote from actual cases, but the précieuses made concerted practical use of the fictions of chivalry. They went to bed in studied objectification of the Virgin Mary. The précieuse was the Virgin made flesh. She dreamed on her couch, unconscious, untouchable, and the emotion evoked by the sight of her was profound respect.

A woman in bed, propped up in the stiff shape of fashion, weighted under her burden of civilization, exposed to a mortality more sinister than a man's because it is hidden within her own body, arouses the man's pity and concern, and this diffuses his brutish desire. He is undone by sentiment. So fragile an object can never be enjoyed, only adored.

A kind of narcissism was engendered in the précieuse by this sentimental image. It was reinforced by the thing behind her physical weakness: her moral strength. For the bed bespeaks not only her womanly functions and her frailty; it also proclaims that one of these functions is being denied: "Here I am in bed; you could climb in with me easily, if I were not so virtuous." The prude—and most of the précieuses were at least pretending to be prudes—is far more tantalizing if she refuses herself from the vantage point of the very bed on which she might be ravished.

NOTES

1. The Place Maubert is the neighborhood where lives Javotte, would-be *précieuse* heroine of Furetière's *Roman bourgeois* (1666).

2. Abbé de Pure, *La Pretieuse*, I, p. 66.

3. Ibid., I, p. 67.

4. Ibid., I, p. 69.

5. Abbé d'Aubignac, *Histoire du temps, ou relation du royaume de coqueterie* (1654).

6. Scarron, "Epitre chagrine à Mgr. le Mareschal d'Albret," in *Poésies diverses*.

7. Somaize, always eager to blow with the wind, ineptly tried to copy Moliere's wit in this play, while in other works he lashes out at Moliere in defense of the précieuses.

8. Somaize, *Dictionnaire*, I, pp. 178–84.

9. Ibid., I, pp. 195–97.

10. Ibid., I, pp. 75–78.

11. Benserade, *Poésies*, ed. O. Uzanne (Librairie des Bibliophiles, 1875).

12. Somaize, *Grand Dictionnaire des Pretieuses, ou la Clef de la langue des ruelles* (1660). This *"Dictionnaire,"* not to be confused with his vaster *Grand Dictionnaire des Pretieuses Historique, Poetique, etc.*, of 1661, is a compendium of *précieux* turns of phrase. We have taken many of our examples of word play from it. Both works appear in the Livet edition mentioned above, p. 26, n.2.

13. *Dictionnaire universel contenant généralement tous les mots françois tant vieux que modernes et les termes de toutes les sciences et les arts. . .* (1690).

14. *"Grace"* rhymes with *"glace"* (mirror), and this figure recalls the word substitution of cockney rhymed slang: "apples and pears" instead of "stairs."

15. As early as 1623, *Les Caquets de l'accouchée*, author unknown, describes the conversation of a group of middle-class ladies gathered around the bed of a recently delivered matron. Entertaining in bed thus had both genteel and bourgeois precedents. See *Les Caquets de l'accouchée*, ed. E. Fournier (1855).

Prudes

As with language so with psychology. The précieuses, recipients of an increasingly impoverished idiom which they sought to enrich by superficial embellishment, were also enveloped in a society that was aiming to unveil the simple universals of human nature, beneath the accidents of particular lives. This society was bent on isolating the essences, the "characters" of mankind, rather than its eccentricities. It looked at everybody through the distorting lens of stereotype: the miser, the irate father, the boastful upstart. And for women, since they could only be thought of in terms of sex, the words *prude, coquette*. This pair of moral opposites swallowed up all women, leaving them with these choices: a libertinage so depraved as to exclude them from the society of desireable people or a chastity so total as to make them totally unhappy.

The précieuses did not invent this dichotomy. The stereotypes were not new. They were simply the current euphemisms for the centuries-old duality of virgins and whores. Chastity had always been the womanly virtue, as valor was the manly one. But chastity had never been stronger than in Catholic Europe where women were assigned just enough freedom to choose to be chaste. For where women live in severe or total enslavement, the burden of chastity is imposed from without, with stone walls and eunuchs. The woman is a thing. But where she is supposed to be free, the stone walls are placed in her conscience; they take the form of virtue.

Where woman is defined in terms of sex alone, as had in fact always been the case, and is then offered a chance to exercise self-control, sexual virtue is the only thing she can call her own. The jewel of her chastity becomes her most valued possession. It is of her own making, the product of her will. It is the only form of freedom there is.

The précieuses had to choose. And they chose, understandably, to be prudes. Or to look like prudes. We have seen how well this choice had worked for Mlle. Paulet and Julie d'Angennes. The hundreds of précieuses who came in their wake in the 1650s found the pattern ready and waiting.

Having found their tongues in an abstract language of psychological stereotypes, the précieuses began to ask questions.

They asked amazing questions: What are my rights, what is my meaning as a maiden, a wife, a mother, a daughter? How should I respond to the demands of the world? And above all, they talked in circles around and around the topic of all topics that haunted them, the unspeakable problem of their bodies. Behind all their coy verbiage about love and friendship these women were obsessed with burning thoughts about what it was that made them female and what they could do about it.

There was nothing they could do about it, except say no. The famous *refus de l'amour*, pronounced from the stronghold of their damask bed-hangings, was a double liberation, both from the bondage of marriage and pregnancy and from the disrespect and ostracism that came as the price of capitulation.

But it was not enough to refuse. In the goldfish bowl of society a lady must be seen to be chaste. She must be constantly tending that chastity like an artificial garden. And it was a good idea to scorn other women less successful at keeping their garden neat.

For the scorned one it was much harder. The lady who had earned the name of *coquette* must do what she could to get rid of it by concealing her lapses. It behooved her to pretend to be a prude. Prudes may band together in a sisterhood of hostility to threatening males. But there was no freemasonry of coquetry. Every coquette was alone.

The celebrated prudery of the précieuses was a source of belly-laughs to frustrated libertines who could not get at the women. But it was still the safest bet, in a world where any doubtful behavior would bring those same libertines shouting the scandal with glee. As women were driven further into their "character" of prudery, the men, glimpsing the real woman underneath this role, fought back with disbelief. Their skepticism is summed up in La Rochefoucauld's acid *maxime:*

Chastity in women is often nothing but a regard for their reputation and their peace of mind.[1]

Or: the prude is a false prude.

Of course she is. It seems a fairly obvious thing to say that there is no such thing as a prude or a coquette. All women are both modest and flirtatious in their moments. But by inventing categories of behavior, a society can force individuals to fall into them forever.

And the précieuses, talking on and on in their *réduits* about the twenty kinds of esteem (*estime d'inclination, estime d'amour, ...*), flirted wildly with the illicit possibilities, idealized, elevated, and worshipped love in the pure state, and kept their knees firmly together under their stiff skirts.

Prudery was every woman's badge, but it was most conspicuous in the most conspicuous ladies. Angélique-Clarisse de Rambouillet (d. 1664),[2] youngest daughter of the marquise, found in a militant and strident prudery the key to her own distinction. Born at some unknown date between 1625 and 1630, she had carrot-colored hair, a flat chest, and smallpox scars. They had named her after that ravishing lady, Angélique Paulet, who knew how to turn her own lion mane into an asset. The younger Angélique, lacking her aplomb, thought best to cover hers up with a wig. She had to make up for her looks by being remarkable in some other way. But first of all this girl must get out of a convent.

All the younger Rambouillet daughters had been placed in convents early, no doubt because their dowries were too small for an acceptable marriage. Two of them became abbesses. Getting a good convent to run could be about as complicated as getting a good husband, if not as expensive. The cloistered Rambouillet girls led fairly worldly lives, filling their residences with works of art, reading profane poetry, receiving visits, and even going home occasionally. They engaged in lawsuits, wrote letters, and enjoyed a pleasant existence, sheltered from the storms of secular life, spared the pangs and pleasures of sex and motherhood.

But Angélique-Clarisse was not happy in her convent. She quarreled frequently with her older sister, the abbesse d'Hierres, and when Julie d'Angennes got married in 1645 she asked to come home. Perhaps she hoped to replace Julie as the most marriageable lady at the *chambre bleue*. Voiture may have planted the idea in her head, for he had already "discovered" her in her convent and was coming to see her there. Her wish was granted. She came home and took up the place vacated by Julie. Now the ever-hopeful Voiture, who could not resist any aristocratic young girl, began a campaign of courtship. He played tennis with Angélique-Clarisse in the garden of the hôtel, heroically disguising his gout. He was often seen whispering in dark corners of the salon with her, and it was obvious that she was listening to his suit. The poet was in his early fifties and working harder than ever on his looks. The grey hair was beginning to show, yet his heart was still young. Perhaps this last Rambouillet daughter would be less cruel than Julie. . . .

This state of affairs, so compromising to the girl, was brought to the attention of the marquise by Chavaroche, the steward of the household. Voiture was subjected to an irate scolding. In a fit of pique, he challenged Chavaroche to a duel and fought it right on the premises. A scandal ensued which had to be hushed up. Everyone in the family, but especially Julie de Montausier, was angry with Voiture. He was discouraged from ever coming back.

All this gave Angélique-Clarisse something to think about. She liked Voiture and wanted to defend him, but he had jeopardized her reputation, and she had come very near to being sent back to her nunnery. She now swung in the opposite direction and became a fierce prude, the fiercest one the *chambre bleue* had ever seen. She gathered around her a little circle of extremely critical, simpering, blushing, and supercilious maidens. Where her mother had been amiably virtuous, where Julie had been sharp-edged but tactful, Angélique-Clarisse was absurdly finicking. She flaunted her new style: she was known to faint at the sound of an improper word. At the same time she professed to be annoyed at the notice she attracted, and once turned on the hapless author Gilles Ménage, a decorous suitor to so many of the précieuses, and snapped, "Monsieur, I hear you have been putting me in your books. Please stop it at once!"

During the Fronde she took care to distinguish herself from the loose-living *frondeuses* by adopting a highly visible pro-Mazarin stand. Once she encountered the notorious Mlle. de Chevreuse with the Duc de Savoie, a wanted rebel, strolling in the Place Royale disguised as a nun. She tried to coax them into her carriage with a view to kidnapping the duke and throwing him into the Seine!

And now, after the Fronde, she was to be seen riding around the Cours-la-Reine with her girlfriends, Mlles. d'Aumale and d'Haucourt, loudly proclaiming that everything *revolted* her.

Her posturing was considered by some to be quite outlandish. Tallemant tells us even that she and Mlle. d'Aumale were the "originals" of the foolish provincial girls in Molière's farce *Les Précieuses ridicules*. This may have been going too far. How could a précieuse so high and mighty as Angélique-Clarisse be satirized in the guise of a lumpen-précieuse from the sticks? Presumably Tallemant did not mean that she was Molière's specific model, but rather of the "original type" which the provincial girls in the play were trying to emulate. The silly maidens of the farce are not to be taken seriously. But Angélique-Clarisse? We can see her as a person in distress: an unattractive girl at the center of a society where she was expected to be distinguished. When she saw what a few coquettish giggles with a middle-class poet in a corner of the *chambre bleue* could lead to, she distinguished herself by an implacable virtue that doubtless did not sit well with her true nature. We can guess that she was a prude in bad faith. But then they all were.

The gentlemen-libertines made her their prime target. In a ballet, *La Déroute des précieuses*, she and her girlfriend were actually named:

> Précieuses, vos maximes
> Tyrannisent nos désirs
> Vous faites passer pour crimes
> Les plus innocens plaisirs.
> Rambouillet et vous d'Aumale,
> Quoy, ne verrons-nous jamais
> L'Amour et votre cabale
> Faire un bon traité de paix? [3]

> (Précieuses, your rules
> are the tyrants of our desires.
> You make our most innocent pleasures
> look like crimes.
> Oh Rambouillet and D'Aumale,
> when will we ever see
> your faction and the God of Love
> sign a peace treaty?)

Curiously, this girl did sign a peace treaty with Love. Mlle. de Rambouillet got married in 1658, at about age thirty, to the Comte de Grignan, a man well known for his sexual prowess.

What happened when this prude became a wife? With the wags snickering on the sidelines, she can hardly have gone to her nuptials in great comfort. In fact, word got out that Angélique-Clarisse's husband performed great exploits on his wedding night. This story occupied not only the song merchants of the Pont-Neuf but also the more delicate chatter of the *ruelles*. Mme. de Montausier wrote drily to her sister, "People are saying awful things about you." Mme. de Grignan, knowing perfectly well what her sister was hinting at, replied that there was only one way to restore the reputation of the précieuses for repugnance to the physical side of love: that was for her friend Mlle. d'Aumale to marry the Marquis de Langey, an unfortunate man who had just been proven impotent in a much-discussed public "trial by congress." Angélique-Clarisse's remark went the rounds of the *ruelles* and was eventually taken, in error, to be a statement of the real intentions of Mlle. d'Aumale and Langey. Langey himself, when he heard the remark, said ruefully, "At least if I married a pure and pious girl like her, when she did have children people wouldn't go around saying they weren't mine." The rumor got out of hand when a town counselor approached the blushing Mlle. d'Aumale and informed her that, if she wished, he could nullify the ban on Langey's remarrying!

Reflected in this story was the masculine opinion of the précieuse as a woman whose elaborate display of prudery was not borne out by the intimate facts of her married life:

If you want to know what the précieuses consider to be their greatest merit, I'll tell you, it's in loving their sighing suitors most tenderly, without physical pleasure, while solidly enjoying their husbands with aversion.[4]

Was Angélique-Clarisse happily married? All we know is that she had two children and died after six years, in 1664. Grignan went on to marry the daughter of another famous précieuse, Mme. Du Plessis-Bellière, and after this second wife died he took a third, still more famous, the daughter of Mme. de Sévigné. Husbands simply outlived wives. The bullets they encountered on battlefields were never so unerring as the worm of childbirth in a woman's loins.

Marriage was clearly no solution to the *précieux* dilemma. It had been depreciated by courtly conventions which had separated love and marriage for centuries. And the poets were still running marriage down, as the more dismal alternative:

L'Amour n'est fait que de mystère,
De respect, de difficultés;
L'hymen est plein d'autorités,
Peut tout, et ne daigne rien faire.
Assembler l'hymen et l'amour,
C'est mêler la nuit et le jour.[5]

(Love is all mystery,
respect, obstacles.
Marriage is all permissions.
You can do anything in marriage
but you no longer want to.
Putting marriage and love together
is like trying to mix night and day.)

La Rochefoucauld put it even more succinctly:

Il y a de bons mariages, mais il n'y en a pas de délicieux.[6]

(There are some good marriages, but no delightful ones.)

And if marriage was a tiresome bore to the enterprising man, it was worse for women; it only reinforced misconceptions about their intimate nature. The prevalence of forced marriages had turned enough women against sex to give currency to the myth that women enjoyed it less than men. The myth was elaborated over centuries: woman's participation in the sexual act was diffuse, passive, romantic, generous, sacrificial—anything but physical or immediate. Women were receptacles of male passion.

Never mind that the contrary was also true. But the lubricious goat theory did not apply to *nice* women.

For all their pride in their prowess, French men of the seventeenth century were taught little about the niceties of mutual pleasure. (Women were taught nothing at all.) The idea that women were undersexed was reinforced by a general sexual incompetence.

But the real enemy of marriage was poetry. Marriage was a materialistic association, an armed truce; love was heroic war. The language of love poetry teems with images drawn from fortifications: the lover attacks the fortress; either the fortress withstands the attack and the lover is utterly miserable, or she gives in and he despises her.

Relations between the sexes, on the testimony of the poets, seem to have been confined to this battle. Love was dissociated not only

Mme. de Brégy

from marriage but also from friendship and even from pleasure. Sex was a source of despair. No wonder that a man felt sad after sex, as in the Roman proverb, because now it was all over and there was nothing more to conquer. A woman felt more deeply bound after the act, because she had "given herself," perhaps sinfully, and was now the possession of the man.

The précieuses believed this mythology. But what makes the *précieux* reaction to it interesting is that for the first time in the history of modern society large numbers of women said no, loudly and with sincere conviction.

Blotting sex out of their lives was a sacrifice costing them more than it cost the man who was denied. He could just try elsewhere. But for the women who were in search of some better form of communion the sacrifice seemed worth it.

The oldest reason of all for being chaste was that it kept you from getting pregnant. Marriage made pregnancy lawful, but it did not make it safe.

Mlle. Charlotte de Saumaize (1619–1693) [7] had started a promising social career in the entourage of the queen-regent. She almost spoiled it at the very outset—by getting pregnant. But she found that when she married the man, the Comte de Brégy, all was forgiven.

Mme. de Brégy was far more intelligent than this husband, clever enough to launch him on a diplomatic career which took him away to foreign lands. When he was off on his ambassadorships she could endure her marriage; her life—a round of intellectual and social pleasures—could go on. But then he would come back to Paris on leave, and bang—she would get pregnant again.

Mme. de Brégy hated having children. There she was, a highly successful précieuse, beautifully gowned and groomed at all times, one of the brightest lights of the Montpensier circle, welcome at the court of the queen-regent, pursued indeed by Queen Christina of Sweden, and above all, talented. She passed for a gracious letter writer and had exchanged phrases with Mme. de Longueville over the sonnets of *Job* and *Uranie* (see pp. 139–140). But these literary disputes were in sharp contrast to the noisy quarrels of Mme. de Brégy's domestic life. Why must she go on and on bearing children? She asked this question after her fourth delivery and was the first précieuse to dare to ask it openly. The problem was publicized in the 1650s, in Loret's *Gazette*,[8] wherein she was bantered for her vanity, as though the only disagreeable thing about childbearing was what it did to your waistline and complexion.

There was nothing new in the filthy, bloodsoaked conditions in which women of all classes brought forth babies in the seventeenth century. They did as they had always done, risking childbed fever, screaming with pain that was intensified by the intervention of superstitious midwives and worse doctors. The prolapsed organs then had to be dragged through the rest of their lives.

What was new was the sensibility of the woman, who had begun to believe the poetic image of herself as a pure and immaculate being, a glittering diamond set forever in the environment of the salon, safe from the obscure terrors of the body. Childbirth turned her into an animal again. Childbirth hurt now more than ever. When you have learned to elevate your thoughts and study your sentiments on a high level of abstraction, the reduction of your whole self to this elemental function is a rude awakening.

But there was only one way out: abstinence. Other wives had chosen it, using illness or piety as their lever. Mme. de Brégy, who was neither sick nor devout, announced that she wanted a separation.

When she tried to get one, the gossips went to work on her. Some said she was looking for adventures elsewhere—otherwise why would she still be painting her face? But it was her husband, not she, who was caught red-handed:

He had started a casual affair with one of her maids. Mme. de Brégy went disguised as this maid to keep a rendezvous with him, and put him to shame in front of all his relatives. This piece of theatre added fuel to the fire of her resentment. A wife, of course, could not permit herself such lapses. She had to be content with smaller vices—rouge, avarice, lawsuits. Sex was a privilege for men, but a duty for wives.

After years of litigation she got her separation.

Mme. de Brégy had already turned from the misery of marriage to the consolation of literature, and became, in the '50s, a celebrated author of society portraits, a form calling for sustained extravagant flattery. Her portraits of Anne of Austria and Louis XIV reflect the honored position she held among the great. Other writings of hers, little *"questions d'amour"* that made pretexts for conversational combat, circulated in the *ruelles:*

Question: whether to be loved by the person one loves causes more joy than his indifference would cause of sorrow.

Of the dilemma one finds oneself in, when one's heart holds one opinion and one's head another.[9]

Such questions seem remote from Mme. de Brégy's real domestic problems, but they are not. Each refers to love as an insoluble dilemma, to be studied for its own sake as a way of transforming the real despair of life. This lady knew very well that, as a woman, she was a victim of a vast biological injustice. Nature had given her passions, but she was not allowed to use them without suffering intolerable consequences. She tried to fight nature, but finding this a useless struggle she discovered in the *question d'amour* a means of summing up the sadness of all human relations.

Later in life she tried to block her daughter's marriage; her refusal to attend the wedding brought scorn on her from every quarter. It was downright mean, they said, to frown on her own daughter's establishment. This vain, painted, and by now middle-aged woman was trying to break the vicious circle of marriage, sex, children, and pain for her daughter by opposing the arranged match. It was a futile gesture.

The libertines made jokes on her dark skin, her age, her cosmetics, her prudery which they did not believe was genuine. But all this could be screened away in the verbal filigree of Mme. de Brégy's *précieux* debates.

Question: Is it better to love a person whose heart is engaged elsewhere or one whose heart is impervious?

For most women, the only alternative to marriage was the convent. An unmarried girl could not run around as she pleased. She must be fixed, *established;* and there was no way of establishing a woman without a husband, except by locking her up. Somaize lists in his *Dictionnaire* various worldly nuns who complained that their convent was a fate worse than death, an enemy of their freedom, a barrier to unlimited social intercourse. One pair of nuns, the La Chesnaie sisters (Clytie and her sister), actually left the convent in their middle forties "to see the world and be seen by it." They broke their vows "only insofar as these conflict with the

Mme. Scarron

freedom necessary to a précieuse," and now they intended to enjoy themselves.[10]

Since most girls succumbed to marriage and so few were able to turn marriage to their advantage, the happiest solution was to become a widow with independent means, however modest. One very shrewd lady who came into her own when she lost her husband was Mme. Scarron (1635–1719).[11]

"She is a widow without having been married," says Somaize, reminding us that her late husband, the burlesque poet, had been a paralytic cripple and had left her "intact."

Françoise d'Aubigné was a distressed gentlewoman and the granddaughter of the great Protestant poet Agrippa d'Aubigné. But her father, a soldier of fortune, had committed violent murder and gone off to India and died, leaving the girl nothing. She married Scarron in desperation, to avoid being buried alive in a nunnery. She was not yet seventeen; he was forty-two. Scarron took pity on this penniless beauty and made her his wife "to keep me company," for it was, by virtue of his illness, an unconsummated marriage, as everyone knew. He trained her to run his house and minister to his needs, and she also learned to tolerate the libertinage of his literary friends, though she herself was already a pious prude.

How prudish, exactly? Living with the famous burlesque writer gave her a certain doubtful publicity. Many men-friends of Scarron came to visit in the hope of winning her favors. Villarceaux, the most important of Ninon's lovers, came bringing banquets, but he had to sit down and eat them with Scarron while Mme. Scarron stayed out of sight. Boisrobert refers to this infatuation in his "Epître à Villarceaux," where he suggests that the real attraction in that household was not Scarron's verses but a certain dark beauty who had come from a far distant land.[12]

Ninon de Lenclos was at this time her best friend. What did this say for Mme. Scarron's prudery? People wondered. Years later Ninon wrote:

Scarron was my friend; I took infinite pleasure in his wife's conversation. In those days I found her too awkward for love. As for the details, I don't know anything, I never saw anything, but I did lend her my yellow room often, to spend some time with Villarceaux.[13]

And a curious letter appears in the Conrart manuscripts, supposedly from Mme. Scarron to an unknown lover:

> I hate to commit sin but I hate poverty even more. I have received your ten thousand écus, and if you will bring me ten thousand more in two days' time I will see what I can do for you. I do not forbid you to hope.[14]

Even a prude may be reduced to trafficking her charms when she is hard up for cash.

Certain it is that when Scarron died in 1660 he left her in a state of utter destitution. The cheerful invalid had battled so hard against his painful ailment that he let his finances run down. She did not regret him. She now had to face the threat of a convent again as the only respectable residence for a poor widow. She did retire to one for a brief time, but was delivered from it by a small pension from Anne of Austria. Scarron had always dunned the queen for handouts, calling himself the "queen's invalid." This pension was the widow Scarron's real inheritance from her husband. With it she was able to live in town modestly, without frills, still visited by the ever-hopeful (and perhaps lucky) Villarceaux, but still a dragon of prudery to all appearances. In 1663, when everybody else went to a masked ball, including the queen mother, Mme. Scarron stayed home, saying that such amusements were unsuitable for an honest woman.

Somaize lists her *ruelle* among the most distinguished *précieux* centers in Paris. She must have been relieved to have a place of her own after the rowdy squalor of Scarron's life, where she had been an inscrutable, ornamental presence, smiling faintly at his rollicking octosyllables and biding her time.

Her time came. Oh my, did it come. Her impeccable reputation earned her a job as nursemaid to the king's four bastards by Mme. de Montespan. She schemed patiently for years to alienate them from their mother, and was thoroughly successful with the eldest, the Duc du Maine, who turned against his mother and became a son to the childless nanny. And much more successful with the king himself, who repudiated Mme. de Montespan and his profligate life to turn to God and Mme. Scarron, now metamorphosed into the all-powerful Mme. de Maintenon. One thing her subsequent career as the morganatic wife of the Sun King has taught us about Mme. Scarron is that she had infinite self-possession of the most calculating kind, an inner coherence which escaped the influence of the tumultuous Scarron milieu. There is no smell of burlesque or libertinage in the later life of Mme. de Maintenon. In fact, Scarron as a writer went down the memory-hole in France. It became a gross lapse of delicacy ever to mention his name again at court.[15]

The only echo of her former days—and it is a very indirect one—was the girls' school of Saint-Cyr, Mme. de Maintenon's favorite charity. She opened this refuge for distressed girls of gentle birth as an alternative to the convent for them. Forty years earlier it might have harbored a girl named Françoise d'Aubigné.

NOTES

1. La Rochefoucauld, *Maximes* (no. 205) in *Oeuvres*, p. 273.

2. Tallemant discusses this lady at length in his *historiette* on Voiture (*Historiettes*, I, pp. 484–500).

3. Bibliothèque Nationale ms. fonds français, 12676, 7, 8, II, p. 110.

4. Saint-Evremond, *Oeuvres en prose*, ed. René Ternois, 4 vols. (Société des Textes français modernes, M. Didier, 1969), IV, p. 407. This fragment first appeared in the Desmaizeaux edition of 1705, under the title of *Le Cercle*.

5. Bussy-Rabutin, "Maximes d'amour," *Histoire amoureuse des Gaules*, I, p. 176.

6. La Rochefoucauld, *Maximes* (no. 113), p. 260.

7. See Tallemant, II, pp. 403–6 et passim; *Lettres et poésies de Mme. la comtesse de Brégy* (Leyden, 1666); Mongrédien, article in *Revue de France*, September 1, 1929; *Galerie des portraits de Mlle. de Montpensier*, ed. Barthélemy, pp. 4–33; Motteville, *Mémoires*; Jean-Frédéric Phelypeaux de Maurepas, *Recueil de Pièces libres, chansons, etc.* (Leyden, 1865); Jean Loret, *La Muze historique*, ed. Ravenel, La Pelouse, Champion (P. Jannet, 1857–91); and Conrart mss., Bibliothèque de l'Arsenal, Paris, folio IX, p. 1165.

Somaize calls her "Belarmis" (*Dictionnaire*, I, p. 38).

8. Loret, *La Muze historique*, 1650–1665, I (Oct.–Nov. 1651), pp. 47, 59.

9. Five of these questions are included in her own book, with answers by Quinault.

10. Somaize, I, p. 51.

11. Françoise d'Aubigné, who married Scarron in 1652, became Mme. de Maintenon in 1674, when Louis XIV gave her this title. She married the king in 1685 after the queen's death. See Tallemant, II, pp. 680–84 et passim.

Somaize calls her "Stratonice" (I, pp. 205, 221).

12. Boisrobert, "Epître à Villarceau" (1657), in *Epîtres en vers*, II, p. 178. Boisrobert thought she had been born in Martinique. She was indeed called "*la belle Indienne*" and may have been a mulatto.

13. Ninon de Lenclos, Lettre à Saint-Evremond, undated, in: *Correspondance authentique de Ninon de Lenclos suivie de la Coquette vengée*, ed. E. Colombey (Dentu, 1886), page 79.

14. Conrart mss. in Bibliothèque de l'Arsenal, Paris, XI, part 1, p. 151.

15. Not only his name but his style of poetry was an embarrassment to the age of the Sun King. Boileau puts the seal of disapproval on the burlesque and *précieux* manners alike in his *Art poétique* of 1674.

Sapho,
the Ultimate Prude

A WOMAN who refused her favors forever could keep men—certain men anyway—forever in her thrall. This triumphant discovery in the field of sentimental blackmail was made by the lady who became, of all the précieuses, the most conspicuous for all her secrecy, the most wildly successful for all her handicaps—indeed, the model, the incarnation of the précieuse. This is Madeleine de Scudéry (1608–1701).[1]

She is usually dismissed by literary critics as a frustrated old maid and a very bad artist, a view which can be traced to Boileau-Despréaux, a misogynist whose bachelor's scorn for women was reinforced by his aesthetic absolutism. Boileau damned the précieuses and all their works because the literature they produced was trivial, self-serving, and untrue. His prejudices became laws in France after the *précieux* manner and world view had been overtaken and supplanted by the more sober classical ones. But he succeeded, not because his own aesthetic opinion was true, or better, or even useful at all, but because it had been demonstrated by Molière's delightful antifeminist plays. Molière made Paris laugh with the best kind of laughter, laughter which is a kind of self-criticism. He won Boileau's battle for him before Boileau had even formulated the issues, because he had genius. Madeleine de Scudéry had only talent.

No one would argue today with the fact that Molière was a better observer of what we still call "human nature" than she was. But Madeleine's life and work were valuable in a way that was beyond the reach of purists of the sublime, upholders of universal truth, or even great artists. She deserves to be judged, not as an artist, but as a humanist, even under the disfiguring mantle of *préciosité*.

She was born in 1608, just a little later than Julie d'Angennes, in the depressing backwater of Le Havre. She grew into an ugly girl, tall and gaunt of figure, dark of complexion, with the long-boned face of an amiable horse and the droning voice of a school-master. While "princesse Julie" was coming to maturity at the center of a host of admirers, Madeleine was tucked up with a book. Her moment of glory came decades later, long after Julie's magic had ceased to work and the Rambouillet daughter had passed on into marriage. Madeleine was in her mid-forties when she blossomed forth as a desirable woman. She had something else to offer than roses and lilies and blue eyes that kill.

Madeleine was not only ugly and poor but an orphan. Normally a girl in her position, with small money and no looks, would have ended up in a mean little convent, the usual refuse bin for un-wanted girls. But she clung to the world by making herself useful to her brother Georges, who took her with him to Paris.

This brother was a swaggering fool. He boasted all his life about their illustrious origins and bemoaned the downfall of their fortune. In fact, their sea captain father had been jailed for piracy in 1610, and it was Georges who squandered their patrimony on his vast col-lection of prints.

Georges was an author. By dint of quarreling with other authors and shouting the praises of his own works, he acquired a literary reputation of sorts. They called him a *matamore des lettres*, a literary militant, always at his happiest on the attack. He was a prolific writer of plays in the pompous declamatory style of tragicomedy. But in the 1640s his pen ran dry.

Madeleine had already ghost-written for him a short novel and a eulogy of women. At the same time she was building up a personal reputation at the *chambre bleue*. They pitied her there for her helpless dependence on the extravagant Georges and liked her for her poise and wit. It was for her sake that Mme. de Rambouillet found Georges a job as governor of a tiny fortress on the southern coast of France, Notre Dame de la Garde, a barren rock perched on a hill near Marseilles. It paid just well enough for brother and sister to survive.

Georges and Madeleine made the journey south in 1644. High on his rock, with the wind in his hair, Georges could strike martial attitudes and look down on everyone else. But it was lonely for Madeleine. She kept up a correspondence with the *chambre bleue*, describing to her Parisian friends, with gentle condescension, the fatuity of the Marseillaise women with whom she had to sit and visit. She was a Parisian herself now, however plain of face, and her sense of conversational proportion and tact were beyond the reach of such provincials.

To while away the long, hot hours, brother and sister began to write a novel, *Le Grand Cyrus*. Novels were popular. La Calprenède had done well in the genre, and there was the great success of the century to aim at: *L'Astrée*. The novel that Georges and Madeleine embarked on was of the conventional type: the adventures of extraordinary heroes in imaginary landscapes, a jumble of episodes leading nowhere. It was escapist entertainment to be read by women.

Their literary partnership was very one-sided. Madeleine did the actual writing and Georges would then "correct" it by changing the color of this one's hair and that one's eyes. He sometimes locked his sister up, lest the public find out he had a ghost writer, for the novel was to appear under his name only. She endured all patiently, and after years of exile the first installment was ready. They returned to Paris to find a printer.

The novel began to appear in 1649, in the midst of the Fronde, and continued regularly at six-month intervals until the Fronde was over: ten stout volumes amounting to about five thousand pages. With Corneille's play *Nicomède*, it was the only major literary production in France at this time, the chief cultural expression of a country torn by civil war.

In 1650 Georges lost his governorship (insurgents had casually walked into the fort in his absence!). But luckily *Cyrus* was now a steady moneymaker. It earned him a chair in the Academy.

Le Grand Cyrus was a runaway best seller. The love story, embroidered with kidnappings, mistaken identities, broken lances and broken hearts—all unfolded in the simpering superlatives that became Madeleine's trademark—touched a chord in the hearts of her contemporaries. And Madeleine had thought up a new and original novelistic device. She filled her story with portraits of her friends, sweetened and veiled by exotic names and settings, but easily recognizable. Her book was, in fact, the first real roman à clef. The heroism of Cyrus, King of Persia, is matched by the beauty of his beloved, Mandane. Anyone could see in this magnificent pair of lovers the rebel Condé and his sister Anne-Geneviève.

The new trick was an instantaneous success. Everyone at the *chambre bleue* rushed to buy each volume on publication day and share in the self-congratulation of a whole society. Ladies and gentlemen schemed to get their portraits into future volumes.

We can hardly evaluate the *Cyrus* as literature today. Madeleine's psychological insight is warped by her desire to see only the virtues (and more rarely the faults) of her sitters. She seizes on the important trait which sums up a personality—pride in the case of Condé—and then plasters it over with sugar. She is too nice to be a first-class writer. Her talent is hemmed in by her social obligations. There is character analysis of a long-winded sort. Madeleine was attempting to do what nobody had yet done in the novel—analyze personality in a real social context. She was on the right track, but the existing novel form, with its clutter of marvels, prevented her from taking a great leap forward and writing a genuine work of art.

The style of her writing is hard to bear. Poor in images, rich in hyperbole, her sentences meander. The monotonous thud of her prose soon wearies the twentieth-century reader, and one wonders how her vast public could endure it for all those thousands of pages. Every hand and bosom so snowy, every sword so invincible, every heart so pure.

Humility was not one of her faults. Here are a few fragments from her own portrait:

As for her complexion, it is not of the greatest whiteness yet it has such a lovely color that one can say it is beautiful.

But the most agreeable part of Sapho's person is her eyes, which are so lovely and bright, so loving and full of wit that one can scarcely bear their brilliance. . . . Indeed they shine with such penetrating fire and are yet so soft and passionate that vivacity and languor are not contradictions in the lovely eyes of Sapho. . . .

Sapho also has such admirable hands that in truth they are hands made for the taking of hearts, or, if you wish to consider her as a girl dearly loved by the Muses, hands worthy to pluck the loveliest flowers of Parnassus. . . .

The charms of her wit surpass by far those of her beauty. . . . She can so well draw the anatomy of a heart in love, if one may be permitted to say so, that she knows how to describe all kinds of jealousy, anxiety, impatience, joy, repulsion, . . . and all the tumultuous sentiments which are never understood but by those who feel them. . . .

But the most admirable thing of all is that this person . . . knows so many difficult things, knows them without playing the knowledgeable one, without pride, and without despising those who do not know. . . .

And that is the marvelous Sapho.[2]

The reader has to make his own adjustments in the interest of reality. If Sapho's complexion is "not of the uttermost whiteness," we can guess that she is really quite sallow. The euphemism turns the reader away from such things to the inner truth of character. But the denial of facts for the sake of truth is a dangerous artistic method. Madeleine de Scudéry failed because she did not have the cunning to flesh out her idealized personages in the body of visual reality. She belonged to an age when literature had little to do with "local color" as we understand it. Her readers were in love with the marvelous, the exorbitant, the sublime. They were fighting the Fronde! And what Sapho sought to give them was reality shaped in an elevated form.

Madeleine de Scudéry, though she was to be scorned by the next generation of truly classical writers, nevertheless shared their search for the sublime essence of things. She also yearned for the appropriate form in which it could be expressed. But the novel had a long tradition of empty heroics. These she accepted uncritically, and so did her readers. What she gave them that was fresh and original, modeling her characters on real, live contemporaries, was enough to delight her public, and, though such a poor artist, she became one of the most popular authors of all time.

But let it not be thought that this artistic poverty was a reflection of an emotionally drab or unfulfilled private life. Madeleine was a social and eventually a personal success.

By 1653 she was an established writer. No one believed that Georges counted for anything in the making of the *Cyrus*. She now took up residence with him in the Marais, where they found a modest house with a garden. Here in the rue de Beauce she was visited by many ladies of the highest rank and an even larger number of ladies of more modest quality but unimpeachable virtue. "Sapho" was now forty-five. The lovers' quarrels, the elopements, the betrayals she wrote about were drawn from observations of her friends, for in the whole course of her life no name had ever been linked romantically with hers.

But now in the pleasant leisure of the postwar calm, she singled out Valentin Conrart, a good grey Protestant Academician whom she had known for twenty-five years at the *chambre bleue*. Conrart, a married man of fifty with grandchildren, rich and devoted to learning and literature, embarked on a literary flirtation with Sapho, sending her little carved crystals and semiprecious stones wrapped up in madrigals. The sentiments expressed in his poems usually referred to the "secret" nature of their friendship. But these delicacies were read aloud by all the ladies and gentlemen of her circle.

No sentimental attachment, however formal and literary, is entirely free of complications. Conrart had a younger colleague, Paul Pellisson, an eminent author in his own right, who was dying to meet Sapho. Conrart brought the two together and Pellisson promptly fell in love with her. Of course, Conrart was jealous, in a manner perhaps too polite to be very painful.

This new admirer was horribly pockmarked and red-eyed. His face oozed pus. Though only twenty-nine, Pellisson was a fit companion to the swarthy Sapho. The middle-aged ugliness of this pair was so remarkable that a number of wags commented on the absurdity of their relationship. But Sapho was not discountenanced.

What did bother her was Georges. He had never minded Conrart's attentions, but Pellisson was another matter. The young man was a threat to Madeleine's peace and to his own bread and butter. A quarrel blew up between brother and sister, and Georges actually thrashed Madeleine. He banned Pellisson from the house and almost destroyed in the bud the one flowering bloom of Madeleine's love life.

At this critical moment Georges' politics caught up with him. He was exiled to Le Havre for the moral support he and Madeleine had given to the Condé family during the Fronde. The Scudérys had never received much assistance from those exalted rebels, though Mme. de Longueville did send them her portrait framed in diamonds during her exile in Normandy. It was just the kind of present she would send: penniless and abandoned, she had only her priceless jewels to give. The present was lovely and useless. And it resulted in exile for Georges.

This exile turned out well for him. In Le Havre he met a bookish girl, Françoise de Martinvast, and married her. The bride became his new ghost writer. He was shortly after reinstated on his rock in Provence, took his wife to live there, and forgot about Madeleine.

The departure of Georges opened the truly experimental period of Madeleine's personal history. She was mistress of her life now, and attended by two "swains," each of whom, though cutting a comic figure as Sapho's lover, was unconcerned with outside opinion. Their drama was an affair of hearts, not bodies.

Madeleine steered a careful course between Conrart and Pellison. She did not want to have to choose between them, but feeling more pressure from the younger man, she decided to keep Pellisson on edge by setting up a six months' trial of his constancy. She would consider admitting him to the land of *Tendre*—that is, her inmost heart—only if he could wait that long in an attitude of submission and devotion. Sapho placed a high price on her affections, but wrapped them in ambiguity and did not promise success:

No one enters my heart the very first day, and Théodamas [Conrart] himself, though he is well established there, cannot neglect me if he wishes to keep what he has gained. . . .

I have hardly any friends who know exactly where they stand in my heart. Judge for yourself, then, if you can, where you stand. For if you cannot guess, you will never know exactly.[3]

She keeps her lover in doubt, and is always in control of the situation, an imperious mistress who can probably never be pleased. Pellisson was often discouraged, and Madeleine sometimes found it hard to keep his ardor from flagging. But she held out for the full six months. Then she felt constrained to give him his prize:

> Enfin Acante, il faut se rendre,
> Votre esprit a charmé le mien.
> Je vous fais citoyen de Tendre,
> Mais, de grace, n'en dites rien.[4]

> (At last, Acante [Pellisson], I must give in.
> Your wit has charmed mine.
> I will make you a citizen of Tendre.
> But please don't tell anyone.)

Pellisson's reply was ecstatic:

> Qu'il est doux d'aimer et d'apprendre
> Que j'arrive à Tendre avec vous!
> Sapho, dans un aveu si tendre
> O dieux! que le secret est doux!

> Mais puis-je sans ingratitude
> Le taire et le dissimuler!

O dieux, que le secret est rude
Et qu'il serait doux de parler! [5]

(How sweet it is to love and learn
that I have arrived at Tendre with you!
Sapho, in such a tender confession,
O God, how sweet is the secret!

But can I without being ungrateful
keep it quiet and disguise it!
O God, how rude is the secret,
And how sweet it would be to speak!)

The secret was not meant to be very well kept, for these poems were also passed around and read by their friends.

But what exactly was Sapho offering Acante? What and where is *Tendre?* This imaginary land had been mapped out by Sapho as an idle fancy, but its allegorical playfulness caught on and became popular with all the précieuses. *Tendre* is filled with towns through which the lover must pass to reach the fulfillment of his passion. Beyond *Tendre* there is a Dangerous Sea and beyond that Unknown Lands. We can imagine Sapho and Acante charting their course on this map but never venturing beyond *Tendre* to the *Terres Inconnues* of a carnal understanding. Madeleine's love was platonic, a harmony of minds only.

On the map there are three towns: the first, *Tendre-sur-Inclination*, is reached by an unimpeded rush down the river. There is no obstacle to love at first sight. But *Tendre-sur-Reconnaissance* (i.e., Gratitude, or recognition of the lover's kindness and constancy) is reached overland by traveling through towns with names like Submission, Eagerness, Obedience. The loyalty, patience, and self-abasement of the lover, if he goes all that long way on his knees, must deserve at least gratitude.

Tendre-sur-Estime, on the other hand, is reached by a more detached, literary approach. The emotional enthralment of the lover is here replaced by talent: Great Wit, Pretty Verses, Sincerity—in short, more comradely virtues. *Reconnaissance* is for slaves of love. *Estime* is for friends.

Still, neither *Estime* nor *Reconnaissance* is any match for *Inclination*. When love hits the beloved, no show of devotion or cleverness is needed. The lover goes straight to his target. *Inclination* is mysterious; we do not understand why we are inclined toward

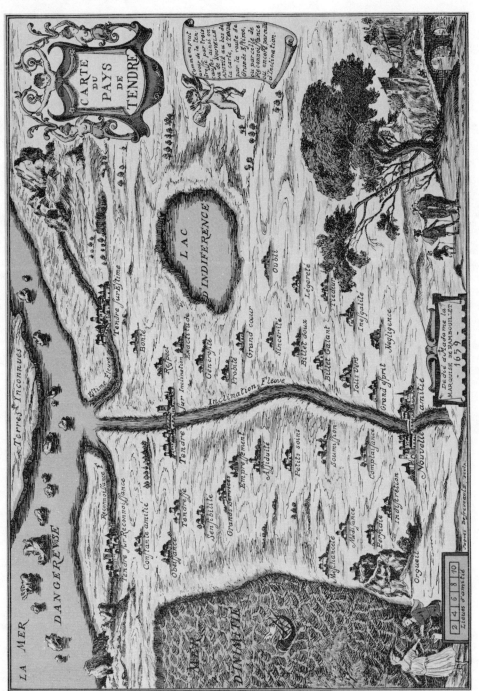

La Carte du pays de Tendre

certain persons. It makes no sense. *Inclination* is also physical. You can swim to it. Indeed, the whole map of *Tendre* is disturbingly suggestive of some improbable biological geography, some mysterious sexual diagram.

Madeleine, of course, was unconscious of this suggestiveness. For her, *Inclination* was the highest, purest kind of love. If the beloved object has inclination for you, it does not matter what virtues or talents you possess. You will get there. But when you do, you will not do anything improper.

Pellisson loved Sapho by inclination, but it was evidently not this sort of love she returned to him, since he had to wait half a year for the right to enter. But he must have been a citizen of both the other towns, for he was both assiduously faithful and archly intellectual in his courtship.

There is room on Sapho's map to get lost in the jungle of egotism. Meanness or pride will lead the traveler to a Sea of Enmity. Luke-warmness will drive him into the Lake of Indifference.

Madeleine was not the first to invent this topography of the heart. There are many other such maps, some cynical and libertine, some antifeminist. But Madeleine's map was plain in its allegory and comforting to the romantic illusions of women. There is no breath of irony in its moral view of the meaning of love.

Madeleine's distinction between love and friendship is vague, but vagueness is essential to her flirting system. Since love never leads to sexual fulfillment but remains in perpetual physical suspension, its gratification, resting on the verbal level, is hard to distinguish from the joys of friendship. Yet it *is* different. For her, love is between a pursuer and a beloved object. She sees herself as the object pursued while her lover tries to please her. She expects to be loved ardently, but her lover must expect nothing in return. He must even hide his sentiments in the depth of his heart, so that she is the only one to know. She is the *belle matineuse* all over again, the cruel Uranie, demanding that her lover suffer in silence.

The Saturday afternoon meetings during which the sentimental cocoon was spun around Pellisson's heart produced an atmosphere which seems too delicate to be handled by the thick sensual fingers of outsiders like ourselves. That atmosphere is preserved in a few rare documents, such as the *Gazette de Tendre*,[6] an allegorical newspaper which tells in mysterious hints, as befits the darkened rooms of women whose looks cannot stand too much light, about arrivals at the town of *Tiédeur* (Lukewarmness) and departures from the town of *Oubli* (Disregard). Its murky allegory is a screen to hide the fact that not very much is going on at all. Item: a *lady of very high quality* has found an island in the river *Inclination*, and settled down on it. But the island breaks loose and floats down the river, bringing her directly to *Tendre*. The lady is Mme. de Saint-Simon, who indeed went by boat to a rendezvous with Mlle. de Scudéry and immediately became her bosom friend.

Pellisson (whom they called the "Apollo of the Saturdays"!) was the editor of this coy journal. He also wrote a *Chronique du samedi*, of which only fragments remain to us. He records that a pet chameleon has died and is to be stuffed, pigeons and parrots are given as presents, Sapho is made queen of *Tendre*. A famous Saturday in the annals of the *Chronique* was the "Day of the Madrigals." Conrart had already launched the fad of sending madrigals wrapped around a small jewel or crystal to his lady love. After Sapho admitted Pellisson-Acante to *Tendre*, Conrart—or "wise Théodamas, who had long burned with an amorous passion for the beautiful and virtuous Philoxène [Mme. Arragonais] but with a passion so discreet that it scandalized no one"—transferred his affections officially to this lady and sent her a poetic message wrapped around a seal. The message was a play on the secrecy of both seals and love.

But how public was this secret courtship! All their friends now got together and began writing impromptu madrigals to help Philoxène reply to Théodamas. The creative paroxysm was contagious. It rained madrigals that day. Even the servants joined in the collective poetic urge and displayed unsuspected talents belowstairs.

The Saturdays continued, nourished by such fragile games, from about 1654 to 1659. Madeleine's friends at this time are largely drawn from the middle class. The Montausiers and Sablés still visited her, along with lesser ladies from the literary world like Mme. Scarron and Mme. de La Calprenède. But the inner circle was comprised of plain names like Robineau and Bocquet and Le Gendre. Mme. Arragonais, wife of a rich financier, often entertained them in her magnificent house. The Marais, where all these ladies lived, became noted as a district where, as Somaize puts it, "the précieuses make the most noise," a playful triple reference to their lute playing, their inexhaustible chatter, and the *"bruit"* of their fame. An occasional libertine showed his face, Lignières or Tallemant des Réaux, but these were only snooping for "material" and Sapho did not welcome them. Charleval and La Rochefoucauld, libertines of another stripe whose tact covered their smiles, were received more readily. They seemed to understand.

One wonders, with amused bystanders like these, what sustained the Saturdays for so long, and why learned and eminent men who must have had better employment engaged in these girlish travesties with unattractive middle-aged prudes. The answer is to be found in Madeleine's own personal magnetism and the novelty and rarity of this kind of idealized intercourse. The Saturdays were an experiment, a feeling of the way in unknown territory. Ordinary identities were laid aside, and with them the common lusts of the flesh. A purer inner self, the real self behind the cruel appearances and base urges, was set free and bloomed with a beauty that was never obscured to the faithful. Sapho's middle-class girlfriends were frustrated women for whom the taming of a few literary lions was compensation for life's emptiness. But Sapho herself seems to have been perfectly at home on her peaks of purity in the land of *Tendre*. She was so convinced of her own value that she was sure it was she who refused to marry, and not marriage which had been refused her. The only real act of union was conversation, for this was the only relationship which guaranteed the absolute freedom of both partners.

The verbal subterfuges which Madeleine de Scudéry employed to control her "lovers" are so transparent as to be harmless. Behind them was something positive and real: her belief in the transformation of personality through love. Love, for her, was a conscious, deliberate gift, to be given, not used. It was an act of will. It elevated the personality, brought forth the best in one, made one intelligent and artistic. Her own apparent egotism at the center of all this affection was in fact a demonstration of self-possession. Her friends and lovers were requited with her love in return, but it was a love that did not lose sight of itself. It was a choice she made of herself and the other person.

That curious interweaving of flirtation and friendship which pervades the relationships of Sapho's circle is a kind of test: a test of the lover's disinterestedness. The members of her circle enjoyed being tested; they liked the idea of surpassing themselves, of showing how the will can dominate the passions.

And not only the old, the ugly, or the rejected were drawn to it. Popular society poets, Sarrasin, du Raincy, and an enterprising lady-killer Ysarn (called Thrasile, the Audacious One), too rich and handsome and young to be attracted to Sapho for any of the obvious charms, which she did not have, came eagerly to her Saturdays and were sincerely fascinated. It is true that these young bloods were forever abandoning the Scudéry circle for fairer game elsewhere, but they came back, not just to be forgiven but to be congratulated on their ability to distinguish their trivial outside liaisons from the real thing in the rue de Beauce. Ysarn, the enterprising one, was, they said, "made for love," and his defections were always excused.

Madeleine's novel *Clélie* [7] was written during these years. It proved to be as long as *Le Grand Cyrus*. With its stagey Roman decor totally unrelated to the personalities, which come of course straight out of a Parisian *ruelle*, it is a worse book than the *Cyrus*. Where the Rambouillet habitués had recognized themselves in *Cyrus*, *Clélie* is heavily populated with Bocquets and Robineaus. Some of her upper-class readers were tiring of her style. They still read Madeleine out of habit, but were more critical than before. Most of *Clélie*'s readers were middle-class. Madeleine had sensed the cultural evolution of her time and brought these women an emotional literature to help them on their way up the ladder.

She committed the error of publishing her *Carte de Tendre* in the first volume of *Clélie*, making public a very private fancy. And the rumble of libertine criticism grew a little louder. The abbé Paul Tallemant said that Sapho's lovers had "soft hearts but never anything hard." And Segrais, who was not above composing *précieux* novels himself, suggested an alternative route to *Tendre*, faster and more certain, via *Bijoux* (Jewels).

It was easy to make fun of Mlle. de Scudéry and her unglamorous friends. But if the Saturdays produced nothing but vapid games and slight poetry, they were at least no worse than what had come out of the hôtel de Rambouillet. But the unselfconscious poise of the aristocracy in the rue Saint-Thomas-du-Louvre was lacking here in the rue de Beauce. Sapho's friends were earnest rather than witty, and above all they had a cause: women's rights. The domination of the Scudéry circle by women was more militant and positive than the mere unavailability of the Rambouillet women. These précieuses chose themselves, rather than merely renouncing men.

When we speak of women's rights in connection with the

Scudéry circle, we do not mean anything like a definite program. Of course, there was wild talk about reforms of all kinds. But neither Sapho nor any of her friends expected to change the hard facts of women's lot. They were more interested in the first step—asserting the intellectual dignity of woman, her moral ascendency over men (it took willpower to refuse physical love while remaining in the ambiguous land of *Tendre*)—than in enlarging women's legal rights or lightening their material burden. They were right. Their first task was to demonstrate that women were positive persons, capable of disinterested friendship and genuine love.

Yet this courageous experiment in delicate human relations looked funny to outsiders. In a society which was beginning to pride itself on not making an issue of anything, it was a little too purposeful to assert that women could break the shell of egotism and create new rules of social behavior. A growing world-weariness, a pessimism born of Jansenism and disillusion, born of absolutism in government and the search for the sublime in art, was becoming more fashionable in the higher salons of Paris. Mme. de Sablé and La Rochefoucauld were the intellectual lights of the new blasé style. The *ruelle* of Sapho, with its optimism about human nature, was beginning to seem rather quaint to these sophisticated *mondaines*.

Mlle. de Scudéry no doubt saw the world through rose-tinted glasses, but her faith in individual human beings was progressive and open to discovery, while the pessimism that was creeping up on French thinkers and writers was closed and final. "Everything's been said," La Bruyère was to say, for to the weary courtier of Louis xiv's court there really was nothing new under the Sun King.

Was Madeleine de Scudéry's affirmativeness shallow and short-sighted compared to the cynicism that could see only the folly and self-delusion of human nature? On the scale of morality perhaps her only error was to believe that a revolution could be effected privately, in the individual heart, without hurting anyone or giving offense. She thought she could demonstrate the power of the will in guiding the passions to a good end. But the new worldly mood emphasized the pernicious irrationality of the passions, and in perfectly rational terms.

And on the scale of art, it is Molière who still makes us laugh at our own folly, Racine who makes us wring our hands in despair. The writings of Madeleine de Scudéry, if we were to read them at all today, could only make us yawn.

By 1659 Sapho had acquired an international reputation, but the Saturdays had begun to sag. A new play, a mere curtain-raiser by a nonentity from the provinces, caught the public fancy at the end of December, suddenly named the unnameable, gave voice to all the latent absurdity that had until then been merely whispered. By reducing the sentimental experiment to the level of two country girls putting on airs of *préceiux* elegance, Molière destroyed it.

And yet, despite the mounting criticism and its own artistic flatulence, *Clélie* went through many editions, was translated into English, Italian, German, even Arabic. Thousands of readers took comfort from the example of Sapho and found a ray of hope for a new kind of woman in her modest spiritual reformation, sugar-coated though it was.

Shortly after the débacle of the Saturdays, Madeleine's attachment for Pellisson was put to a real test. In 1661 the minister Fouquet was disgraced and thrown into prison for having misused public funds and built himself a palace grander than the king's. Paul Pellisson was Fouquet's secretary. Pellisson suddenly found himself in jail with his master. Fouquet never emerged from prison alive. But Madeleine de Scudéry devoted all her energies during the next four years to freeing her hapless friend, and succeeded.

The *tendre amitié* of Sapho and Acante blossomed into a genuine friendship that stood the test of three more decades.

Sapho now took to other kinds of writing, more strictly "correct" and edifying than her novels had been. She delivered an address to the Academy on *La Gloire* in 1671, having been awarded the first Prix Balzac.

Now and to the end of her days famous and honored, she immersed herself in a large correspondence with distinguished persons.

Her last work, *Conversations morales*, displays both her gift for conversation and her new stricter morality, in line with the spirit of the age. Mme. de Maintenon saw to it that they were read often by the young ladies of Saint-Cyr.

NOTES

1. See Tallemant, *Historiettes*, II, pp. 684–96 et passim; Conrart mss. in Bibliothèque de l'Arsenal; and Mlle. de Scudéry's own novels. The best of the biographies is still that of Georges Mongrédien, *Madeleine de Scudéry et son salon* (Tallendier, 1946).

Somaize calls her "Sophie" (*Dictionnaire*, I, pp. 27, 61, 63, 111, 117, 151 171, 173, 198–99, 205–6, 212, 214, 227, 234).

2. Scudéry, *Le Grand Cyrus*, cited in Mongrédien, *Madeleine de Scudéry et son salon*, pp. 57–59.

3. Ibid., p. 82.

4. "Menagiana," in *Ana ou Collection de bons mots, etc.* (Amsterdam, 1789) 4 vols. (of which vols. II, III, and IV are the recorded sayings of Ménage, or "Menagiana"), III, p. 83.

5. Cited by L. Belmont in *Revue d'Histoire Littéraire de la France*, 1902, p. 673, "Documents inédits sur la société et la littérature précieuses."

6. Reprinted with other documents of the Saturdays in *La Journée des Madrigaux, suivie de la Gazette de Tendre et du Carnaval des Prétieuses* ed. E. Colombey (A. Aubry, 1856).

7. *Clélie, histoire romaine* (1660–62), 5 vols.

Coquettes

A NY LADY in the public eye would have liked to pass for a prude and share in the moral glory of the précieuses. But if her natural inclinations were in the other direction, the effort required was stupendous. A lady who heeded the claims of reputation might never have any fun. On the other hand, a coquette had to be very clever to have her cake and eat it too. She might meet a likeable gentleman at a friend's *ruelle*. He can openly court her, but she can only respond covertly. "*Le jeu des oeillades*," the language of sidelong glances, as subtle as that of smiles and sighs, is the only form of communication that will not be overheard. But the eyes of the other guests, bored, perhaps jealous, are in the game too. The conversation evolves, a declaration is made in the form of a madrigal or a sonnet, addressed to the company at large, and the lady must have the wit to recognize that it is meant for her alone and not some other!

Then, assuming that an understanding has been arrived at, where and how do you meet your lover? Everyone is surrounded by armies of talkative servants. Every valet has a cousin in service in the house of one's enemies. The lady and her suitor must be very astute at finding pretexts to meet, and eventually a private space on which to lie down. The arrangements are infinitely complex and precarious.

The "*Dames de Noyon*," Mmes. de Ménardeau-Champré, d'Ecqueville, and de Turgis, were three Parisian ladies who put their heads together and devised a clever scheme for a day's outing with their suitors. Each of them would tell her husband that the three were going to the country for the day with one of the other husbands as chaperone. Instead, they got into a carriage with their respective "*soupirants*" and drove to Noyon. A picnic in the fields.

A stroll into the woods. A pairing off. A hurried tumble in the bushes, and then back to Paris, all six together, in the stuffy, jiggling carriage. So much effort for so little? Yet it must have been worth it. But alas! the outing turned out very badly indeed. Their carriage was stopped by a platoon of Gaston d'Orléans' soldiers, who roughed up the swains and took their places in the carriage, enjoying the ladies' company as soldiers will. Could anything be worse? Yes! The whole escapade was found out by the husbands, who happened to meet at the Town Hall and compare notes on the whereabouts of their wives. And when the wags heard of it! These poor ladies were the talk of Paris for months, and were called the *Dames de Noyon* for years after—totally discredited not just because they had slipped from their duty, but because they had been so inept about it.

We expect to know less about the smart coquettes who hid their exploits more adroitly. But the libertines seemed to smoke out everybody's secrets.

For one thing, a lady's secret was obviously not very safe with her own lover. He was likely to be one of those very libertines, for they were the men most assiduously courting the ladies. And such men had a compulsion to blab their successes. Not all were as perfidious as the Marquis de Roquelaure, who would leave a lady's boudoir and rush straight to the Louvre to tell everyone. But it came to the same thing. To be savored, a victory must be announced, if only to one's dearest friend. And from there it went irresistibly to another and another.

Love letters were a further weakness peculiar to that century. We may wonder why so many ladies took the risk of putting their amorous thoughts on paper. Most love affairs came to an end; and then the letters had to be got back before they could be flaunted.

Love letters were common because it was a century of letter writing. Pompous and grand like Balzac's, arty and frivolous like Voiture's, relaxed and newsy like Mme. de Sévigné's, letters were an important expression of personality. Everyone had to learn to write them. It was an indispensable social grace. Love letters, a more intimate subvariety, were a way of artfully formulating, and therefore discovering, one's feelings. They were a substitute for the meetings that were so hard to set up; a relief for lovers unable to fly casually into one another's arms.

Nothing was casual about courtship in the seventeenth century.

Love was rigorously patterned—disciplined, we might say—to meet standards of civilization, dignity, and honor, even when (especially when) it was illicit. The love letter was an indispensable element in the pattern. Bussy's "Maximes d'amour," studied by courtly lovers right up to the level of the king, show us how love was ritualized. He deals with questions like these:

How should ladies behave in love so as not to lose their reputations?

How can you tell a true lover from a false one?

Are the great pleasures in love of the head or of the senses? (*Answer:* of the head, of course)

Which is the best kind of mistress, a prude or a coquette? (*Answer:* the prude's love gives you glory; the coquette's gives you pleasure)

Is it true that lovers are never satisfied?

Can one stay in love without hope? (*Answer:* no)

What are the tools of the lover?
(*Answer:* pen and paper!) [1]

Bussy wrote over a hundred madrigals to answer such questions. One could not simply fall in love; one had to do it right. Love was a geometry, to be learned and followed through to its logical conclusion, from first flickering eyelash to *dernier bien.*

Bussy-Rabutin, the great exponent of seduction according to the rules, was also responsible for much of the recorded gossip, for he was the best of the libertine writers. *"Ecrire comme Bussy"* was to write with style and verve, the supreme gift. His scandal sheets were passed around in manuscript, lovingly copied by hand, and often embroidered on. His *Histoire amoureuse des Gaules* is famous as a description of the naughty behavior of the d'Olonnes and Châtillons, but he is also probably the author of at least one version of the *Carte du pays de Braquerie,* [2] an allegorical map which was a libertine answer to the *Carte de Tendre.* In the *Pays de Braquerie,* or *Braquesidraques* (the word might be translated as Codpieceland) there are many fortified towns each bearing the name of some lady in the public eye. The manuscript is a tourist's guide to these "fortresses":

Saint-Loup, a small town, fairly strongly fortified, but more by the infantry than by the strength of its own battlements. [3]

Mme. de Saint-Loup was faithful to her lover, the Duc de Candale, only because he was there.

From there you come to Comminge, a small town where the houses are all painted on the outside, making them look newly built. However, the town is really fairly old. The present governor is an old Satrap of the Ruffians, who only governs by proxy, and who, because of his age, is about to be kicked out.[4]

Mme. de Comminges, a lady much in evidence at court, did paint and even Somaize mentions the "Spanish product" she wore on her face.

More damning than Bussy were the anonymous pornographic song books. A lady whose name appeared in one of those could expect to be talked about for years. A favorite theme was mercenariness in love:

> On fait tout pour de l'argent
> A la cour comme à la ville.
> Voyez comme Menneville
> Baise le surintendent.
> La Motte à la d'Angoulème
> Ne le faisait pas pour rien,
> Et la Monaco de même
> S'abandonnait pour le bien.[5]

> ([Women] will do anything for money,
> at court or in town.
> Look how Menneville
> is screwed by the finance minister [Fouquet].
> La Motte didn't do it for nothing
> to Mme. d'Angoulème
> and the Princesse de Monaco also
> surrendered herself for cash.)

Another is inconstancy:

> Maréchale pour Jeannin
> Votre amour est peu ferme.
> On dit qu'il tire à sa fin
> Et qu'il est pour le certain
> A Terme, à Terme, à Terme.[6]

> (Mme. la Maréchale [de Castelnau],
> your love for Jeannin [the counselor] is shaky.
> They say it's come to an end,

and has definitely been given over
to [the Marquis de] Termes, Termes, Termes.)

(*Etre à terme* = to be completed, ended)

Sometimes the point is quite crude:

> Que Deodatus est heureux
> De baiser ce bec amoureux
> Qui d'une oreille à l'autre va
>   Alléluia! [7]

> (How glad is Dieudonné (Louis xiv)
> to kiss this amorous mouth
> which stretches from ear to ear.)

There is real malevolence in the libertine attitude toward both the prudes and the coquettes. The coquettes, being more open to exposure, could be thrown to the wolves, their prudish sisters. But of course it was especially pleasurable if the lady exposed was one who passed for a prude.

It is not for us to place the blame in this dialectic of mutual frustration. A prude, seeing how badly the songwriters treated the coquette, became ever more careful in her behavior. The libertine man, finding the women ever more inaccessible, where both men and women were living the verbal stereotypes, exploded with joy when he could catch one of them doing anything illicit.

The antifeminism of Bussy and his friends was a corrective to the indiscriminate dithyrambs of the *précieux* idolaters and a kind of revenge on women for having claimed their independence. Anti-feminism also became a characteristic of the classical age, which was bent on exposing the foibles, the inadequacies of "human nature." Women were a splendid target. When we come upon such maxims as the following, we see what the précieuses were up against:

Most women use their wits more to bolster their follies than their reason.[8]

When a woman ceases to love a man, she forgets even the favors he has received from her.[9]

Women were not so much hated as despised by the great moralists. La Rochefoucauld wrote: "A woman is to be pitied when she is both in love and virtuous!" [10] because he did not see much chance for sexual or even emotional fulfillment for a woman. It never occurred to this bitter cynic that the intolerable burden of chastity might be as gaily laid aside by a woman as by a man, were it not for the even more intolerable burden of social censure. In defining them so neatly he only confined women more firmly in their character. They were what they were and, like men, they got what they deserved. They deluded themselves, like men; they were sentimental, self-indulgent, like men. Let them pay for their weaknesses, as men had to pay, but in their womanly way.

It was not moralists like this who could help women in search of communion.

Only a few coquettes survived the combined censure of prudes and libertines without being extremely careful to cover their tracks. Henriette de Coligny (b. 1618), later Mme. de La Suze,[11] was one. This lady would have liked to compose for herself an impeccable public image, but life and love pressed in on her, and she lived from day to day, in scatterbrained bad faith, cunning and clever but plainly promiscuous. Everyone knew.

Not everyone blamed her. She was a Coligny, the great-grand-daughter of the famous general who had led the Protestants against the Ligue a century earlier. The Coligny-Châtillon clan was the most distinguished Protestant family in France and still very much committed to their faith. Her pious mother had married Henriette in 1643 to a Presbyterian Scottish laird, the Earl of Haddington. This husband was handsome and loving but not robust. He died of tuberculosis a year after their marriage ("And she certainly hadn't spared him," says Tallemant). She came back to France a young widow just as her brother Gaspard was eloping with the beautiful Catholic Isabelle-Angélique de Montmorency. Now Isabelle tried to convert Henriette to Catholicism. But Henriette's mother, having failed to stop the marriage of her son to Isabelle, was determined to save Henriette from those dissolute papists by finding another husband for her. She chose the Comte de La Suze, and got the girl off her hands in 1647. La Suze was one-eyed, alcoholic, and loaded with debts, but a Protestant.

It was a disastrous marriage. The uncouth husband was drunk all the time. After one orgy he fell on his face in the public thoroughfare and a troop of pigs ran over him before he was picked up and dispatched home. Not much there to keep a pretty wife in line. Mme. de La Suze launched herself as a lady of letters and took lovers.

She busied herself with poets and poetry, and was a great success in literary circles. She collaborated with the author Pellisson in a series of anthologies, and attracted the flattery of all the lightweight authors who hoped to get their verses into her collections. Alcovists collected like flies around her bed.

But most of them seem to have let her down. She wrote elegies about faithless hearts to mark the termination of one disappointing love affair after another. The most prominent of them was with the Comte du Lude, a man who also flirted with Mmes. de Sévigné and Scarron. But such prudes were deaf to his moans; Mme. de La Suze consoled him. When her relationship with him came to an end she was thrown into real despair.[12]

Meanwhile her sisters-in-law, the sinister La Suze women, were intercepting her love letters and trying to break up her marriage. A repudiation by her husband would have finished her socially. She headed this off by coolly accusing La Suze of impotence and forcing him to submit to that most dreadful of legal dramas, a public trial of his manhood. The trial attracted almost as much publicity as that of Langey had done. The poor man sweated over his wife for hours in front of the leering eyes of a row of judges, but failed to prove himself capable.[13] Mme. de La Suze later confided the truth to her lawyer: La Suze was not impotent at all, but annoyingly assiduous at his procreative task. Had she, like Mme. de Langey, put a spell on her husband? She got her annulment in any case. It was the only way to freedom. To consolidate it, she now made a showy conversion to Catholicism, bowing to the trend of the time, and spent a few weeks in a convent to publicize her new virtue. But the nuns found she consulted her mirrors more than her prayer books and were glad when she returned to the world.

Freedom did not bring joy to Mme. de La Suze. She was always yearning for real love, such as poets sang of. But with the succession of lovers this dreamer became callous and indifferent to the finer aspects of intimacy. At least that is how it looked to Tallemant, who says that after seducing his brother-in-law, a boy seventeen years younger than herself, she shrugged him off and behaved in his presence as if nothing had ever happened between them.

By the time she reached forty she was a fat courtesan, affected of speech, vain of her accomplishments. Ménage had the misfortune to say one day that her sister-in-law, Isabelle de Châtillon, was beautiful, a "Grace," while she, La Suze, was clever, a "Muse." Mme. de La Suze replied tartly that she considered herself both clever and beautiful. The poet extricated himself by saying, "Madame, Erato, one of the Nine Muses, was so called only because of her charms."

At fifty, she became religious in her fashion and fell in love for the last time, with Christ, whom she imagined as a tall, dark man. The aging Ninon de Lenclos, chatting with her one day about God, said in jest that she thought He must be blond (Ninon preferred blond men). Mme. de La Suze replied solemnly, "Not at all, my dear, you are mistaken. I know from first-hand experience that He is dark-haired."

A coquette who did not try at all to cover her lapses was the Comtesse d'Olonne.[14] She seemed to suffer none of the sentimental distress of Mme. de La Suze. With only a thin layer of culture to distract her, this lady went after men with a resolute lust and an eye for their pocketbooks that occupied the gossips for decades.

But Mme. d'Olonne had begun her social life as Catherine-Henriette de La Loupe, a virtuous teenager and apprentice précieuse. The Cardinal de Retz tells candidly in his memoirs how he tried to seduce this juicy nymphet and failed, and was even rendered speechless by her severity.[15] After her marriage to d'Olonne in 1652 her behavior changed dramatically. Her husband, a libertine more interested in food and drink than sex, became the most celebrated cuckold of his day.

There was an outcry when she masqueraded at a ball in a nun's habit. She got into Bussy's *Histoire amoureuse des Gaules* as one of the star attractions. Her name appears in all the licentious allegories so popular in the 1650s: *Les Vins de la cour* (hers is "common"); *Les Logements de la cour* (her address is on "Money-Changers' Bridge," or "Codpiece Street by the sign of the Cupid, where all comers are welcome"); *Les Métiers de la cour* (where her trade is to "keep furnished rooms"); *Les Proverbes de la cour* (her proverb is "Lose one, catch two"). The street peddlers hawked song sheets rhyming her name:

> La d'Olonne
> n'est plus bonne
> Qu'à ragoûter les laquais.[16]

Mme. d'Olonne and her sister

(Mme. d'Olonne
is no longer good for anything
but inflaming jaded lackeys.)

The *Carte du pays de Braquerie* says:

Olonne is on the river Précieuse. The town is very considerable for the beauty of its buildings. It is a well-trod thoroughfare. Anybody is welcome there, provided they pay the price. You have to pay either with your person or your purse.[17]

Her friends warned this sensual beauty about her passionate nature, her failure to accept discipline or observe the decorum of the day. "You know, Madame, that people accuse you of being eccentric," says the Marquis de Vineuil,[18] and he notes that her temperament is unstable, flickering between joy and depression. He is afraid for her. Another libertine friend, Saint-Evremond, sees her as an innocent, and admires her hedonism, her animal energy.[19] But he too is afraid, more for himself than for the lady. He announces that he has decided to avoid Mme. d'Olonne, lest he be burned by her fire.

Mme. d'Olonne was a phenomenon rather than a personality in her day. Stupid rather than brave, she faced the disapproval of her contemporaries with only indiscriminate appetite. Her coquetry is insensitive and perhaps vulgar. But her sensuality is real. Unfortunately, there was no place for such sensuality in the polite world. The huge gap between what was expected of a lady by reasonable people and what she was accounts perhaps for her occasional moods of depression. She had no hope of being taken for anything remotely resembling a prude, and this came home to her and made her feel bad, at least momentarily.

Saint-Simon tells us that in her old age when her lovers were all gone, she developed a craving for food and became very stingy. One day she went to church and was so terrified by a sermon on fasting that she came home resolved to do penance. But how? She found a solution which suited both her *gourmandise* and her avarice: "I'll have my servants fast." [20]

No discussion of the coquette in the world of the précieuses can fail to mention Ninon de Lenclos (1620–1705),[21] that most successful of all courtesans, whose life is almost more fable than reality,

Ninon de Lenclos

whose story has collected entertaining apocrypha like barnacles. Who is there who does not know at least one Ninon de Lenclos anecdote? My own favorite is that of the young chevalier who comes daily to Ninon's salon in the hope of gaining her favors, only to be told that he must wait until a certain date in a few weeks' time. He counts the days impatiently, and at last the appointed one dawns. He perfumes himself, dons his best lace and ribbons, arrives and is requited. Requited for hours, with a style and sensitivity and verve that is beyond his wildest dreams. Falling back exhausted on the pillows, the boy asks, "Why, Ninon, why did you make me wait so long?" The amiable answer: "Because today is my seventy-fifth birthday."

The real Ninon, we are glad to say, was quite as charming as all the legends. She is still one of the most appealing figures in that age of tight-lipped, guilt-ridden sex: a heroine of the boudoir.

Perhaps the most startling fact in Ninon's history is that her age tolerated her at all. Prudes and libertines alike who condemned or laughed at other coquettes allowed Ninon to flourish and respected her as their glorious exception, a kind of one-woman safety valve on a sealed society where decorum and orthodoxy had shut down most of the exits. Other coquettes had to try to cover up their libertinage or take the consequences. Ninon never did this.

Even more astonishing: not only men but women were drawn to Ninon, and this included women who were extremely virtuous. Mlle. de Scudéry describes her in the *Clélie:*

Delightful Clarice is undoubtedly one of the most charming of social beings, whose wit and humor have a most special style.[22]

Sapho does not elaborate on what that style is, but of course she knew. Another lady who had reason enough to hate Ninon was Mme. de Sévigné, for Ninon had counted her husband, the Marquis de Sévigné among her lovers in the 1640s and twenty years later took on the son. Mme. de Sévigné seems to blame her men rather than Ninon for these liaisons. In later years she had occasion to be tenderly solicitous for the health of the aging Mlle. de Lenclos. And another pillar of virtue, who was fated to become the most highly placed of all prudes, Mme. de Maintenon, was Ninon's best friend in her youth! This friendship dates, it is true, from the lady's shabbiest period, when she was only the wife of the poor cripple Scarron. But the story is also told (though it may be apocryphal) that

214

half a century later the sober seventy-year-old Mlle. de Lenclos was invited by the all-powerful Mme. de Maintenon to take up residence at Versailles and contribute to the amusement of Louis xiv. Mlle. de Lenclos is said to have declined this offer from her old girlfriend, preferring the independence of the Marais and the company of her old libertine friends of the rue des Tournelles. And perhaps also she had not grown as sober as Mme. de Maintenon thought.

Ninon was born into a household where the father was a free-thinker and the mother excessively devout. They fought over this child, and the father won the battle for her morals while teaching her to play the lute. It must have been a very early victory, for when Ninon was barely into her teens her father killed a man in a duel and had to flee the country, leaving her to her mother's tutelage. But Ninon had already decided to live by the rule of pleasure. She soon got into "bad company," that of Marion de Lorme, a high-class prostitute who counted Richelieu among her clients, and of all the young rakes who frequented Marion. Ninon herself was never technically a prostitute, for she managed to live on her own independent means, taking only such presents as a lover may honestly offer his beloved. She was also extremely lucky with the law, being incarcerated in the Madelonnettes only once, and that for refusing to observe the dietary laws: A friar had happened to pass under her window during Lent and was hit by a chicken bone thrown down into the street by one of her feasting guests. The friar complained to the queen. This sacrilege seems to have caused more indignation than her promiscuity. On another occasion, the anecdote goes, Queen Anne proposed to place Ninon in a convent for a while, to meditate on her sins, and offered the girl her choice of religious orders to withdraw to. "Oh, in that case, I choose to go to the Franciscans!" The matter was quietly dropped.

Ninon was different from the other coquettes of her time, arty romantics like Mme. de La Suze and disheveled trollopes like Mme. d'Olonne. The tarnished précieuse had to put up with a great deal of scorn. Why was Ninon spared? No doubt because she possessed one special rare gift, which for other women was a psychological luxury beyond their means: a truly disinterested honesty in her relations with men. She saw early in life that men enjoyed a thousand liberties which were denied to women. But she was the only woman who thought of this solution: "Well, then, I'm going to be a man, too." That is, she would ignore the restrictions of modesty imposed on other women. At the same time, she would put aside the sentimental blackmail that was woman's time-honored weapon of defense in the unequal battle of the sexes. She would not be coy or ambiguous. She approached her lovers with a lucidity and forthrightness that sometimes they were not able to bear. Even hardened libertines were not prepared for a woman who demanded absolute equality and who absolutely refused to cheat. A famous case was that of the Grand Condé, who like everyone else made the pilgrimage to Ninon's bedroom expecting to do wonders. The prince was very hairy, and according to the Latin proverb, "A hairy man is either very brave or highly sexed." His performance was so undistinguished that Ninon remarked, "Monseigneur, how brave you must be!" Was he unmanned by her clear-eyed, rational, "masculine" lovemaking?

However, it was generally agreed that her directness and clarity in defining the terms of her relationships never detracted from her feminine charms. She had a softness and tact to go with her sharp wits that made an irresistible combination. And her underclothes were the finest and cleanest in Paris! (That sheer, close-woven fabric we still call ninon was first worn by her.) Never indelicate or gross, as even the most noble man could be, she provided an elegant haven for refined upper-class freethinkers. The most talented and exalted courtiers considered it an honor to be invited to her home, as Saint-Evremond testifies:

> L'indulgente et sage Nature
> a formé l'âme de Ninon
> de la volupté d'Epicure
> et de la vertu de Caton.[23]

> (Wise and indulgent Nature
> has shaped the soul of Ninon
> out of the voluptuousness of Epicurus
> and the virtue of Cato.)

These are surely noble ancestors on which to base a philosophy of life. We see that she was a woman with enormous self-control, able to regulate her pleasures, which she studied and fashioned with deliberation, limiting them so as to avoid disagreeable excesses, diversifying them to avoid boredom, balancing the intellectual and the physical.

Ninon believed in the golden mean. Her values of the spirit were as precious to her as her body. Her hedonism is indeed essentially of the mind; while pursuing pleasure, she did not renounce decorum. She was as far from the old *gauloiserie* as possible, and the members of her circle preferred to think of themselves as civilized Romans rather than as lusty animals. Not sex in all its anarchic energy, but civilized sex, the body used reasonably, was their choice. After the initial fever of the senses came the calm pleasures of conversation, and conversation of the best quality.

We may wonder whether she got as much out of her physical relationships as she should have. "I am on my twentieth caprice," she said casually one day, meaning her twentieth quick lay. Does this indicate true sexual detachment and fulfillment? It sounds more like another tiresome masculine boast. Most young men felt they had to prove something about their virility; it was their social duty to take mistresses, and in the battle of the sexes their norm of success was always performance, while the woman's norm was some degree of withholding or refusal. A woman always "surrendered" with a certain sense of defeat. Ninon's charm must have been subtle indeed to bridge the gap between these masculine and feminine attitudes. For Ninon to "perform" like a man while at the same time "surrendering" with all the charm of a woman meant that she had to keep her head and approach sex as an artist, rather than merely submerge herself in pleasure.

However unique and miraculous Ninon may be in her century, we do know that she had one serious attachment for the Marquis de Villarceaux, with whom she ran off to a country retreat and stayed several years. She bore him at least one child during their idyll, and was perfectly happy to surrender herself to him entirely, beyond caring, fearlessly, helplessly in love. But this man turned out to be a shallow, unsympathetic rake. When he abandoned her she shrugged him off and went back to Paris to resume her life of well-organized and civilized pleasure. Henceforth she stuck to her program.

Was Ninon de Lenclos by any stretch of the imagination a précieuse? One day, chatting with Queen Christina of Sweden, another original untrammeled by the modesty of ordinary ladies, Ninon called the précieuses the "Jansenists of love," and made Christina smile. Clearly the coquette to end all coquettes had little in common with those iron maidens of the rue de Beauce, or even the lighthearted virgins of the *chambre bleue*. And yet ... Somaize places Ninon confidently in his *Dictionnaire des pretieuses* and gives her a fairly lengthy comment, saying that we should not judge her by appearances, because her numerous admirers are only dancing attendance on her brilliant mind! Somaize tells us blandly that Ninon is really a perfectly chaste lady. Is this claim made with a straight face? Evidently not. His heavy innuendo ("Of course, if I were to write down all that they say about her, I would never be finished ...") makes it plain that he does not believe she is chaste in the usual sense. Why, then, does he include her among the précieuses in his catalogue? He says that, pretty as her face may be, her intellectual attractions are much greater. Could even this vaporous society writer really appreciate the mind of Ninon?

She was a woman not only deeply committed to intellectual values but determined to be happy. She kept a *ruelle*, wrote poetry, discussed ideas, played the lute, even wrote a little book, *La Coquette vengée*, in which she exposed a sanctimonious priest who tried to seduce one of her girlfriends. And if Ninon did not form sublimated attachments of the normal *précieux* type, that is nevertheless what many of her love affairs eventually turned out to be.

In spite of all the obvious differences, there is an affinity between the coquette Ninon de Lenclos and the prude Madeleine de Scudéry. Seemingly at opposite poles of the moral code, they were yet both remarkable women going against the prejudices of their time, and for much the same reasons. The one all mental flirtation, the other resolute in her epicureanism, both were out to prove something about their intellectual and spiritual distinction. Each demonstrated in her own person the dignity of their sex, the one by refusing, the other by consciously using her body. It may seem to us that Ninon, recognizing the unnaturalness of the *refus de l'amour*, lived a more complete and wholesome life (although the quality of her sexual activity, judging by the men she had to deal with, may have been quite poor by the standards of twentieth-century adepts), but in her time she was just as isolated by her uniqueness as Sapho. The best quality of these two women was the gift of self-control, a talent of the will.

Ninon desired, and got, the freedom to choose herself. This purposeful claim was enough to make her a précieuse, and in this sense at least, Somaize is right to call her one. But she is the only précieuse of her kind.

The difference between Ninon and the précieuses must also be told. It lies in that sense of proportion which so many of the précieuses lost in the intensity of their enthusiasms. Ninon's closest friend, the moralist Saint-Evremond, remarks on the lopsidedness of *précieux* extremism when he says:

Indeed love is a God to the précieuses. It does not excite passion in their souls. It becomes a kind of religion for them. But to speak less mysteriously, the *précieux* band is none other than a little group among whom a few truly refined women have thrown their imitators into a ridiculous affectation of refinement. These falsely finicking women have taken all that's natural out of love, thinking to give it some more precious quality. They have taken all the sensitivity out of the heart and put it in the head, and converted emotions into ideas.

This purification has its origins in an honest disgust for sensuality. But they have departed just as far from our true nature as the most sensual of women; for love is neither exclusively of the reasoning process nor entirely a matter of brute appetites.[24]

Being a genial epicurean himself, more intellectual than sensual, Saint-Evremond puts his finger on the "illness" of the précieuses: it is the seventeenth-century form of the disease which D. H. Lawrence would one day call "sex in the head," an attempt to divorce body and mind, to deny the essential unity of life. As such it is a moral sickness, a profound corruption, like unbridled lust.

Ninon and Saint-Evremond were immune to this disease by virtue of their sense of the fitness of things. But they were not therefore antiprécieuses. Saint-Evremond is careful to distinguish the truly refined women from the host of imitators. We are back in the land of the true and false précieuses. The true ones for him and Ninon are the ones who are sincerely devoted to their idea of love and distinction, just as they themselves are devoted to pleasure. The false ones are those who do not understand the deep meaning of their choice and therefore overdo their prudery. What Saint-Evremond is attacking here is only one aspect of *préciosité*—the error of excess. Believing in moderation, he and Ninon felt that the error of the false précieuses was not in sublimating but in sublimating too much— and without comprehending the liberating value of the sacrifice. We have to presume that D. H. Lawrence, Henry Miller, and all our other modern apostles of sexual liberation would have been far from approving of Ninon's measured pleasures, and would probably have preferred Mme. d'Olonne.

Saint-Evremond speaks of his friend Ninon as a "singularity" such as nature is pleased to give us once in a while, by design or caprice. He says we must not judge the generality of women by such isolated cases. In borrowing the virtue of men, passing from her natural condition to the "advantages" of the opposite sex, Ninon has committed a kind of infidelity to her own sex.

It is interesting that Saint-Evremond thought of Ninon as an eccentricity of Nature, which only served to confirm him in his low opinion of women as a class. She was the exception which proved his rule of what women were like: naturally, this was a betrayal of her sex.

The unconscious revelation implicit in this tribute to his friend is that Saint-Evremond learned little about women in general from his long association with Ninon. He seems not to have guessed that what she had the strength to become (a woman with a "man's" mind) other women wished dimly to be. They were prevented by their own weakness and confusion and by a society that wanted them the way they were. There was room for only one Ninon de Lenclos in this narrowing world.

NOTES

1. Bussy-Rabutin, "Maximes d'amour," *Histoire amoureuse des Gaules,* I, pp. 149-89.

2. This literary map was first printed in 1668 at Cologne, under the title *Carte géographique de la cour,* but it had been composed in 1654 by Bussy and the Prince de Conty. Several variant versions exist. We follow the reprint in Bussy-Rabutin, I, p. 203. (Mongrédien's edition includes several works by Bussy or attributed to him.) Another version, probably earlier, lies in the Conrart mss. at the Bibliòtheque de l'Arsenal, Paris, folio vol. V, pp. 501 ff.

3. Bussy-Rabutin, I, p. 204.

4. Ibid., I, p. 209.

5. Bibliothèque Nationale, fonds français, ms. 12676, 7, 8, I, p. 429 (1653).

6. Ibid., II, p. 177.

7. There is a double meaning here, of course! *Baiser* and *bec* were both used in another sense. The lady being "kissed" by the king in this madrigal is Marie Mancini, one of Mazarin's nieces, whom Louis fell in love with and actually wanted to marry. It is not thought that he ever made her his mistress. She was the patroness of Somaize, who dedicated his *Grand Dictionnaire* of 1661 to her, and then went to Rome as her secretary. This poem is from one of the *Alléluias* of Bussy.

8. La Rochefoucauld, *Maximes* (No. 340), in *Oeuvres,* p. 295.

9. La Bruyère, "Des femmes," *Caractères,* p. 116.

10. La Rochefoucauld, *Maximes* (No. 548), p. 329.

11. See Tallemant, *Historiettes*, II, pp. 105–13. See also E. Magne, *Mme. de la Suze et la société précieuse* (Mercure de France, 1908).

Somaize calls her "Doralize" (*Dictionnaire*, I, pp. 46, 66–67, 206).

12. Her grief at losing du Lude may have been the occasion of this sonnet:

> Ah, l'on m'avait bien dit qu'il était dangereux.
> L'honneur de nos hameaux, la divine Climène,
> Au soir que nos troupeaux paissaient parmi la plaine,
> Voyant qu'il m'abordait me vint dire tout bas:
>
> Si vous craignez d'aimer, ah! ne l'écoutez pas!
> Son adresse en cet art n'eut jamais de pareille.
> Il sait comme on attire une âme par l'oreille,
> Fuyez, fuyez, bergère, un si mortel hazard.
>
> Je ne saurais, lui dis-je, il est un peu trop tard!
> Et tous les traits d'Amour ensemble me blessèrent.
> Un agréable trouble, une douce langueur
>
> Surprit en même temps, et mes sens et mon coeur.
> Au lieu de repousser cette atteinte imprévue
> De lui-même il s'ouvrit au poison qui me tue.
>
> (Ah! they told me he was dangerous.
> Lovely Climene, the honor of our villages,
> one evening when our flocks were grazing on the plain,
> seeing him approach me, whispered in my ear,
>
> Don't listen to him, if you're susceptible!
> His cleverness in the art of love is unequaled.
> He knows how to draw a soul out by the ear.
> Flee, flee, shepherdess, this mortal risk.
>
> I can't, said I, it's already too late!
> And I was wounded by all Love's darts at once.
> A delightful anxiety, a sweet weakness
>
> Overcame my senses and my heart all at once.
> Instead of repelling this unlooked-for assault,
> my heart opened to the poison which is killing me.)

The sonnet was published in the *Recueil des plus beaux vers,* ed. Sercy (1659), III, p. 5.

13. Such trials were not uncommon, and could even be discussed openly by respectable people. Mme. de Sévigné said to the Marquis de Langey, who also had to face this test, "The outcome of your trial is in your breeches." Or so Tallemant reports her to have said (II, p. 891).

14. Her birth and death dates are unknown. See Tallemant, I, p. 515; II, pp. 431, 439, 730, 891 et passim; Montpensier, *Mémoires,* II, pp. 79, 430; Bussy-Rabutin, "Histoire d'Ardélise," I, p. 1. Also see E. Magne, *La Comtesse d'Olonne* (1929).

Somaize calls her "Dorimenide" (I, p. 97).

15. Retz, *Mémoires*, pp. 635–36.

16. Maurepas, *Recueil de pièces libres, chansons, etc.* (1668), I, p. 130.

17. Bussy-Rabutin, I, p. 203. However, an earlier version, the *Pays des Braquesi-*

draques, Conrart mss. in Bibliothèque de l'Arsenal, folio vol. V, p. 501, describes her as a fortress "difficult to take."

18. *Galerie des portraits de Mlle. de Montpensier,* pp. 461–65.

19. Ibid., p. 145.

20. Quoted in Saint-Simon, *Mémoires,* IV, pp. 281–82.

21. Ninon was Anne de Lenclos (nicknamed Ninon). Regarding her, see Tallemant, I, pp. 440–49 et passim. See also Bussy, Sévigné, Saint-Evremond. Numerous eighteenth-century documents, many of them specious, have given way to E. Magne, *Ninon de Lenclos* (Emile Paul, 1948) and Lillian Day, *Ninon: a Courtesan of Quality* (London, 1958).

22. Scudéry, *Clélie* (1658 edition), I, p. 234.

23. Saint-Evremond, quoted in Ninon de Lenclos, *Correspondence authentique de Ninon de Lenclos, suivie de la Coquette vengée,* ed. E. Colombey (Dentu, 1886), p. 108. This poem appears in a letter dated 1686 (when she was sixty-six!).

24. Saint-Evremond, *Oeuvres en prose,* IV, p. 407.

The Jansenists of Love

T HE PRÉCIEUSES, however chaste and pious they might be or seem to be, were remarkably little interested in religion. Church-going was a formal obligation, an occasion for meeting one's be-loved, a chance to wear one's best clothes.

And yet the seventeenth century was growing more pious with each decade. It came to be called the Christian century by free-thinkers of a later age who looked back with nostalgia on its untroubled piety.

We cannot say how Christian the century really was, for after the first few decades it was not safe to be anything else. After about 1660 it was not even comfortable to be a Protestant. From Henri IV's Edict of Nantes (1596) declaring religious freedom in France until Louis XIV's revocation of the edict (1685) and the expulsion or forci-ble conversion of the Protestants, it was a century of hardening orthodoxy.

Freethinkers had flourished openly around 1620, when the tav-erns were loud with the blasphemous songs of Théophile de Viau. But after the trial and incarceration of Théophile, the others had second thoughts. Some of his best friends pretended they had never known him. When Richelieu came to power, free thought had to go underground. Intelligent men of speculative bent continued to think for themselves. But they wrapped their thoughts in Latin or they published abroad. As the piety of Louis XIII increased, so did that of his courtiers. The aging regent Anne was a model of devo-tion for ladies to copy. Even the young Louis XIV, for all his sexual adventures, had his front to keep up. He did what he could to avoid offending his mother. Much later, when Louis himself had sunk to his knees, the religious conformism of France was complete. Piety was in. But was it sincere? La Bruyère wrote in 1688: "A devout person is one who, under an atheist king, would be an atheist." [1]

Behind the pious show the libertines were still there. But they had become invisible. The real battle of the century in the field of religious opinion was not the conflict between belief and disbelief, or even that between Catholic and Protestant, but a curious argument between the devout and the more devout within the Catholic church.

That peculiar form of piety known as Jansenism was the height of fashion in the 1640s and 1650s. The Jansenist quarrel with the Jesuits absorbed the passionate interest of ladies and gentlemen not normally accustomed to theological disputes, and had them debating the differences between Sufficient and Actual Grace, the "five propositions" of Jansenius, and ultimately the value of orthodoxy.

The quarrel was complicated, but the issues boiled down to: predestination or free will. The argument was an old one; it had started in the fifth century when Saint Augustine condemned Pelagius for claiming that man could gain heaven without God's special help, or grace. The church fathers took up the question, and Saint Thomas Aquinas softened the Augustinian concept of grace, to give man the incentive to use his own willpower in resisting evil. But the Protestants went back to Augustine. Calvin preached the necessity of divine intervention and warned that God chooses those he will help.

The Catholic church rejected this pessimistic view and tried to give man the benefit of both divine grace and his own will. But within the church the Jansenists (after Jansenius, Bishop of Yprès) emphasized Grace. The Molinists, on the other hand (after a Spanish Jesuit, Molina), emphasized man's personal effort to earn heaven, through good works and the practice of the sacraments. The Molinists tried to make it easier for the rich and worldly to get into heaven. The Jansenists were making it harder.

The Jansenists said: grace is not given to all men. God elects only a very small number of them. God may deny grace even to a saint. He denied to the apostle Peter the grace (in the form of courage) to stand up for his lord in time of peril: on Holy Thursday Peter denied Christ three times.

This looked like Protestantism to a good many people, and created the controversy which ended in the Jansenists being declared heretics by the Sorbonne in 1653, then persecuted for decades by Louis xiv, and eventually destroyed officially by the pope in the *Bulle Unigenitis* of 1715. But the Jansenists always maintained that

Mme. de Sablé

they were the real Catholics and that the casuistry of the Jesuits was the real heresy. As Pascal put it, the Molinists would dispense us even from the necessity to love God.

Another "Protestant" element in the Jansenist persuasion was their asceticism. They took it upon themselves to be holier than everybody else. Mère Angélique Arnauld began the reformation of her convent of Port-Royal by shutting the door of the visitors' parlor in her own father's face—and she was only seventeen! The saintly men of culture and learning—Saint-Cyran, the Arnaulds, Nicole, Le Maître, Pascal—who became the famous solitaries of Port-Royal made Louis XIV uncomfortable at a time when he was trotting around Paris in his carriage in the company of *two* mistresses *and* his queen. But later, to the older Louis XIV, the Jansenists were a more obscure kind of threat. They were arrogant. He wanted submission and conformity. They were remarkable. He wanted mediocrity. Jansenism was doomed.

When Ninon de Lenclos called the précieuses the "Jansenists of love," she meant it no doubt as a playful slap at the unattractive ladies who flocked around Mlle. de Scudéry and talked piously about "love's mysteries." These ladies, however, are known to have been anything but Jansenists. Mlle. de Scudéry was not even particularly devout in the 1650s, at the height of her fame as *Sapho, Reine de Tendre*.

But we know the names of a number of other ladies—no magistrates' wives with long noses and dark complexions, but beautiful princesses at the top of the social ladder, just as worldly and sophisticated as Ninon herself—who were in fact literally both Jansenists and précieuses. The most prominent of these were the Marquise de Sablé and her friends the Princesse de Guimené and the Duchesse de Longueville.

Précieuses they certainly were, but not prudes, though of course they kept appearances above reproach.

Mme. de Sablé (1599–1678) [2] is the most original of them. The life of this lady is a pattern on which many others may be traced, a model of the *précieux* achievement and dilemma from beginning to end. She went through all the basic experiences: a premature arranged marriage at fifteen; disenchantment with a brutal husband who not only flouted his marriage vows, but also ruined her financially; numerous love affairs of her own; political maneuvers against Richelieu; involvement in the Fronde; a deep interest in all kinds of literature and intellectual matters. She added to these fashionable experiences a charming hypochondria which grew steadily worse over the years and produced a thousand anecdotes. Illness was her trademark: it absorbed her attention so much that eventually she lived in constant dread of the shadow of death. But what exactly was wrong with her we do not know, and she lived to be seventy-nine years old, under the assiduous care of many doctors. No doubt rich foods and frequent doses of medicine contributed to her condition. But she was hardy enough to withstand them. Perhaps her illnesses were essentially of the *précieux* kind: a mixture of real organic female disorders resulting from multiple pregnancies in insanitary conditions and psychological aberrations which eventually developed into a refusal to get out of bed at all, a form of feminist protest. Mme. de Sablé bore seven children, but her cult of friendship placed her affection for them in the shade. She was the very incarnation of an ideal of *"politesse mondaine,"* and her friendships were monuments of psychological refinement.

In her younger days at the *chambre bleue* she admired the poetry of Voiture and was much courted by that tireless gallant. He even spread the rumor that she had not been cruel to him. But her other lovers were much grander than he, though he probably stimulated her with his literary flirting. This lady dabbled in hair-splitting discussions about the varieties of sentimental experience, and started a vogue for *"tendre amitié,"* intellectual and pure, as early as the 1630s, twenty years before Madeleine de Scudéry was to elaborate this theme. Mme. de Motteville writes about this younger Mme. de Sablé:

She was convinced that a man could have a tender but virtuous feeling toward a woman, and that the desire to please her would lead him to great and heroic deeds, would make him intelligent and would inspire generosity and all sorts of other virtues in him: but that woman, who was the ornament of society and meant to be served and adored by men, must permit only the most respectful attentions.[3]

This courtly view, so out of keeping with the real facts of her private life, derive from her readings in Spanish heroic literature. Her good friend La Rochefoucauld tried to cure her of this romantic taste and eventually succeeded, for she had the wit to tackle more challenging writers like Montaigne. She was not afraid of abstract learning and gradually developed a neat, diamantine writing style of her own.

Her table was one of the richest in Paris. A large portion of La Rochefoucauld's letters to her are devoted to recipes for jam, which seem to be as important to her as his moral observations.

Another of her hobbies was home remedies and charlatans' miracle drugs. She presents an endearing combination of scientific progressivism and superstition, both colored by her feminine vanity. She opposed bleeding and antimony, the current medical curealls, on scientific grounds that do her credit. But she consulted astrologers for her own health.

She was morbidly frightened of contagion. When Mlle. de Montpensier had smallpox and the Duc de Nemours came to see Mme. de Sablé after having been to see that princess, she turned him out of the house and fumigated everything. When there was talk of plague in Paris, she called in her three doctors but would not allow them into her room. They had to hold their consultations outside the door with her maid scurrying back and forth between them and their patient.

Before moving into a new house she always inquired whether someone had died there. She frequently went into seclusion, and her friend the abbé de la Victoire, after knocking on her door several times, finally began talking to her friends about "the late Mme. de Sablé" until she relented and admitted him again.

After her Jansenist conversion in 1645, she built herself a house opposite the town convent of Port-Royal in the Faubourg Saint-Jacques. It was here that the Comtesse de Maure came to live with her. These two ladies stuck to their beds in separate rooms, keeping contact by letter, writing sometimes six notes or more to each other in a day. Once the abbé de la Victoire told Mme. de Sablé that Mme. de Maure was having serious marital difficulties and might even come to a separation from her husband. He thought Mme. de Sablé ought to go and see her. But how? There was a big staircase, a drafty gallery, and several antechambers to pass through in order to reach that part of the house. What if she caught a chill along the way? The abbé then suggested that she wrap herself in a large counterpane. Thus bundled up she made the odyssey to her friend's bedside, only to find that there was no problem in the de Maure household at all. Mme. de Sablé refused to forgive the abbé this time, until he threatened to place a choir under her window to sing a *De Profundis*. She had to make peace with him.

This eccentric lady had a friend and fellow in amorous exploits and theological disputes in the Princesse de Guimené (1604–1685).[4] The illustrious house of Rohan had produced great Protestant generals two generations before. But the Rohan granddaughters, Mmes. de Chevreuse and Guimené, were Catholics, beautiful hoydens who inherited from their warrior forebears an independence and willfulness that sometimes did nobody any good.

The Prince de Guimené was fortunately never bothered by his wife's countless youthful infidelities. Nearly all her lovers came to a bad end anyway: Montmorency, Soissons, Bouteville, de Thou went one after another to the block for conspiring against Richelieu. Mme. de Guimené herself knew nothing of politics, but had a gift for passionate involvements with rebels.

She also flourished a considerable culture, read widely, and even studied Hebrew! Her tutor was a ragged savant named des Vallées. Once her husband asked what this beggar was doing in the house. She replied, *"Il me montre l'Hébreu"* ("He exposes the Hebrew language to me"). "He will soon expose his ass to you," replied the prince, looking at the tattered breeches of the poor scholar.

She shared the total thoughtlessness of her class for anyone beneath her. Although she enjoyed doing sporadic deeds of kindness for poor writers—thus, she "protected" La Calprenède, that is, got him a job in the royal household—she was impatient of bores. Once when riding in her carriage with a certain Nevelet, a pedant of little renown, she dropped her glove out of the window. When he jumped down to retrieve it for her, she slammed the carriage door shut and drove off, leaving him stranded.

These précieuses, whose taste and manners were shaped in the *chambre bleue* and who did what they pleased with the greatest possible decorum, were evidently of a different breed from the plain Janes of the Scudéry circle. Yet they were just as vulnerable. They, too, would grow old, feel their charms dwindling, and like many women of their condition discover the cold comfort of religion.

Each of these ladies reached a moment in her early forties when it could not go on, and we may speak of a conversion—sometimes followed by backsliding, but nevertheless an unequivocal decision to change their moral state from vice to virtue forever.

They had learned, from their psychology of "characters," that piety was the natural refuge of old women, as avarice was that of old men. A nice pile of money or prayers replaced the capital of youth-ful energies and confidence. Piety was seemly for older women, like higher necklines.

The menopause conversion was often quite genuine, but La Rochefoucauld saw it only as another form of self-delusion:

We think we are taking leave of our vices when it is only our vices which are taking leave of us.[5]

It was Mme. de Guimené who first touched bottom, so to speak, and who was then torn between her lengthy confessional sessions with her *directeur de conscience*, Arnauld d'Andilly, and her stormy love affair with the Cardinal de Retz. This lady's conversion was a subject of cruel amusement to others. The Chevalier de Méré spoke of "Mme. la princesse de Guimené who has been thirty times pious and thirty times a libertine." [6] The Marquis de Roquelaure boasted that she had entertained him in her bedroom three times on the same day that she "was playing the bigot with d'Andilly." And Retz perfidiously describes how Arnauld terrified her with images of hellfire and devils, while he himself, after six weeks of this, was able to evoke "more agreeable devils" and to entice her away from Port-Royal, "to which, from time to time, she made escapades rather than retreats." [7]

And yet it was this lady who guided Mme. de Sablé toward the Jan-senist form of piety. It was during her struggles with her conscience in the early 1640s that the affair of Antoine Arnauld's *La Fréquente Communion* made her and Mme. de Sablé the "founders of Jan-senism," as La Rochefoucauld put it.

This is how it happened. Mme. de Sablé was accustomed to taking communion about once a month, being under the direction of a Jesuit, the père de Sesmaisons, and that was the socially acceptable thing to do. One day, Mme. de Guimené, seeing her preparing to go to a ball on a day when she had taken communion, was scandalized at this "profane" act so soon after an act of sanctification. The prin-cess thought once a month too often for a *mondaine* to go to com-munion. Mme. de Sablé promptly referred this matter to her own confessor, who tried to put her mind at rest by giving her some written advice based on the teachings of Molina. This brought on a confrontation of Jansenism and Molinism, for Mme. de Sablé then showed her Jesuit confessor's advice to Mme. de Guimené, who put it into the hands of Arnauld. Arnauld responded by writing his book about communion, in 1643, as a Jansenist retort to the relaxed morality of the Jesuits. According to Arnauld, communion should be taken rarely, only when one is in a true state of grace. Worldliness is antithetical to grace. Therefore, a worldly person who takes communion is probably committing a sacrilege and also giving scandal to others. The Molinist view, on the other hand, more human—all too human for the exacting Jansenists—encouraged frequent communion as long as the communicant was technically not in a state of sin, in the hope that the sacrament would lead to greater virtue.

Mme. de Sablé blocked publication of the book for six months in order to defend Sesmaisons from public rebuttal. But a year or two later, by dint of fighting it, she was won over to Jansenism herself.

It was ten years later that Mme. de Longueville also turned seriously to this sect, following the collapse of the Fronde. She was thirty-five. Mme. de Longueville already knew a great deal about the controversy, and had made a show of virtuosity in threading her conversation with its thorny polemics. Jansenism stimulated her, just as the quarrel of *Job* and *Uranie* did. But it was only when her personal life began to fall apart, when the Fronde was lost, La Rochefoucauld turned enemy, Turenne fled, Nemours dead, her brother Condé beyond the law, her own rebellious heroism looking like ordinary shabby treason—only then did she turn to her faith in earnest. And she plunged deep.

Now a question is raised by the Jansenist conversions of these three beautiful society women who had lived life to the hilt: Why did this form of piety appeal to them? Was there something in Jansenism that was particularly attractive to the précieuse, or at least to this type of précieuse?

The obvious answer is that Jansenism was the *distinct* form of piety. The précieuses, already conscious of their superiority as literary critics, felt they had a special sensibility that raised them above the common herd. Therefore, when they decided to "humble themselves" before God, they were inclined to go to the same extreme lengths in piety that they had reached in self-cultivation. As Jansenists they went right on cultivating themselves, no longer as literati now but as mystics. It is one of the painful paradoxes of the spiritual life that extreme humility can also be a disguised form of pride. Jansenism was attractive because it *was* so exacting; it proved their moral worth to be able to abnegate themselves so much.

But Mme. de Sablé, although she found distinction in her Jansenist faith, was, it must be admitted, an uncertain Jansenist. Her chief reason for withdrawing to the convent of Port-Royal was not really piety but financial straits. Mère Angélique was glad to have her in the movement. With her social position, she made wonderful window dressing. She brought highly placed friends along who were able to stave off the persecution of the sect for a time. But Mme. de Sablé proved to be more of a burden than she was worth. Her hypochondria was a great strain. She feared contagion from the nuns at the Port-Royal chapel. And she had no mystical talent, no naïve, spontaneous faith. To sustain her religious sentiment she needed to read and reason.

In 1661, as part of the persecution of the Jansenists, her private doorway to the monastery of Port-Royal was boarded up by the civil authorities. Her "tribune," or private gallery in the church, was also suppressed. It had been her only means of going to mass without coming into contact with the infectious mob. It was at this time that her Jansenist faith began to falter.

She took part in the peace negotiations between the Jansenists and the Jesuits, but found that the intransigence of Antoine Arnauld prevented any settlement. A lifelong admirer of Montaigne, Mme. de Sablé could only be of the party of moderation and compromise. The extremism of the Jansenists pleased her, but her common sense was against it. And she never found the grace to follow their hard road to the end: *"Que cela est beau! Que cela est beau! Mais je ne sais pas si cela est beau . . ."* Later her fear of reprisals caused her to detach herself from the Jansenists.

We are not surprised at the turning away from Jansenism of this great précieuse. Jansenism was attractive because of its distinction as an extreme form of piety. But it goes quite against the *précieux* notion of civilization.

Consider the *précieux* style of life: It is above all gregarious. The ladies who flocked together on all levels in the 1650s were feverishly given to talk and visiting. *Préciosité* feeds on *divertissement*, which to the Jansenist is nothing but an occasion of sin. Jansenism prescribes silence, withdrawal, and meditation. It is antisocial. Mme. de Sablé withdrew into herself from time to time, but nobody took this seriously. Her withdrawal was prompted more by a fear of contagion than by a true desire to be alone. Her natural bent was sociable.

Jansenism may have appealed to the prudery or would-be prudery of the précieuses also, but their prudery had its origin in practical, not theological or moral, needs. Prudish or not, they all wanted to have fun, a little pleasant conversation, a few romantic daydreams, in the cracks of the walled prison of their real lives. Jansenism could only present their most innocent pleasures to them as the bottomless pit of sin.

But there is a deeper cleavage. *Préciosité* is optimistic. The précieuses believed in self-improvement, in progress, in women's rights, in being young and lovely forever, in using poetry to secure them a little power in a precarious world dominated by men. The disdain of the unattainable goddess for her *soupirant*, affirmed by *précieux* poetry, was better than the truth: it was a means to self-respect, and thus a step toward freedom. *Préciosité* affirms that women have a future, that something can be done for them. And that something should be done, for they are morally better than men. This last was a useful formula: the précieuses believed deeply in their own innocence.

Jansenism, on the other hand, is pessimistic, not only about human prospects, but about our very nature. The Jansenists say we are born evil. Without divine intervention we are as nothing.

How, then, could Jansenism ever have taken hold of the imagination of the précieuses—and the best and most intelligent ones at that? Only by an appeal to that very worldliness that defines them as précieuses. Nicole, Arnauld, Pascal all recognized this principle: you must entertain worldly people with worldly images, if you want to catch them in your net. *"Il faut placer la balle,"* as Pascal put it; you must hit the mark with a delightful phrase, a compelling or frightening metaphor. The Jansenist confessors of these ladies were subtle, tactful men, at home in the atmosphere of the salons. And a précieuse could be led anywhere by a book. *La Fréquente Communion* was such a book. But another book written to justify the Jansenist cause to society people was to be far more famous and effective: Pascal's *Lettres provinciales*. Appearing anonymously at the height of the *précieux* fashion, in 1656–57, these eighteen letters describe the Jansenist-Jesuit controversy in terms that can be easily understood by well-bred amateurs. Using the weapons of irony, satire, and sarcasm, Pascal demolishes the reasoning of the Molinists by cajoling the reader, appealing not only to his reason and common sense but to his admiration for harmony and elegance. Ultimately the triumph of Pascal's arguments rests on aesthetic rather than theological persuasion. And that was Jansenism's appeal to the ladies. *"Que cela est beau. . ."*

This theological gamesmanship won over a number of précieuses in the entourage of Mme. de Sablé who would not otherwise have cared to know what a casuist was. Suddenly theology was fun. Religion became a conversation piece.

But the *précieux* alliance with Jansenism could never be more than a flirtation. A lady must either cease to be a précieuse when she became devout in this fashion (and this was the case with Mme. de Longueville) or cease to be a true Jansenist (and this was the case with Mme. de Sablé). Mme. de Longueville sank deeper into narrow piety, Mme. de Sablé became more broadminded and humane as she retreated from Jansenism. Mme. de Longueville became a true solitary, without actually having to leave the court. Mme. de Sablé became more gregarious, opening her salon to discussions of medicine, education, and science.

Mme. de Sablé undoubtedly had the best mind of her generation of women and was serious enough to appreciate both Pascal and La Rochefoucauld, that "Jansenist without God." The long friendship with the latter was based on a shared disenchantment, a philosophical bent, a taste for worldly intrigue. They were not lovers. He was fourteen years her junior; she had been his father's mistress. He was still obsessed with Mme. de Longueville, whom he could talk about freely to Mme. de Sablé. He could also share in the passionate discussions of a very wide range of subjects at her salon. Cartesian philosophy, welcomed by some Jansenists, was much discussed there. Mme. de Sablé had many other interests, made experiments in physics, and dictated an attack on the medical profession to her long-suffering doctor, Vallant.

At the same time, her salon was still the scene of many *précieux* discussions about love. They played the game of the *question d'amour* there. A typical question: Is it better to lose one's beloved by death or by infidelity? Or: Are love and desire two contradictory feelings? Or this thoroughly feminine question: Which is better, to hold a woman by the head or by the heart?

As much discussed as love was friendship. Mme. de Sablé was an expert on this, and wrote a little treatise on the subject in the form of maxims. The game of *maximes* originated in her salon and was played by all the regulars, as well as by the hostess and La Rochefoucauld. The classical propensity for rolling the universe up into a ball as tightly compressed as possible was neatly expressed in the lapidary sentences which were formulated and polished by these friends. But the pessimism of La Rochefoucauld's vision was, in the last analysis, too bleak for Mme. de Sablé and the other women of her circle. She had to find a loophole for herself in the terrible indictment of all our virtues as disguised vices. In the *Portefeuilles Vallant*, her doctor's private papers which contain some of the *maximes* in their early form, we find:

Virtue is a figment produced by our passions whose name we use in order to do whatever we like with impunity.

This dreadful condemnation is modified in the 1665 edition of La Rochefoucauld's *Maximes* to read:

What the world calls virtue is commonly no more than a figment created by our passions, to which we give a respectable name in order to do whatever we like with impunity.[8]

Evidently Mme. de Sablé demanded and got her loophole.

A letter from Mme. de Guimené sums up the reaction of the précieuses to his *Maximes:*

What I have seen of them seems more founded on the character of the author than on truth, for he does not believe there is any generosity without interest, or piety either. He judges the whole of society by himself. As for the many, he is right. But certainly there are some people whose only wish is to do good.[9]

And among those "some people" she placed herself.

These ladies remained précieuses in their outlook—optimistic, feminist, sociable, inquiring, sensitive to the nuances in human intercourse. Perhaps La Rochefoucauld's cynical condemnations were true, but it was not *useful* to say such things.

Were these précieuses, then, "Jansenists of love"? In their extremism, in their passion for distinction, in their defiance of the physical laws of love, yes. But in their humanism, in their desire for happiness, no. Ninon's whimsical remark recognizes the lopsided heroic extremism of both *préciosité* and Jansenism, but does not notice that they are irreconcilable ways of seeing life.

The dilemma of these intelligent Jansenist précieuses was that their *préciosité* was affirmative and suited their nature, but they lived in a world where ideas were becoming more and more negative and pessimistic. Their affirmation of women's possibilities was contradicted by the trend of the times, and Jansenism was a part of that trend. The world-weariness of La Rochefoucauld overtook their need for joy.

THE PRECIOUS DECADE

The précieuses were eventually to be engulfed in the pessimism of the classical world view. Jansenism was a step in that process, a step away from the wishful affirmations of *préciosité*.

It is interesting that when the Jansenist "fashion" blew over in its turn, these same women relaxed into more conventional forms of piety. For when the précieuses grew older, old enough to see all their vices and vanities and hopes abandon them, they sought a more commonplace consolation in the religious attitudes of conformism. In the long run, they were devout in the manner of their king. They were devout as old ladies should be devout, without disturbing the balance of society. They put on devotion like a neat black dress. Neither Jansenism nor *préciosité*, two extremes of idealism, have anything to do with this piety of conformism, which found its place, like the classical ideal of mediocrity, in the France of the Sun King.

NOTES

1. La Bruyère, "De la Mode," *Caractères*, p. 405.
2. Born Madeleine de Souvré. Regarding her, see Tallemant, *Historiettes*, I, pp. 514–21 et passim. See also numerous references in Motteville, *Mémoires;* Sévigné, *Lettres*, ed. Gérard-Gailly (Pléiade, 1953–1963); Montpensier, *Mémoires;* and a modern study by N. Ivanoff, *La Marquise de Sablé et son salon* (Presses Modernes, 1927).
   Somaize calls her "Stephanie" (*Dictionnaire*, I, pp. 166, 241).
3. Motteville, I, p. 13.
4. Born Anne de Rohan; she married her first cousin Guimené in 1617, when she was thirteen. See Tallemant, II, pp. 225–30 et passim; Retz, *Mémoires*.
   Somaize calls her "Gelinte" (I, p. 106).
5. La Rochefoucauld, *Maximes* (No. 192), in *Oeuvres*, p. 271.
6. Le Chevalier de Méré, "Divers propos," in *Revue d'Histoire Littéraire de la France* (1922), p. 219, reported by Adam in Tallemant, II, p. 1231n.
7. Retz, p. 13.
8. *Les Portefeuilles Vallant* contain forty-five Maxims which La Rochefoucauld sent to the Marquise before 1665. Seven of them were never printed during the life of the author. Of the others, four were altered radically, in meaning or moral content, when they appeared in the first edition; the other corrections are all purely stylistic. Mme. de Sablé had little real effect on the *Maximes*. (See Ivanoff, pp. 175–76). The quoted example is one of the four most radically altered. Dr. Noel Vallant was Mme. de Sablé's physician from 1658 onward. His notes were first opened by Victor Cousin, and remain in manuscript in the Bibliothèque Nationale.
9. Quoted in La Rochefoucauld, p. 689.

Bourgeoisie and Worse

*P*réciosité was more and less than an idealism. It was also a practical, progressive movement, and not only because of its focus on women's right to personal value, but also in general terms of egalitarianism. Emerging slowly from feudalism, France had to develop a middle class, not only rich and knowledgeable but also socially viable, before she could discover, in the eighteenth century, anything so sophisticated as the idea of the brotherhood of man.

That middle class was there, had been there for centuries, getting richer and more self-assured. Now it was to learn manners as well, in the *précieux ruelles*.

Throughout the seventeenth century the nobility felt increasingly threatened, and with reason. There was constant pressure from below. By the late 1650s it seemed as if every ambitious housewife who had a little money could launch herself into some sort of genteel society by calling herself a précieuse.

The ennobling of the rich in France was a process which had been going on for centuries. Such social mobility is found in any hierarchy based on birth. The families at the top wear out and have to be replaced. The military exploits, the diplomatic talents which first placed them in privileged positions diminish in succeeding generations. The fortunes they accumulated are spent by idle grandsons. The titles are sold for cash.

The surge upward of the bourgeoisie was unremitting. The first thing a rich family must do was acquire a few pieces of land. Tallemant, a banker's son, adds to his name the title of a small property at Réaux. Or the family disposes of the old name by a few judicious marriages. Matthieu Garnier, a businessman who made an enormous fortune as a "partisan"—that is, a financier exploiting government contracts—was the father of three noted précieuses who traded their plebeian name for fancier ones: D'Oradour, d'Orgères, and even a Brancas. We notice that Mme. de Sévigné wrote frequently to the Comte de Brancas but ignored his wife. Was it because of Mme. de Brancas' numerous love affairs, or because she used to be plain Susanne Garnier?

The aristocracy in France, with its roots still mainly in the soil, regarded the *partisans*, the overnight millionnaires, with envy and disgust. They had to offer their sons and daughters to these magnates to make ends meet. But they despised their rich in-laws, and their children often despised their own spouses. "We have to manure our lands," said Mme. de Grignan, née Sévigné, when she married her son to an untitled heiress to pay her husband's debts.

They set up artificial distinctions, but these were always breaking down. The *tabouret* was one. You had to be a duchess to sit down in the presence of the queen. Duchesses fought to keep mere countesses off their territory. But now any pretty girl from nowhere might have the luck to marry a duke.

Another obvious distinction, between the sword and the robe, was growing fuzzier: the *noblesse d'épée* was nobler than the *noblesse de robe* because of the symbolic heroism implicit in exposing one's body on the battlefield. This was a moral quality to which the sword-bearing class had a unique claim. But there was no money in it. The gifts given by the monarch to loyal soldiers were usually in the form of governorships or courtly functions—splendid marks of esteem, but it took another kind of enterprise to convert such favors into wealth. The loyal soldier had to traffic his privileges for money, bleed his peasants with taxes, marry his daughter to the bailiff.

The *noblesse de robe* had its own form of honor, that of unselfishly and intelligently administering the government according to the royal will; but how did you make a living out of a magistracy? Why, from bribes, of course. This abuse became so normal as to put the whole *robe* on a moral level with the profiteering *partisans*.

It was not only intermarriage and land speculation that eroded the old class patterns. There was a falling off in the ethical assumptions which had justified the hierarchy. In the absence of any real basis for righteousness, everyone clung helplessly to the outward signs. The right to use gilt on carriages or braid on servants' uniforms, the number of Swiss guards in front of one's door, the length of one's train in a royal procession, the degree of intimacy of one's ceremonial position in the king's household—these things mattered more and more, and it was precisely these things which were now constantly being usurped. The laws restricting the use of gilt and braid were broken. The education of middle-class girls was as good or better than that of young ladies with the *tabouret*. Even the snobbery worked in reverse. Sometimes it is the bourgeois parent who rejects a noble suitor for his daughter's hand because the title is just not worth all the money it will cost him. The most celebrated example is that of the Chancellor Séguier, who refused Mme. de Sablé's son. The boy had to resort to an elopement. Another case is that of Mlle. de Chemerault, a girl of noble birth who married Macé La Bazinière, a man far beneath her. His mother did not welcome this daughter-in-law who had no dowry but her name.

A couple of decades later, Louis XIV was to exploit the deep insecurity of his nobility by giving them a superficial outlet for the expression of their pretensions as courtiers at Versailles. There they could show him their devout, submissive faces, dressed up in expensive wigs, while he gave the important tasks of government to selected experts of a lower class. But what was happening now, in the 1650s—the sudden social arrival of the bourgeoisie (and worse) —was a consequence of forces beyond anyone's control.

We find ladies like Mme. d'Oradour (a Garnier daughter) and Mme. Paget represented in the *Galerie des portraits*. They were guests of the Grande Mademoiselle. Such ladies could be accepted into her circle solely by virtue of their social graces. New hostesses take up fashionable authors, new plays are performed at their magnificent salons. These ladies have not only money but a kind of energy that makes them enthusiasts of the new even as they forge their links with the old.

The *précieux* authors loved these aggressive, faddish women. Somaize, Saint-Gabriel, and Beauchasteau rattle on about their perfections. But the tone is different from that in which they eulogize duchesses. Somaize seems to have more to say about the lapses of taste and morals of these ladies, not because they are more promiscuous or vulgar than their betters, but because he can get away with it. He tells their ages. He notices the paint on their faces.

These ladies spend less on cultural patronage for its own sake. Writers are their personal friends rather than their houseboys. The ladies seek their advice, borrow their pens, pick out favorites to applaud at the theatre; but when the printed works come out, the dedications continue to be addressed more often to dukes and princes who can get these authors jobs.

The aristocracy liked to think that there was still a certain something, a *je ne sais quoi*, that made all the difference between true refinement and its bourgeois imitation. Society writers, to please them, were often ambiguous in writing about these newly rich middle-class ladies.

There is little actual difference, however, in the plight of these up-and-coming matrons. They all seem to have equally horrible husbands. But the reaction is resolute and practical: cuckold them. And those who are not coquettes are busy counting their money.

Of Mme. de Launay-Gravé [1] Somaize says that her dominant passions are literature and gambling. He also tells us she is thirty-seven years old in 1660.

She was Françoise Desmarais, and she came from Brittany as a young girl to live with her uncle de Launay, a rich *partisan*. Tallemant des Réaux fell in love with this pretty cousin of his when he saw her in a faded and soiled blue dress serving the table in her uncle's house. The young man was sorry to see her so exploited by these uncouth newly rich Parisians. The lady of the house was only a Breton peasant herself under layers of finery. Tallemant took Françoise by the hand and brought her out of the servants' quarters into the salon where he felt she belonged. He taught her Italian at a fee of one kiss a month, but never got any farther with his virtuous cousin despite his many ruses. He had to content himself with being her first friend.

Then Mme. de Launay died. M. de Launay began to look hard at this niece who already knew the ways of his house and could run it efficiently for him. Besides, he had promised Françoise a dowry of ten thousand écus, and by marrying her himself he could keep the money. To bring matters to a head, she cleverly asked her brother to say that it was not proper for a young girl to continue to live under the same roof with a youngish (under-fifty) widower like de Launay. De Launay did marry her, secretly, in 1646, and the secret was kept for two months, though he often forgot himself and murmured endearments to her in public. Then she became pregnant and they had to announce the fact. Tallemant who had predicted to her when old Mme. de Launay was dying that she, Mlle. Desmarais, would "sleep in the big bed," now reminded her of his prediction. He was piqued that a prude like her could marry and sleep with the man for two months without saying a word to anyone, while a shameless rascal like himself had to get married in church with all public ceremony.

The new Mme. de Launay now began to live very well, spent a lot of money on clothes, and took to the gaming table. Her husband gave her a regular betting allowance, and her house became a lively place where no gambler was ever turned away. To attract better-class guests she also held parties at which elaborate ballets were sung and danced. But her friends talked all through the performances, and the cultural benefit was small. When she had the *Ballet des Romans* performed, the house filled up with so many guests that a prince who had been invited was inadvertently turned away.

She went every day to gamble with ladies like Mme. Fouquet. Once when playing cards at the home of the Duchesse de Nemours, she won ten pistoles and grandly left them on the table when she departed. The Duc de Nemours remarked gaily, "Really, this Mme. de Launay is the most generous person in the world; she knows we aren't rich and gives us back what she wins from us." The blood-elite was irked by this lady's pointed disregard for money.

Mme. de Launay made a killing at society balls, where she danced well, but the higher-up ladies kept her out of court for years. A courtly libertine named Roquelaure told her that the way to get invited to the Louvre was to go there on the arm of Mme. du Lude. She took his advice and went to court with that lady. Mme. du Lude was admitted, but Mme. de Launay suffered the humiliation of being turned away. The next day Roquelaure protested to Gaston d'Orléans: "Look here, we queue up to bring you beautiful girls and you shut the door in their faces!" At last she got invited to a ball where the king was present. She went up to Roquelaure to ask him to dance. The king, sitting beside Roquelaure, stood up. Mme. de Launay thoughtlessly told Louis xiv that it was not he but his companion she had chosen.

Despite such small disasters, she made her way steadily. When de Launay died in 1655 she claimed that he had married her for her provincial title (she let it be known that she was the daughter of a country squire). She still ran a tidy household, married off her sisters, took care of her numerous children. But her friends were now all people with entrée at the court. She affected the *précieux* mannerisms and was very condescending. Her conversation became intelligent and easy, if not witty.

One of her schemes was to marry the Duc de l'Esdiguières. He was a flirt. He led her on for a while, but she made a false move. Having contrived to be taken out for a drive in his carriage, she placed one of her own footmen behind, along with his. Someone called out in the street, "Hey lackey, has Monseiur de L'Esdiguières gone and married Mme. de Launay?" The duke did not like this and dropped her. It made many a fine lady laugh with relief at Mme. de Launay. For there had been real alarm at the possibility of a marriage which would have given her the *tabouret*. Mme. de La Fayette wrote in 1657, "I have the greatest esteem for Mme. de Launay-Gravé, although I do not know her, but it would give me great displeasure to see her taking the place of the late Mme. de l'Esdiguières." [2] However, four years later, she did marry the Marquis de Piennes, a match at least as grand as one with l'Esdiguières would have been. And the ultimate honor came to her: Mlle. de Montpensier once stayed overnight at her house, and mentions it in her memoirs.

She had come a long way from that stained blue dress in de Launay's kitchen. She now went to church in masculine hunting attire and knelt down on one knee, which Mme. de Montausier found quite scandalous: this lady was even invading the upper-class prerogative of bizarre behavior!

She lost her figure and grew pious, in the manner of Mme. de Sablé. But not pious enough to give up gambling. Many years later the king singled her out at a carnival where he saw her betting for high stakes at the royal card table. Did he remember that she had once been gauche enough to turn him down on the dance floor?

If Mme. de Launay (née Desmarais) was able to claim a modest gentility that nobody contested, the name of Mme. Cornuel (1609–1694) [3] was totally common by birth and marriage. There was money behind the name. But money was not enough. She also had *précieux* connections. She and her three stepdaughters (who were about her own age) were habituées of the Saturdays of Mlle. de Scudéry.

Mme. Cornuel was a witty freethinker with a malicious style that delighted the wags. Shortly after her marriage she dressed up as the ghost of her husband's previous wife and visited him in bed at midnight, reproaching him for his ingratitude. Then she burst out laughing at his terrified reaction. She deceived this rich old husband with a number of prominent men, chaffing gaily about a husband's horns, which are like teeth: "When they first begin to come out it hurts, but then they laugh about it." The Marquis de Sourdis had a liaison with her, and when she kept him waiting for a long time in her antechambre he amused himself with her chambermaid and got the girl pregnant. Mme. Cornuel raised this child as her own, because "he was produced in my service."

The Cornuel ladies were accepted everywhere despite their low birth and easy morals, largely because of their association with Sapho, even when they earned her criticism, for it placed them in the public eye as précieuses. They were also forgiven their lapses because they were fun:

"Oh, Mme. de Fiesque," says Mme. Cornuel to that lady who has been trying to prove that a certain mutual friend of theirs is not mad, "you are like someone who has eaten garlic."

Nicolas de Bailleul was a shrewd commoner who had risen in the world by a series of royal promotions until in 1643 Anne of Austria appointed him finance minister, a post far beyond his capacities. He accepted it unwillingly, being honest enough to admit that his command of arithmetic was inadequate. In 1647 he was relieved of the job, and Particelli d'Emery, his former assistant who had been doing his work, replaced him.

Bailleul's father had been a sort of chiropractor, a "resetter of broken or dislocated bones," and Nicolas inherited an aptitude for putting bones right. He was more comfortable in this humble occupation than in controlling the finances of France. After him, all bone setters were called "*Bailleuls*."

Such was the background of the Bailleul daughters,[4] all three of them born in the 1620s and each eulogized by the *précieux* authors. All three were also notorious enough to earn a place on the *Carte du pays de Braquerie* but nevertheless all three got married on the cheap, without dowries, to men far above their station.

How did they do it? We know that the Marquis du Tillet and the Marquis de Saint-Germain-Beaupré married, respectively, Elizabeth and Agnès de Bailleul because they hoped their father-in-law's position would be advantageous to them. But when Bailleul lost his job, these husbands were no longer so pleased with their merchandise. Du Tillet sent Elizabeth back to her father when he found out about her adulteries.

Somaize admires this lady but remarks that he will not discuss

her private life "for fear of saying too much." And Boisrobert
warns her to simmer down in his *Adieu des Forges:*

> Adieu parfaite Présidente;
> Modérez cette soif ardente
> Qui brûle toutes vos humeurs
> Et le vôtre et les autres coeurs
> Sans autre plus prompte allégence
> Que celle qui fait l'espérance.
> Espérez pourtant de guérir;
> Et nous espérons de mourir
> Si vous voulez être cruelle
> Tout autant que vous serez belle
> Et qu'aurez le teint d'un oeillet.
> Adieu la dame du Tillet.[5]

> (Adieu most perfect President,
> restrain that ardent thirst
> which burns up your body
> and your heart,
> and for which there is no relief
> save that which raised our hopes.
> Yet go on hoping to recover,
> and we will go on hoping to die,
> if you are as unyielding
> as you are lovely
> and flower-tinted.
> Adieu Mme. du Tillet.)

Evidently Boisrobert, who preferred boys, was frightened by her
aggressive sensuality and tried to hide politely behind a conventional pose as her "hopeless admirer."

The *Carte de Braquerie* finished her off:

Le Tillet, a big town open on all sides. The inhabitants are coarse, the soil
rich and quite beautiful; however, we notice that no man in his senses
has ever been able to stay there two days running. But as the world is more
full of fools than decent folk, the place is never empty.[6]

The situation of her sister Agnès was more complicated, for this
lady's husband, the Marquis de Saint-Germain-Beaupré, was a violent
man who forced her to submit to sexual "indignities." The *Carte
de Braquerie* tells what they are: *Saint-Germain-Beaupré* is a town
where the river *Coquette* joins the river *Carogne* (tramp). The
"governor" of this town has been trying to enter the fortress "by

the back door, and frankly I think it was not without reason." But the town refused, "thinking that if she allowed this she would forfeit all the rights associated with the front door" (i.e., the rights associated with having children).

This ogre spied on his wife and beat and kicked her when her alibis were proved false. Yet Somaize rhapsodizes thus:

> She has a beautiful bosom which has no blemish; and as we can judge from this the other delights of her body, which I have not seen, and of which no one can speak but by conjecture, I leave others to their conjectures, and I admit only that, if I were her husband, I would be just as jealous as he is of all the delightful treasures of which he is the master.[7]

Somaize would not have dared to talk in this way about the physical "delights" of a more noble précieuse.

Agnès fought hard against her husband's cruelty. She filed suit for separation and won her case. Her "bestial" husband had to let her go home to her father with a pension of eight thousand livres. She took a lover, the Marquis d'Alluye, and her husband went back to the country and occupied himself rebuilding his chateau and terrorizing his peasants.

Of all the Bailleul daughters only Marie made a truly brilliant success of her life. She married a marquis like her sisters, lost him a few months later, and promptly married another. This second brilliant marriage, to the Marquis d'Uxelles, ended when he was killed in battle in 1658. But by this date she was well launched in polite society. Mme. d'Uxelles was just as relaxed morally as her sisters, but somehow she rose above the gossip. For one thing, she was lucky enough to become a widow early and could sigh regretfully over her late husband ever after instead of fighting him. But more important, she promoted herself by putting into action her own devouring thirst for gossip. She circulated a newsletter to keep in touch with friends and exchanged a well-publicized correspondence with upper-class men of culture, such as Bussy-Rabutin, the young Condé, the Prince de Conty, and La Rochefoucauld. Women, too—Mlle. de Montpensier and Mme. de La Fayette were glad to hear from her. The *précieux* authors handle her with greatest delicacy. Saint-Gabriel calls her "L'Archangélique. I place her above the angels."[8]

Her literary talents served this lady well. Mme. de Sévigné wrote her one of her earliest letters, a charming one in Italian. The

Sévigné–d'Uxelles friendship lasted over three decades. They became the bright lights of a group which Mme. de Sévigné calls "the virtuous widows." They went to church and did their social rounds together.

But the *chansonniers* are sardonic about Mme. d'Uxelles, right to the end: "*Cessez, vieille marquise, de vouloir avoir des amants . . .*" ("Stop looking for lovers, old marquise . . ."). They objected to her relations with very young men, such as the Comte de Saint-Paul, Mme. de Longueville's illegitimate son by La Rochefoucauld.

Never mind. Mme. de Sévigné never once mentions the youthful and not-so-youthful errors of her friend—or her maiden name of Bailleul.

How low could a lady be at the start of her career and still climb to the pinnacle of the *précieux* hierarchy? The Maréchale de l'Hospital (d. 1711), née Françoise Mignon,[9] was a provincial girl whose father was probably a laborer, her mother a laundress. She rose from this humble starting point by stages, perhaps fortified by a prediction she had heard that she would marry three times, each time higher until she reached royalty. First Françoise Mignon secured the love of an underling of Des Portes d'Ambérieux, treasurer of the province of Dauphiné. Then she ensnared Des Portes himself, who married her. When this husband died, she came to Paris with her lawsuits and met the secretary of the Maréchal de l'Hospital. This secretary, on learning that she was well-to-do, decided to marry her. The old maréchal, out of consideration for his secretary, did all he could to further her legal cases. She went to see the maréchal to thank him and promptly set her cap for him.

Now Loret the newshound, in one of the liveliest and longest news items of his *Gazette Burlesque*, had reported the death of the maréchal's first wife. M. de l'Hospital was far from sad at her passing (she was in her sixties) and had immediately begun looking around for a younger wife (he himself was practically in his dotage). The chronicler, in his bouncing doggerel, suggests scores of possibilities, virtually all the reigning beauties of the court season. The maréchal may have his pick; they would all accept him eagerly. But the maréchal waited, until in 1653 Loret reports the marriage to our Françoise Mignon, now the rich widow Des Portes. Eight months later a lovely boy is born, and l'Hospital, to share his joy

Mme. de l'Hospital

with his friends and neighbors, sets out great vats of wine in the street. But three days later the child is dead.[10]

In the 1650s, there are several more mentions of balls and parties where Loret observed this couple whirling on the dance floor, the young woman growing stouter, the old husband unsteady on his legs. Mlle. de Montpensier watched from the sidelines with pursed lips:

Mme. la maréchale de l'Hospital has a handsome face but she is so fat that she looks quite ridiculous on the dancefloor. She dances well. She has the most beautiful jewels in the world. Her pearls are bigger than the queen's. She is lavish both with her personal finery and in her house furnishings, and the surprising thing about all this is that she was once a seamstress in Grenoble. . . .

She's a good sort, not unintelligent, but she has that countrified sort of intelligence, which blurts out the kind of words one doesn't use at court, where she is often seen. You can imagine how successful she is.[11]

Somaize puts the *ruelle* of this glamorized country woman among the top *précieux* centers of Paris. He says she likes music and supports authors, especially dramatic authors. We can see her glittering entrance at the théâtre de l'hôtel de Bourgogne; she settles down in her place in the gallery, masked, bejeweled, laughing out loud, open and easy among her friends. And when the play begins, wide-eyed and candid in her admiration for the fulsome *tirades* of Scudéry, Boisrobert, Rotrou, and Corneille.

In 1661 l'Hospital died. Françoise Mignon, the washerwoman's daughter from Dauphiné, would marry again, in 1672. Her third husband was Jean-Casimir, former King of Poland, who had abdicated and settled in France. The prediction had come true.

Dozens of bohemians, would-be genteel ladies of no fixed position and low estate, down-to-earth and down-at-the-heels women of pleasure, actresses, even prostitutes are represented in the *précieux* directories. They had little or no social prestige, or their fame did them no good. One or two were truly talented, others cashed in on the movement, still others were true originals, like Mme. de Saintot, Voiture's mistress, who wrote excellent letters which were passed around and admired at the *chambre bleue*. But the lady herself was not welcome there, because of her irregular connection with their star. She loved Voiture deeply, smothered him in sometimes embarrassing attentions, and when he died she moaned her grief loud enough for all Paris to hear. Her moans were duly recorded in Somaize's *Dictionnaire*, to the discomfiture of her family, who tried to hide the scandal by declaring her insane.[12]

A more interesting girl, Marie-Catherine Desjardins (1632–1683),[13] was probably an actress in Molière's company in the provinces around 1657, just before he came to try his luck in Paris. Perhaps she even acted the part of Cathos in an earlier provincial production of *Les Précieuses ridicules*. She moved in the more-or-less anti-précieuse libertine circles of Gilles Boileau, Sauval, d'Aubignac, and Colletet. Yet this lady's own poetry is *précieux*, however unconventional.

She preferred to call herself by her boyfriend's name of Villedieu, but was never married to Villedieu or anyone else. The liaison with this young army officer was quite public. Everyone knew the circumstances: He had met her at a dance, then found himself locked out of his own house afterward and accepted her offer of a bed at her home. He then fell sick and had to stay there three weeks. She took care of him and became his mistress while he was convalescing, all in the vain hope that he would marry her. It is possible he was already married. They lived openly together for another several months. Then he tired of her and went back to the army. She insisted he was her husband and always called herself Mme. de Villedieu after that.

This emancipated girl who was so unlucky in love wrote a number of erotic sonnets of the type called *jouissances* (physical pleasures) and recited them before large mixed audiences, with amorous looks and gestures which offended the sense of decorum of many a well-behaved lady and even a few libertines. (Tallemant, who objects to her style, is not easy to embarrass!) Here is the best one:

> Aujourd'hui dans tes bras j'ai demeuré pâmée,
> Aujourd'hui, cher Tirsis, ton amoureuse ardeur
> Triomphe impunément de toute ma pudeur
> Et je cède aux transports dont mon âme est charmée.
>
> Ta flamme et ton respect m'ont enfin désarmée,
> Dans nos embrassements je mets tout mon bonheur,
> Et je ne connais plus de vertu ni d'honneur
> Puisque j'aime Tirsis et que j'en suis aimée.

O vous, faibles esprits, qui ne connaissez pas
Les plaisirs les plus doux que l'on goûte ici-bas,
Apprenez les transports dont mon âme est ravie.

Une douce langueur m'ôte le sentiment;
Je meurs entre les bras de mon fidèle amant,
Et c'est dans cette mort que je trouve la vie.[14]

(Today I lay swooning in your arms,
Thyrsis, today your loving ardor
triumphs freely over my modesty
and I give in to the transports which bewitch my soul.

Your flame and your respect have disarmed me at last.
In our embraces I find all my happiness,
and for me there is no more virtue or honor,
now that I love Thyrsis and he loves me.

Oh, all you weaklings who do not know
the sweetest pleasures to be tasted here below,
let me tell you the transports that ravish my soul.

A sweet languor takes me from my senses,
I die away in the arms of my faithful lover,
and in this death I rediscover life.)

Her bohemianism closed surprisingly few doors to her. Despite her outspoken sonnets, she was respectable enough to have her self-portrait included in the *Galerie des portraits*. In it she is honest about her looks ("I am not a beautiful girl but I'm no fright either"), but disingenuous about her passionate nature. She says she loves Paris, but pretends to prefer country pleasures, such as hunting, to society balls (a typical *précieux* myth). She claims to be unambitious and unenvious, more sensitive to the distress of others than her own, and would only accept the friendship of a man of like sentimental nature. Unfortunately, neither Villedieu nor Sauval, her two closest men friends, fits this description.

But this girl was more than a casualty of love and dabbler in poetry. She was also a successful writer who lived by her pen. Besides poetry she wrote fables and popular second-rate plays, and she was a regular contributor to the *recueils*.

But her true talent was for the novel. She began turning out workmanlike ones by 1661. Her chief topic was love, in all its forms: solitary love, peaceful love, flirtatious love, and above all, *amour d'inclination*. Mlle. Desjardins was fascinated by the irrational, the indefinable, the *je ne sais quoi* in love. She was fond of describing betrayed women and the disorders and ravages of love, no doubt drawn from her own bitter experiences. We are still in the land of *Tendre*. But unlike Mlle. de Scudéry, Mlle. Desjardins describes relationships that have a physical basis, and this adds an urgency and aggressivity to the arguments of her characters.

Mlle. Desjardins catered to an enormous public of not very refined sentiments. She was constantly working under financial pressure and had no time to write a masterpiece like *La Princesse de Clèves*. We can only guess what her talents might have produced if she had had the chance to develop them in the leisurely sheltered atmosphere of Mme. de La Fayette's *ruelle* on the rue de Vaugirard. Or what she might have made of the friendship of a La Rochefoucauld, in place of that of Colletet, d'Aubignac, Sauval, and Gilles Boileau, the "pests" of the literary underworld.

Mlle. Desjardins is unique in the seventeenth century: a literary bluestocking without fear of appearances, without means, without moral support, living by her wits and sustained only by a romantic image of love. She has been called a "seventeenth-century George Sand." But she was far more exposed than that nineteenth-century liberated lady. We like her bravery and enthusiasm. What a pity she did not write at least one good book.

A few more steps down and we are at the bottom: Mlle. Colletet.[15] Somaize says that this lady has been married twice and "used to keep a second-class *ruelle*" where Gilles Boileau was her alcovist. He gives her age, thirty-four or thirty-five, and avoids even the slightest gesture of praise or approval. This puts her in the category of the poorest précieuses in his *Dictionnaire*. Somaize was Boileau's enemy. He seized this chance to strike at him by disparaging his defenseless lady friend.

She was indeed defenseless, and belonged to the lowest social stratum, being a servant girl. The Academician Guillaume Colletet, who lived with three of his female servants, did not disdain to make her his wife. And although only a servant, she wrote verses, some of them considered by their friends to be rather better than his. But there is doubt as to their authenticity. When Colletet died, she wrote a last tearful poem to announce that she would now bury both her heart and her pen with her husband.[16] It is more than likely that Colletet had guided her pen even in this epitaph. Her verses express great tenderness to her elderly husband, but Boisrobert whispered that she earned their keep by a little friendly prostitution. Gilles Boileau, however, affirmed that she was an honest woman. As she was always in the company of the rather scruffy bohemian men of Colletet's circle and they were extremely poor, we can assume that she did what she could to make ends meet. When Colletet died in 1659, Chapelain wrote that it must have been a relief to him. He had lived from hand to mouth, "between Apollo and Bacchus," all his life. Yet he was among the first Academicians, a poet admired by the older generation of Chapelain and Conrart. Tallemant des Réaux writing in the 1650s is curiously unsympathetic to this old-fashioned poet, whose humanistic realism seemed ugly to him. Tallemant cites a remark of Colletet in the presence of ladies at the home of Conrart:

"When we wake up at night, Claudine and I, what do you suppose we do?" The ladies lower their eyes. "We read *L'Astrée!*" he said.

Still later, Boileau-Déspréaux looks back on old Colletet with superior pity:

> Tandis que Colletet, crotté jusqu'à l'échine,
> S'en va chercher son pain de cuisine en cuisine. . . .[17]

> (While Colletet, mud-spattered to the spine,
> goes hunting for bread, from kitchen to kitchen. . . .)

La Fontaine, that eternal butterfly among the ladies, was briefly caught in the web of Mlle. Colletet's charms, and the charms of her talent; in one poem he offers her a crown of laurel for her verses which echo from one end of Parnassus to the other. But his eyes were opened when he discovered the limitations of her muse:

> Les oracles ont cessé:
> Colletet est trépassé.

> Dès qu'il eut la bouche close,
> Sa femme ne dit plus rien;
> Elle enterra vers et prose
> Avec le pauvre chrétien.

> En cela je plains son zèle,
> Et ne sais au pardessus
> Si les Grâces sont chez elle;
> Mais les Muses n'y sont plus.

Sans gloser sur le mystère,
Des madrigaux qu'elle a faits,
Ne lui parlons désormais
Qu'en la langue de sa mère.

Les oracles ont cessé.
Colletet est trépassé.[18]

(The oracles have ceased.
Colletet is dead.

As soon as his mouth was closed
his wife fell silent too.
She buried verse and prose
with the poor Christian.

It's a pity she's so scrupulous.
I don't know
whether the Graces reside with her.
But the Muses have moved out.

Without probing the mystery too much,
let us just say no more about the madrigals she has written,
and speak to her hereafter
in her mother's tongue.

The oracles have ceased.
Colletet is dead.)

This seems an unkind conclusion to his infatuation. Perhaps his vanity was wounded at having been "duped" by a literary woman.

After her husband's death, Claudine went rapidly downhill and tried to borrow from her friends using various subterfuges. Gilles Boileau and Furetière were among the unamused victims. She lost all these literary friends and was reduced to begging in the streets. She married one Jean Morain in 1660, but kept her name of *la veuve* Colletet. She had a shabby affair with the abbé Tallemant, among others, and drank herself to death, dying in the paupers' hospital.

The little neighborhood people of Paris had their précieuses, too, simple women whose hearts fluttered at the enormous horizons opening out before them. An interesting document preserved by Conrart in his voluminous papers is an advertisement for a

"Précieux Palace" [19] setting forth the entertainments available at a new club about to be opened in 1655 in the rue Béthisy. Anyone may belong to this club who can pay the dues of three pistoles, but "unworthy persons" will be kept out. This brochure offers daily entertainment at the Précieux Palace of a type to help cultivate the wits of very ordinary people: dances, concerts, philosophy lectures, orangeade parties, and practical services such as notice boards where one may look for a good maidservant or tutor—or even husband. Conrart no doubt saw this curio as an item of low-brow *préciosité ridicule*. That anonymous crowd of would-be ladies of fashion which is called in the brochure "the most distinguished assembly ever brought together in Paris" came to the club clutching their three pistoles, each lady hoping to be transformed into a priceless jewel for this modest price.

If the species *Précieuse* was to be found in all classes and neighborhoods of Paris, it soon cropped up in Lyon, Toulouse, and other towns with cultural pretensions as well.

Two young Parisian cavaliers, Chapelle and Bachaumont, went junketing around France in the 1650s and wrote a book about their travels. When they came to Montpellier, they found

a great number of ladies who were said to be the most polite in town, the best informed, the wittiest, though they were not the prettiest, nor the best-dressed. We gathered from their simpering speech, their little flirty gestures, their extraordinary remarks, that we had fallen on the *précieux* club of Montpellier.

But though they did their best to impress us, they were only country précieuses, a poor imitation of our Parisian ones. They purposely turned the conversation to writers and writing, to show us how much they knew.[20]

Some fifty of the names in Somaize's *Dictionnaire* are of such persons living in the provincial towns of France. They appear to be of the local bourgeoisie and small rural nobility. Somaize gives many unseemly details on these women, hidden away from the center of things, unsure of themselves, yearning for the excitement and the new freedom they have heard about in Paris. He does not hesitate to say that Mme. Camot ("Camestris") has been abandoned by her lover who has run off to Paris, and that she wishes she could get him back but pretends to be indifferent. Or that Mme. Chartier

("Coriolane") has tried putting menstrual blood as a charm into the hair and the soup of her various alcovists, to hold their affection. She is now such a laughingstock that she dares not go out of the house, but has become, as a result of her ostracism, a most well-read and learned lady. Or that Mme. de L'Angalerie's ("Damestriane's") husband has tired of her and suggests she take up with her former alcovist so that he can resume his own affair with an old girlfriend. Mme. de Monlo ("Medace") has been confronted in court by her husband, who accuses her of cuckolding him. Mlle. Jeuzet ("Icaire") has married a man who had to put a hundred guards around her house to keep off the competition while he was courting her. She is now so *précieuse* that her friends have to study up all the latest books before they dare to visit her.

The ladies Somaize knows in the provinces are heavily bookish, but most of the anecdotes about them are of love and intrigue; usually the man runs off and eludes the lady's efforts to trap him. Somaize does not bother to hide his Parisian prejudice. These provincial women cannot hope to fool anybody into thinking they are the real thing. Only Paris and the court are real.

NOTES

1. See Tallemant, *Historiettes,* II, pp. 830–40.
   Somaize calls her "Ligdaride" (*Dictionnaire,* I, p. 141).
2. Lettre à Ménage, August 17, 1657, *Lettres de Mme. de La Fayette et de Gilles Ménage,* ed. H. Ashton (Liverpool: University Press, 1924), p. 83.
3. Née Anne Bigot, she married Jacques Cornuel in 1627. On Mme. Cornuel and her daughters, see Tallemant, II, pp. 286–91 et passim.
   Somaize calls them "Cleophile et ses deux filles" (I, p. 58).
4. On the Bailleul girls, see Tallemant, II, pp. 383–84, 390, 394–99 (*Historiette de Bailleul*) et passim.
   Somaize calls them "Theodamie" (Mme. du Tillet) (I, pp. 223, 232), "Domitia" (Mme. d'Uxelles) (I, p. 223), and "Spagaris de Britonide" (Mme. de Saint-Germain-Beaupré) (I, p. 223).
5. Boisrobert, *Epîtres en vers,* I, p. 290.
6. Bussy-Rabutin, *Histoire amoureuse des Gaules,* I, p. 209.
7. Somaize, I, p. 225.
8. Saint-Gabriel, *Mérite des dames,* p. 314.
9. See Tallemant, II, pp. 71–75. She is not, as some commentators think, related to Mignot, the cook who ruined so many dinners and was immortalized by Boileau.
   Somaize calls her "Lisimène" (I, p. 142).
10. Loret, *Muze Historique,* I, p. 137, Letter of July 1651. Also December 1651, September 1653.

11. Montpensier, *Mémoires*, III, (1658), p. 202.

12. On Mme. de Saintot: Tallemant, I, pp. 485–88, 497–98, 500; II, pp. 560–61, et passim.

Somaize calls her "Statenoïde" I, p. 220.

13. Also called Mme. de Villedieu. See Tallemant, II, pp. 900–09 et passim. See also E. Magne, *Mme. de Villedieu* (Mercure de France, 1907) and B. A. Morrissette, *The Life and Works of Marie-Catherine Desjardins* (Ph.D. dissertation, Washington University, 1947).

Somaize calls her "Dinamise" (I, pp. 72, 167).

14. Quoted in *Recueil La Suze-Pellisson* (1633). Reprinted in G. Mongrédien, *Les Précieux et les précieuses*, p. 312.

15. See Tallemant, II, pp. 712–20 et passim. Claudine Le Nain did not qualify for the title of *Madame* Colletet when she married, but was still only *Mademoiselle*, like most lower-class wives.

Somaize calls her "Cleophe" (I, p. 55).

16.
> Le coeur gros de soupirs, les yeux noyez de larmes,
> Plus triste que la mort, dont je sens les allarmes,
> Jusques dans le tombeau je vous suy, cher époux.
> Comme je vous aimay d'une amour sans seconde,
> Et que je vous loüay d'un langage assez doux,
> Pour ne plus rien aimer, ny rien loüer au monde,
> J'ensevelis mon coeur et ma plume avec vous.

> (With a heart full of sighs, eyes full of tears,
> sadder than death, whose warnings I hear,
> I follow you, dear husband, right into the tomb.
> As I loved you with a love second to none,
> and praised you in sweet words,
> I will never love or praise again,
> but bury my heart and my pen with you.)

Quoted in Tallemant, II, p. 719.

17. Boileau, *Satire I*, in *Oeuvres complètes*, ed. A. Adam (Pléiade, 1966), p. 14.

18. La Fontaine, *Oeuvres diverses*, ed. Clarac (Pléiade, 1942), II, p. 487.

19. "Avis au public pour l'établissement de la société précieuse" (1655), in Conrart mss., Bibliothèque de l'Arsenal, ms. 5427, folio vol. XVIII, p. 33.

20. Chapelle and Bachaumont, *Oeuvres*, ed. M. Tenant de Latour (Bibliothèque Elzevirienne, 1854), p. 81.

III

Grandes Mondaines

The Decline

THE *précieux* movement had evidently lost some of its momentum when the wrecking crew of Molière and Boileau came along. There was a moment toward the end of the decade when the very word "*prècieux*" was exhausted, like any other transitory expression invented by these ladies. The word had been finally usurped by too many. When serving girls and nobodies from the woods could call themselves précieuses, it was time for the true originals to move on.

The first stage in the destruction of *préciosité* can be seen in the very efforts made to preserve the value of the word. To keep out the mob a barrier is set up between the "true" précieuses and the "false" ones. This artificial barrier was meant to stave off the equalizing process, which rendered all ladies the same in their "distinction."

But then as some ladies felt they were still more distinct than others, they had to find another name for themselves. They became *dames illustres*, or *dames de mérite*, or *femmes savantes*. As soon as a lady had graduated, in her own eyes, from *précieuse* to *dame illustre* she could consider all other ladies still calling themselves précieuses as dated or provincial. From there to the final abandonment of the concept of précieuse by the whole society is a very rapid step. A stylish lady might wear something really old, but she will not be seen dead in last year's gown.

When Molière attacked the précieuses at the end of 1659 he was demolishing a fashion already cheapened by overexposure to the lower orders. But what exactly did happen when his little farce appeared?

The play was first performed on November 18, as a curtain-raiser to Corneille's *Cinna*. Molière was a newcomer to the Paris stage, and he knew the competition was going to be tough. He had chosen this of all topics because it was in the air, a highly visible life style in process of being questioned and criticized, and ineptly defended. He wanted to make an impression with something that would scandalize as well as amuse the public.[1] He certainly did. The play was successful beyond his reckoning.

Somaize tells us that an *"alcoviste de qualité"* succeeded in having the play removed after the sixth performance. We guess that Somaize himself may have been that alcovist. He was already preparing his own *Grand Dictionnaire des pretieuses* and did not like the prospect of seeing the whole movement laughed at in scorn before he could get his book into print.

In any case, enough important people felt personally threatened or insulted by the play to cause it to be suppressed. However, Molière had already made his mark. The popularity of the play won out over the objections of those who wished to defend the précieuses. Performances were resumed December 26, 1659. It ran for ten months and was acted forty-four times, a record for the period.

Many ladies, seeing the way the wind was blowing, found it wiser to go to Molière's play and laugh, thus placing themselves in the category of the genuine. Mme. de Rambouillet herself was reported to have enjoyed the farce at a private performance. Nevertheless, there was a growing uneasiness in the heart of every woman who had ever allowed herself to be called a précieuse.

It was at this time, in 1660, that the mood of the highest society began to change. No doubt the most important factor in that change was the new king. Louis XIV got married that year. An arranged match to his first cousin, the infanta Marie Thérèse, the marriage had been written into the treaty of the Pyrénées. Louis made a ceremonial journey to Spain, with all pomp and leisure, to meet his bride and sign the documents of peace and love. It was a first opportunity for the handsome young king to display himself in full panoply to a large number of his subjects. Mazarin, the queen mother, and every other person of consequence at court went along.

Upon his return to Paris with his bride, Louis ordered a series of monumental entertainments to illuminate further the splendor of the new reign. He was indeed, at twenty-three, far more powerful than his father had ever been. The spirit of the Fronde was dead.

The Protestants were cowed. The foreign enemies were at bay. When Mazarin died soon after, Louis began, with resolution and energy, the personal absolute rule which was to last more than half a century.

He had qualities of majesty and dignity to match his political power. This is why the focus of elegant society began to shift back to the court and away from the town. The privacy of the *ruelle* gave way to the showy publicity of the royal presence.

Louis embarked on a conscious program of collecting his nobility around him and putting the town at a distance. He began enlarging his father's hunting lodge at Versailles to accommodate this throng of courtiers. Construction of the new wings began in 1661. The court moved to Versailles in 1682. And now began that dance of mechanical dolls around the king's person, that ritualization of court life which was fixed for the remainder of his reign. Louis' aristocracy could consider themselves fortunate to belong to the most magnificent court in Europe. But their magnificence was only an extension of the king's. They were his prisoners.

This movement toward political unity in despotism had its counterpart in literature. The great writers of the classical period describe a confined, unoriginal humanity stuck forever in its own nature and unable to change. The pessimism of Racine, Molière, La Bruyère would be unsupportable if it were not expressed with infinite grace and harmony, and in some cases even gaiety. André Gide has called this a literature of modesty and reserve. How different from the wordy and often tasteless heroics of the *précieux* era.

A new social style was forming at the court of the young king and at the hôtels of the great ladies who had access to this court. It was reminiscent of the style of the Marquise de Rambouillet in its decorum and delicacy. *Bienséance*, polite and politic behavior, avoiding any offensive allusion was now a universal requirement. So was a great show of culture and sobriety. The extravagant fancies of the précieuses, their militant prudery, their verbal excesses, their crystalline poetry were to be left behind. The new paragon was the courtier who never gets excited about anything. The *juste milieu*, the golden mean of all pessimists and epicureans—which was for Molière a kind of normalcy of Nature—ousted the excitement and faddishness of *préciosité*. Anything overdone, lopsided, overflowing was now bad, a sin against Nature.

But the women were still there, under their new mask, still burdened with their grievances, still in need of intellectual support and stimulation. In the course of the next decade many précieuses regrouped their energies and emerged again as learned ladies. They took up Cartesian astronomy. They measured lenses. They studied Greek.

And Molière attacked again. In 1672 his *Femmes savantes* aimed at the précieuses reincarnate. As he presents them to us, they are the same old false prudes, simpering over shallow poets like Cotin, impressed by pretentious pedants like Ménage. They have become more shrill than ever in their determination to organize the world anew to suit themselves.

> Nous serons par nos lois les juges des ouvrages.
> Par nos lois, prose et vers, tout nous sera soumis:
> Nul n'aura de l'esprit, hors nous et nos amis.
> Nous chercherons partout à trouver à redire,
> Et ne verrons que nous qui sache bien écrire.[2]

> (We will be the only judges of anyone's work.
> Everything, prose or verse, will be submitted to our laws.
> Nobody will be considered witty except us and our friends.
> We will find fault with everyone else,
> And only we will be seen to know how to write.)
>   —*Les Femmes Savantes*
>   Act III, Scene ii

These ladies are dogmatic enthusiasts, and enthusiasm is passé in 1672. They are also usurpers of men's prerogatives in the domain of knowledge and wisdom. Molière's hero Clitandre sums up the masculine attitude thus:

> Je consens qu'une femme ait des clartés de tout
> Mais je ne lui veux point la passion choquante
> De se rendre savante afin d'être savante;
> Et j'aime que souvent, aux questions qu'on fait,
> Elle sache ignorer les choses qu'elle sait;
> De son étude enfin je veux qu'elle se cache,
> Et qu'elle ait du savoir sans vouloir qu'on le sache.[3]

> (I grant that a woman may have knowledge of everything
> but I would not wish on her that shocking passion
> for being learned just for the sake of being learned.
> I like a woman to know how to plead ignorant of

the things she knows.
I like her to hide her studies, and have
knowledge without wanting me to know it.)
—Act I, Scene iii

We can see that not much progress had been made since 1628 when
Balzac warned Mme. des Loges about overstepping the limits of her
womanly province (see above, pp. 112–113). In fact, men had
learned nothing in fifty years of feminine progress about the intellectual capacities and needs of women. A woman who would
be knowledgeable for its own sake is abnormal.

All of Molière's great madmen—miserly, misanthropic, sick, obsessed with cuckoldry—suffer from the same abnormality. They
lose their sense of balance, which to the classical mind is a sense of
the limited size of human possibilities. They search, in their madness,
for some monstrous self-realization. They suffer from hubris.

The précieuses, even after they had shaken off the label of
préciosité, went on committing their own special form of this "error,"
of believing that human nature is still full of surprises, that the
possibilities are endless, that not everything has been said or done
before.

But doubts had set in among the highborn who had something to
gain by conforming to the new courtly mood. Was it not after all
enough to be a social success? Respected and admired by men?
Why reach for independence? Men, after all, were not free either.

The grandest ladies who decorated the early years of the court
of Louis xiv were innocent snobs who now took their worth for
granted. They were no longer agitated seekers of answers to questions which proved insoluble; they relinquished the extrava-
gances of their own youth and opted for smoothness. They are the
women we think of when we speak of *mondanité:* Mme. de Sablé,
the Grande Mademoiselle, Mme. de La Fayette.

Mondanité—worldliness—is at first simply an absorbing interest in,
and love for, the things of the world. But inevitably it grows self-
conscious, informed, and discriminating, and from there it becomes
a more negative kind of interest in the world, a denial of wonder
or excitement. *"L'honnête homme est celui qui ne se pique de rien."*
La Rochefoucauld's dictum translates as, "A gentleman is one who
does not get upset over anything." This disabusement of experience,

this refusal to be surprised, became the norm after about 1660, with the fading of the *précieux* enthusiasm. The new *mondanité* was more of a worldly-wise, or world-weary smartness—the correct countenance to assume in the royal presence, the way to behave at the theatre (indeed, which plays to be seen seeing), the right topics to discuss, or avoid. This detached smoothness never quite became a reality, for everyone cried buckets of tears over Racine's heroines, everyone schemed passionately to get invited to the king's intimate picnics. But an unruffled morgue was the prescription.

The *grandes mondaines* of the 1660s are among the first who thought of putting some distance between themselves and the other précieuses. But it was only the name they rejected. The lure of freedom and their own tender sentiments enticed them into *précieux* habits of thought, and a few of them even took up their pens for relief. One (Mlle. de Montpensier) wrote valuable memoirs while dashing off elegant portraits of her friends. Another (Mme. de Sévigné) wrote letters more artful and interesting than any others produced in her century. And one (Mme. de La Fayette) finally wrote a great book, a genuine *précieux* masterpiece, the first and last of its kind.

NOTES

1. The two country maidens of his play, Cathos and Magdelon, have names suspiciously reminiscent of Catherine (de Rambouillet) and Madeleine (de Scudéry).
2. Molière, *Oeuvres*, II, p. 785.
3. Ibid., pp. 750–51.

The Most Precious Princess

Mademoiselle, la Grande Mademoiselle, Mademoiselle daughter of the late Monsieur; Mademoiselle granddaughter of Henri iv, Mademoiselle d'Eu, Mademoiselle de Dombes, Mademoiselle de Montpensier, Mademoiselle d'Orléans, Mademoiselle first cousin of the king, Mademoiselle destined to sit on the throne; Mademoiselle the only match in France worthy of the king's brother.[1]

—Mme. de Sévigné

RICHEST and most eligible woman in France, and a true daughter of Gaston d'Orléans in willfulness and vanity, the Grande Mademoiselle (1627–1693) had been brought up in the conviction that a magnificent destiny awaited her. Only half a dozen reigning monarchs were good enough to ask for her hand. From as far back as she could remember, she was encouraged to entertain dreams of glory about her future husband: would he be the King of Portugal, England, or Spain? A Lorraine, a Guise, or the Holy Roman Emperor? Or perhaps the young Monsieur, Philippe d'Anjou, the king's brother; or why not her cousin Louis xiv himself? It had to be a marriage of state, of course, an "establishment." Love was a secondary consideration.

But the years passed. The charming princess reached twenty, thirty, forty, and for one reason or another all of the possibilities dwindled to zero.

In her twenties she had shared with a whole generation of princes the delusory heroism of the Fronde. Her father Gaston was up to his neck in it, and he expected her to support him with money and resolution.

In March 1652, without knowing exactly what she was about, the twenty-five-year-old Mademoiselle had led a small army to the town of Orléans and demanded entry in the name of Monsieur. Technically, Orléans belonged to Gaston, but as he was in rebellion against the crown, the townspeople thought best to lock the gates against her. Undeterred, and full of her exciting mission, Mademoiselle crawled through a small window in the ramparts and declared the city for Gaston against Mazarin. Although she was "welcomed" by the city fathers and allowed to make a speech, her army was not permitted entry. Taking the town by escalade was a fine gesture, but wars are not won with gestures. Later in the same year, having retreated to Paris, she did something even more extraordinary for a woman and a first cousin of the king, when she gave the order for the gates of Paris to be opened and for the cannon of the Bastille to fire on the king's troops. Condé was enabled to break into the city and reverse the outcome of the battle. Mademoiselle was ecstatic. She had saved the day. But someone murmured on the sidelines: "That cost you a brilliant marriage—to Louis XIV."

And what had she saved exactly? That was not very clear. Again it was only a gesture. The rebels lost the war anyway.

Mademoiselle went from the Fronde into exile like everyone else, and settled down to write her memoirs. These pages give a good indication of the nature of that rebellion for the women involved. She discusses the intrigues of Retz, Condé, Gaston, and their mistresses in the same tone she uses for her spats with her girlfriends. And she, the big rosy-cheeked princess, a political innocent and sacrificial lamb, unspeculative and sociable, autocratic as she would be to the end of her days—she is at the center of this personal world. It is hard for this ingenuous girl to conceal her satisfaction with herself. It was her Orléans pride that made her fire on the royal troops.

She spent these years of exile (1652–57) at her various country houses—Saint-Fargeau, Forges, Champigny. Banishment to a many-chambered mansion in the country may seem like very mild punishment for high treason. But these cold, dank, decaying estates offered little comfort, let alone elegance, suitable for a princess. When she arrived at Saint-Fargeau she found grass up to her knees in the courtyard and a gibbet in her bedroom!

Mademoiselle set about cleaning up her retreat and gathered around her a small circle of girlfriends. The idea was to duplicate as closely as possible the luxury and refinement of the society she had left behind. Many visitors came. She entertained them liberally with food and wine, but the real entertainment was their gift to her: gossip and news of Paris and the court.

Entertainment—that was the biggest problem during this exile. The ladies who had come to share her isolation felt as deprived, unstimulated, and ingrown as she. Few of them were genuine friends. She was such a valuable piece of property that no one could resist trying to draw some advantage from their association with her.

The Countesses of Fiesque and Frontenac had been through the Fronde with Mademoiselle, and Gaston had dubbed them "field marshals in the army of my daughter against Mazarin." But now after the escapades of war these ladies found life at Saint-Fargeau too tame. Boredom made them insolent as they came to realise that the princess had no real power. The petty intrigues were endless, whsiperings behind hands at the banquet table, plots against other favorites. They persecuted Mademoiselle's special protégée Mlle. Vandy. This Vandy was a prude whom Mademoiselle had made the heroine of her short novel *La Princesse de Paphlagonie*. One day Mlle. Vandy's fashionable Parisian girlfriends, Mlles. d'Aumale and d'Haucourt, came to visit her at Saint-Fargeau. It was an event for Vandy that these ladies of distinction, of the circle of Angélique-Clarisse de Rambouillet, should favor her with their company. But no sooner arrived but they immediately displayed their distinction by joining forces with the Countesses Fiesque and Frontenac and abandoning Vandy to her hostess. Mademoiselle found these simpering, affected girls insupportable. At her distance in exile, she could not evaluate precisely all the goings-on in Paris, and her idea of the précieuse was limited to such ladies.

This visitation from Paris put a great strain on Mademoiselle's relations with her resident précieuses, the ladies Fiesque and Frontenac. She felt like an excluded bystander in her own home, where she, not they, was supposed to be the center of all the happenings. She wrote:

When a précieuse finds herself alone in any company, she becomes extremely bored and weary; she yawns, does not answer when spoken to, or if she answers, it is all off the point, as if to show that she is not paying attention to what is being said.

If she does this to people who have the courage to rebuke her, or to put it better, who are charitable enough to tell her what she has just said, she will just burst into a laugh and say, "Ah Madame, it's because one has not been thinking about what one has been saying. Oh, it's just too much! Oh, Lord! How to endure. . . ?"

But if another précieuse arrives in the same company, they rally together, and without realizing that they are not immune to criticism, they criticize others, sparing nobody, and quite brazenly, for they display their ridicule by laughing in other people's faces intolerably. They have almost a language of their own, for unless you frequent them a lot, you cannot understand them. They manage to find fault with everything one does and everything one says and generally disapprove of everybody else's behavior.[2]

The *précieux* affectations of her companions were not limited to censorious gestures and speech, however. In 1655 there was an astonishing scene between Mme. de Frontenac and her husband who came for a brief sojourn and naturally expected to sleep with his wife. The lady refused, making a great outcry. Mademoiselle witnessed this noisy marital squabble with its indecent confrontation of sex-starved husband and unwilling wife, and was mystified. She herself was, she thought, too reasonable for such passionate dissentions.

I had always had a great aversion for love, even the legitimate kind, it seemed an unworthy passion for a well-born soul! This scene confirmed my view; I could see that reason is rarely associated with the creation of passion, and passion never lasts very long. Such fugitive feelings, when they lead to marriage, can leave you unhappy the rest of your life. Lucky are they who marry for more solid reasons, even with a little aversion. Love can always come afterwards, I think. I am only judging by Mme. de Frontenac's situation.[3]

The Comte de Frontenac packed his bags and went off to Quebec, leaving his wife to vent her ill temper on Mademoiselle.

Another runaway wife arrived, Mme. de Thianges, and Mademoiselle soon regretted having welcomed her so warmly. This one sat up all night playing cards with the servants, and then came uncombed in her dressing gown to the dining table. When Mademoiselle tried to rebuke her, the replies were flippant. "I really don't care who sees me like this. Let them take me as I am." But the day this lady got drunk and threw a glass of wine at a gentleman guest, Mademoiselle left the table to show her displeasure.[4]

On New Year's Day 1657 in was Mme. de Fiesque who picked a quarrel with the princess and flounced out of the house after a bout of name-calling that left Mademoiselle prostrate with emotional fatigue. This restless lady was too fast for the company of the princess. Although her reputation as a virtuous précieuse was sealed by numerous literary flunkies who praised her in extravagant terms, she was more familiarly "*la reine Gilette*" to her boyfriends.

The authors Mademoiselle entertained were more docile than these girls. Segrais and Cotin were among her "*domestiques*," and to please her, seeing the way the wind was blowing, they occasionally wrote "anti-*précieux*" couplets. But their sporadic anti-*préciosité* was in fact an extension of the style, a bid for further distinction through witty contrast. This is very different from the anti-*préciosité* that was to come later and which would be aimed at the very Cotins of the *ruelles*.

Mademoiselle liked to think of herself as launching rather than following fashions. But she was actually less independent than she supposed and did want and need to belong, to be loved on an equal footing by her friends. That is why she put up with all those troublesome ladies. That is why she wrote her little novel, to show that she could do easily what others had to sweat to achieve.

And that is why she had her greatest social and literary success when she compiled, with the help of the author Segrais, her *Galerie des portraits*.

This collection of literary profiles was the most modish document to come out of the 1650s. It is a gallery of undisciplined feminine egoes, each striving to look remarkable but at the same time to promote a generalized image of herself, *banale*, unassailable in its correctness.

Mademoiselle was staying at her chateau at Champigny in 1657 when two of her girlfriends, the Princesse de Tarente and Mlle. de La Trimouille, arrived from a tour of Holland where "portraits" were all the rage. Mademoiselle sat down to write her own, with a speed and spontaneity that only a princess could command. Before long everyone was doing it.

This new parlor game entertained the ladies in precisely the way they wished: it challenged their wits and flattered their looks. It answered to the need for concentrated psychological analysis, proceeding from externals of face and figure to generalities about the character. Just as the etchings of the time presented ladies in invariable positions of elegance, the face glancing sideways at the spectator, the coiffure and gown stiffly stylish, these portraits obscure more than they reveal. They are the perfect *précieux* mask:

To begin the description of Iris [Mlle. Saumaize], I will tell you that her figure is neither large nor small, that her hair is not of a shocking color, but only as bright as necessary to provide contrast to the whiteness of her skin, which is rosy with youthfulness. Her eyes are blue and soft, her mouth is pink, her nose very well-shaped, her bosom shapely and very white, her arms and hands of the color of her bosom.

That is, more or less, the person of Iris, whose wit is most judicious; in this she is helped by many things in which she has been carefully educated, and which her modesty prevents her from showing off, having been born as wise as others may learn to become.[5]

The *Galerie des portraits* has the same faults as the fictionalized portraits in the novels of Mlle. de Scudéry. Nearly all the sitters are beautiful, clever, and virtuous. Eyes, hair, nose, and mouth are described with the same small fund of overworked adjectives; virtues and vices appear in a parade of congratulatory clichés.

Yet a few sarcasms slip through, smuggled between the layers of cotton-wool. Mme. de Fiesque's portrait is written (probably by Bussy) in sweetened acid:

Amaryllis has a sharp wit; there never was a freer one than hers. She laughs with the mad, cries with the sad, howls with the wolves.[6]

One or two unusual portraits leap to our notice, especially that of Mme. de La Grenouillère, who describes the ugliness of her own person with all its unsightly fat and unpleasant odors, right down to the corns on her toes, and then proceeds to her libertine thoughts and sexual adventures. But such portraits look suspicious by the very fact that they do not aim for the harmonious banality of the others. Mme. de La Grenouillère is unknown to us. She writes like an inelegant Ninon de Lenclos or a less worldly Mme. Cornuel. Her portrait may have been included in the collection through malice and treated as a joke.

The whole gamut of feminine high society, several middle-class women, and a few writers are represented in the *Galerie*. From this collection we get a glimpse of their conversation and aspirations, for though they do not tell many plain facts of their lives, they at least make us familiar with life as they think it ought to be. The

Galerie des portraits fixes subjective images as precious to us as any objective truth.

The subjective image is one of "unoriginal distinction," a genuineness somewhat like that of classic smartness in dress. The lady in the portrait is never meant to be truly unique, only unique within a recognizable type. These ladies did not try to attract attention by being different, but by being perfectly ordinary, supremely natural, ideally human. This is a subtler form of distinction than that cultivated by Mlle. de Scudéry in the rue de Beauce. Already it partakes of the exquisite superiority of an unassailable caste. What a thrill it must have been for a bourgeoise like Mme. Paget to get her portrait into this select company. To appear in Mademoiselle's *Galerie* meant that she belonged forever to the best and the newest of worldly societies.

When her term of exile was over Mademoiselle returned to the court and took on the sleek plumage of a very important person there, forgiven, eminent, still marriageable, still on the lookout for an acceptable husband. Her wistful, lifelong desire for love and friendship seems pathetic in one so rich and proud. A glimpse of the secret romantic girl underneath the grandeur of the princess is found in a passage from her memoirs. It is 1660. She is at the border town of Saint-Jean-de-Luz, in the royal entourage, participating in the huge affair of the wedding of Louis XIV to the infanta of Spain. The festivities have been going on for weeks and Mademoiselle, now thirty-three, has been in the thick of it. But one day, she finds herself looking out of a window at the Pyrénées, musing on the pleasures of solitude, the charm of the "desert," where one might be so happy alone, away from the bother and effort of her formal life, free of the jealousies and in-fighting of the court. She runs down to the seashore to pursue this train of thought and, strolling in the sand, she constructs a bucolic utopia: a small group of courtiers decides to leave the world voluntarily, to live apart in harmony and simplicity; they live chastely as friends; there will be no marriages. Mademoiselle rushes indoors to write to her friend Mme. de Motteville about it, and exchanges several letters with the older lady about her wonderful idea.

What could be more appealing than this literate exchange between two utterly courtly ladies, both pretending to be willing to retreat to a simple life in the country? But it was not all pretense. The imagination of Mademoiselle conceived during that seaside stroll an ideal society, far from the intrigues of court (at that moment she had lost the most exalted of her possible husbands to the infanta), where the freedom was of a kind that any précieuse would delight in. She chose an older woman, Mme. de Motteville, for the confidante of her imaginary commune, because she knew this cultivated, sensitive woman would understand her urge to formulate a difficult idea, and would not laugh at her search for a better world in the purified self, above and beyond the gross disappointments of real life.

The rest of the Grande Mademoiselle's story belongs to the annals of love in the best romantic tradition. At forty-three, being thoroughly disenchanted with her marital prospects, Mademoiselle suddenly fell deeply in love with a certain Chevalier de Lauzun, a mere gentleman of the French court. And she tried to marry him. The princess was so great, her beloved so far beneath her, that even a trivial opportunist and skirt-chaser like Lauzun was embarrassed at his good fortune. He avoided her. She pursued him. He capitulated gracefully. But marriage was unthinkable without the permission of the king. Louis granted it, without thinking too much about the matter. The princess was in a state of utter bliss; the heavens opened before her. A few days later, having had second thoughts, the king changed his mind, forbade the marriage, and locked her gallant up in Pignerol prison.

We cannot help pitying this proud princess who was constantly manipulated by others for reasons beyond her control or understanding. Her father had used her during the Fronde. And now, even long after she had ceased to be an international bargaining counter and there were no more kings or princes for her to marry, the king refused to allow her to have her little chevalier. Why? Chiefly because the king wanted her money. The most sordid blackmail was employed to get her to bequeath a substantial part of her enormous fortune to the Duc du Maine, Louis' eldest illegitimate son by Mme. de Montespan, in exchange for freeing Lauzun from prison. Even so, the man was set free only after the princess had passed childbearing age and could not possibly have an heir. To cap it all, Louis himself soon married a woman at least as common as Lauzun—Mme. Scarron.

Mlle. de Montpensier married Lauzun secretly at age fifty-four. And the big innocent princess, no longer apple-cheeked but still a maiden, learned in her turn that marriage could be hell. Lauzun treated his middle-aged bride with contempt. She swallowed her pride and submitted for a time. But legend has it that one day he ordered her to kneel down and pull off his boots. That was the last straw. Mme. de Lauzun reasserted her dignity and turned him out of her house. She became again *La Grande Mademoiselle*, and lived the rest of her life in pomp and glory at Versailles, devout, charitable, a Bourbon princess, whose heart was invisible under the gilded coronets of her position.

NOTES

1. Sévigné, Lettre à Coulanges, December 15, 1670, in *Lettres*, I, p. 181. This is Mme. de Sévigné's description of Anne-Marie-Louise d'Orléans, Duchesse de Montpensier. On Mlle. de Montpensier, see her own *Galerie des portraits*, edited in 1659 under her direction by Segrais and reprinted in 1860 by E. Barthélemy. Also her *Mémoires*, ed. Chéruel (Charpentier, 1857), 4 vols.

Of the numerous popular biographies of Mademoiselle, that of F. Steegmuller, *La Grande Mademoiselle* (New York: Farrar Straus & Cudahy, 1955), is the best.

Somaize calls her "La Princesse Cassandane" (*Dictionnaire*, I, p. 56).

2. *Galerie des portraits*, pp. 515–19.

3. *Mémoires*, II, pp. 265–66.

4. Ibid., III, pp. 8 ff. (1656). This lady was the sister of Mme. de Montespan, and would one day cash in on her sister's liaison with the king and be a powerful courtly exponent of the "sublime," a patroness of Boileau, and an antiprécieuse of note.

5. *Galerie des portraits*, p. 207.

6. Ibid., p. 91.

The Passionate Mother

I N 1653 there appeared at the *chambre bleue* an attractive and jovial extrovert, Marie-Chantal de Rabutin, Marquise de Sévigné (1626–1696).[1] She might be called a "natural prude," for her virtuous demeanor seemed not to be a painfully imposed discipline but a happy normalcy.

As a bright teenager studying Italian and Latin with Chapelain and Ménage, as a newlywed wife mildly wondering where her husband might be spending the night, as a charming and relieved widow at last in charge of her own person and destiny, the young Mme. de Sévigné presents a serenely sociable profile, relaxed among the stiff-boned women who were her friends, witty without pedantry, devout without trying. There was a saint among her grandmothers, Sainte Chantal, of whom she was said to be a "living relic," though her own piety was not of saintly proportions.

In her girlhood, the *précieux* abbé Ménage became her tutor and "*galant.*" She was sixteen; Ménage was twenty-eight. Courting her was to some extent a professional courtesy, but this flirtatious pedant did fall in love with his pretty pupil. He was given to kissing the bare arms of Marie-Chantal, and she permitted this, saying her arms were not "all that valuable." Mme. de Sévigné's earliest extant letter chides him for his jealousy. Later this courtship settled into a conventional habit, for she just never took him seriously. One day years later he murmured, "I am your confessor now, and I have been your martyr!" She quipped back, "And I am your virgin."

When Marie-Chantal was eighteen and very pretty she married Henri de Sévigné, a typical upper-class cavalier. Sévigné gambled, he drank, he threw his money to the winds, he ran with the pack of layabouts who circled around Ninon de Lenclos, and, worse, he crossed swords with his friends for the favors of various actresses

MARIE DE RAB⋯UTIN CHANTAL
MARQUISE DE SÉVIGNÉ
Née à Paris en 1626   Morte à Grignan en 1696

Mme. de Sévigné

and trulls. It was in one such duel, in 1651, brought on by a dispute over the beautiful eyes of a certain "belle Lolo" (Mme. de Gondran), that he lost his life.

This left Mme. de Sévigné a free woman of twenty-five, with a young son and daughter to raise, her husband's lawsuits to settle, and half a dozen eager admirers to fight off. The list of hopefuls grew long and distinguished throughout the 1650s. There was a Rohan-Chabot, a Comte du Lude, a Prince de Conty, the finance minister Fouquet himself, and above all, her cousin, the Marquis de Bussy-Rabutin. She was impervious to all these handsome gentlemen's proposals, most of which were far from honorable. She wanted to enjoy her freedom in her own way: reading novels, writing letters to girlfriends in Italian, going to hear the *tirades* of Corneille, but above all, nurturing and educating her beautiful, poised, learned little prodigy, Françoise-Marguerite, an absolute miracle for any doting mother to marvel at. Other people said that Françoise was vain, spoiled, and dull. But they did not say it in Mme. de Sévigné's hearing.

This fond mother kept her eye on the world. She found a welcome in all the *ruelles*. She got invited to every ball. For, after her daughter, the greatest pleasure in life was people and getting ahead socially.

Her cousin Bussy was a seducer. Mme. de Sévigné rejected his advances both before and after her husband's death, even in the full knowledge (supplied by Bussy himself) of her husband's affairs with Ninon and others. She was fond of this literate rake, for all his vanity and bad faith. She flirted with him gaily, but adultery was unthinkable. When he failed to seduce Marie-Chantal, Bussy suffered a certain pique. But when she neglected to send him a sum of money in an hour of need, he felt that family honor and friendship had been betrayed. He then did a most ungentlemanly thing. He revenged himself on his cousin by including a portrait of her in his infamous *Histoire amoureuse des Gaules*. This portrait breezily sketches her small, mismatched eyes, her pointy chin, her button nose, and tells the worst: she is too physically cold to be anything but a prude. How does he know? Why, her late husband told him so. But Bussy goes even further:

All her warmth is of the mind. To tell the truth, this compensates for her cold temperament. Judging by her actions, I believe her conjugal vows have never been violated. But if you judge by the intention, it's another story. Frankly, I think her husband came off all right in the eyes of men, but was a cuckold before God.[2]

Well! So Bussy has had her after all, in some obscure mental way, if not in fact. Mme. de Sévigné was furious at finding her virtue so vulgarly interpreted in a manuscript that was going around to dozens of acquaintances. It was as bad as if he had accused her of fornication. The rupture that resulted was a long time mending.[3]

Was it true? This healthy girl, whose tongue was so free, who could parry the propositions of the most attractive libertines in France but who never deviated from her wifely duty, and even went on refusing offers long after her husband had died so ignobly, was she merely an intellectual tease, a précieuse in the worst sense?

Mme. de Sévigné's character was certainly more complex than that. No doubt the repression of sex begun in her pious upbringing was reinforced by the indignities of her bad marriage. Sévigné's profligacy must have made the whole business of love utterly repellent to her. No one can know what intimate outrages turned Mme. de Sévigné against normal sex.

But there was all that enormous emotional energy going unused. Where could it find a decent outlet?

You are naturally tender and passionate, but to the shame of our sex [that is, the male sex—although written by a woman, this portrait is signed "an unknown man"] this tenderness has been useless to you and you have therefore confined it to your own. . . . Your heart is a treasure of which no one is worthy.[4]

This is Mme. de La Fayette on Mme. de Sévigné in the *Galerie des portraits*. Somaize echoes her view in his *Dictionnaire*, where he admires her joyous nature and says:

Yet it is easy to judge by her conduct that joy does not lead to love in her; for she reserves her love for her own sex and is content to give only her esteem to men.[5]

These observations by Mme. de Sévigné's contemporaries were composed at about the same time Bussy was writing his devastating profile (1657–60). It was thus common knowledge that Mme. de Sévigné preferred her women friends to the men in her life. No one thought this was strange.

But only one woman could be legitimately *adored*, and that was the beautiful daughter, the little marvel of grace and wit (Françoise was fourteen in 1660) to whom Mme. de Sévigné would write years later, "If I have remained an honest woman it is because of my passion for you." All the unclaimed longings of Mme. de Sévigné's heart, then, were settled on this girl.

The girl reacted by withdrawing into a shell of Cartesian philosophy, and eventually, after her marriage to the Comte de Grignan, by moving away to Provence. Mme. de Grignan is often viewed as a selfish person who did not respond to her wonderful mother's sacrificial affection. But all that white heat of feeling, all that displaced sexual drive! Who would not flee from such a mother?

The clergymen-psychologists of her time saw plainly that Mme. de Sévigné's mother-love was not noble but sinful. Arnauld d'Andilly actually refused her absolution once because she loved her daughter more than God. Such love was consuming, unreasoning, and surely abnormal.

When her daughter left her the separation was like an amputation. The one thing that sustained this passionate mother throughout the long years which followed was the letters she could pour out, week after week, a dozen pages at a time, in the hope of eliciting a response. This need grew into a happier habit, as Mme. de Sévigné discovered what a flair she had. The talent grew; the letters were preserved; the rest is literary history.

And the other child, the boy? Charles called his mother *"maman mignonne,"* attended faithfully on her illnesses, told her all his secrets. She worried sometimes about his vices, but she supposed all young men were like that. We do not know what comfort or advice she ever gave him, for her letters to him, if any, have not been preserved. All we have are the wry jokes about his failings in her letters to Mme. de Grignan:

I can't think what he does with his money. . . . He finds ways of spending without getting anything in return, of losing without actually gaming, of paying without acquitting his debts. He's a bottomless pit. . . . His hand is a crucible that melts money.[6]

And this malicious and perhaps triumphant remark:

Ninon said the other day that my son was a pumpkin [*citrouille* = pumpkin, fathead] stewed in snow. You see what it does for you to frequent distinguished company: you learn a thousand elegant expressions.[7]

Charles had performed badly in Ninon's boudoir, and she had sent him packing. When the boy ran to *"maman mignonne"* to confess his failure, Mme. de Sévigné coolly passed the news on to his sister.

Mme. de Sévigné's curious maternal fixation did not warp or embitter her character, or lessen her interest in the world around her. She was, like Tallemant des Réaux, a genuine observer of individual people and things. These letters, artful pearls from a gifted amateur who knows she must write well, are also a treasure of factual reality. She was the most natural writer of her century; she wrote what she saw: the leafy fastnesses of Brittany, the midnight burning of a town house, this week's society marriage, last week's play. She wrote what she felt: birthpangs when she became a grandmother, her daughter's near-drowning in a storm on the Rhône, her son-in-law's "excessive" sexual appetite.

Her literary taste evolved with the century. She came to prefer poetry grand rather than clever, and outgrew the conceits of the *précieux* style. But she was loyal to Corneille, and for a long time preferred him to his young rival Racine. She believed in an open universe, and Corneille's heroes lived in such a universe, with limitless moral horizons. How unlike the claustrophobia of Racine's antechambers, where all the characters are churning around inside their rotten selves. Mme. de Sévigné could still look out from her worldly frame and find the sights fresh and entertaining.

In 1671, long after the précieuses had become an absurdity of the past like the flat-topped hairstyles and the enormous sleeves of the regency, Mme. de Sévigné, by now a respected widow with a secure social position at court, wrote to Mme. de Grignan, "I was sitting alone in my chamber with a book *preciously* in hand...." [8] This little flying phrase sums up the précieuse as one who strikes attitudes toward literature. Mme. de Sévigné had never been one of these. Her own "*préciosité*" was an unselfconscious fervor for life. She was a woman true to the wonder and delight of the world, who found a respectable repository for her passionate love and out of it, as though by accident, made literature.

NOTES

1. The documentation is vast and accessible on Mme. de Sévigné, the best of it being of course her own thousand-odd letters, and after them the Walckenaer *Mémoires* (Didot, 1843–56).

Somaize calls her "Sophronie" (I, pp. 55, 61, 96, 205, 221).

2. Bussy-Rabutin, "Histoire de Mme. de Cheneville," *Histoire amoureuse des Gaules*, I, pp. 124–25.

3. The *Histoire amoureuse*, composed in 1658, was not intended for publication. But seven years later a lady friend of Bussy's handed a copy over to the printers, and Mme. de Sévigné's intimate psychology became a conversation piece for bourgeois strangers. No wonder she was furious.

4. *Galerie des portraits*, p. 95.

5. Somaize, I, p. 221.

6. Letter of Mme. de Sévigné to her daughter, May 27, 1680, in Sévigné, *Lettres*, II, p. 720.

7. Letter of April 8, 1671, ibid., I, p. 250.

8. Letter of July 26, 1671, ibid., I, p. 342.

The Lady behind the Book

*L*a *Princesse de Clèves* we have always with us. But the lady behind it eludes us.

Mme. de Sévigné had a younger girlfriend, Marie-Madeleine Pioche de La Vergne (later Comtesse de La Fayette, 1634–1692),[1] who also enjoyed the services of the abbé Ménage as her tutor. The flirtatious abbé went from one young lady to the other, adopting the same literary attitude of unrequited swain in both cases, a kind of one-man finishing school for girls too highly placed above him to care how he felt. It was during the years that Mlle. de La Vergne was looking for a suitable husband that she studied literature with Ménage. He pursued her with poetry and Latin verbs. But it was said that she never learned to conjugate the verb *amo*—except in the future tense!

A sensible girl aiming for a superb establishment that would provide social and material advantages, she waited and landed a big one: the Comte de La Fayette married her when she was twenty-one. This man had large tracts of land in Auvergne to match his very old name. She went there with him in 1655, leaving behind forever the petty nobility of magistrates from which she came and entering the nobility of the sword.

She wrote back letters to Ménage, letting him know she did not miss him:

You know, when one thinks oneself happy then one really is, and as I'm persuaded that I am, I live a more contented life than perhaps all the queens of Europe.[2]

This qualified bliss was based on *estime* rather than *inclination*. She looked out from the safety of her new position on the madness of others with ladylike curiosity. The couple came back often to Paris, where Mme. de La Fayette enjoyed a reputation as one of the most sought-after précieuses. After five years and two sons, her husband returned to Auvergne to work out his own destiny, and she remained in Paris to pursue her social career. The marriage was not a broken one, merely in permanent suspension.

This separation has been scrutinized by Mme. de La Fayette's biographers, because one of the things one would like to know about the author of *La Princesse de Clèves* is how she felt about this husband and what parallels may have existed between herself and the unhappily married heroine of her great novel. The novel, with its eternal triangle (devoted but unloved husband, virtuous wife, and the other man whom she desires but refuses) presents a situation that might correspond to her own—if we knew more about it.

Mme. de Clèves' *refus de l'amour* is inflicted on both husband and lover: she esteems her husband but has no passion for him. She flees her lover, and though driven to confess that she adores him, will never swerve from her duty and be his, not even after the death of the husband. She is frightened of love, the real love that she has discovered too late, and would rather live out her days in reposeful seclusion than risk the exposure of her heart to an unreasoning, defenseless passion that could kill her if she gave in to it. Mme. de Clèves clings to her self-possession, and her final renunciation of happiness is a triumph of her will.

If Mme. de La Fayette's fictional theme is related to some passionate disappointment in her own life, we cannot pin it down. Whatever went wrong with her *mariage de raison*, she covered the clues well. There was a good pretext for her to remain in Paris away from her husband. She had acquired the friendship of no less a person than the king's sister-in-law.

A remark of hers culled by Somaize for his *Dictionnaire* gives an insight into the character of this woman:

I am reproached for being unfeeling and hardhearted; but to tell the truth it is more laziness and absence of heart than hardness or lack of feeling.[3]

Her "emotional laziness" could only do her good. She handled her connections so well that she was soon to be seen riding in the carriage of Louis XIV himself. We know that she was a good businesswoman. She won her lawsuits. She married her son well.

Her youthful letters to Ménage reveal a woman who knew how to

Mme. de La Fayette

manipulate people. At twenty she could write to him safe in the belief that he was crazy about her:

I am glad you are not being capricious; I am so convinced that love is a nuisance that I rejoice to find that not only I but my friends are immune to it.[4]

But in certain other letters she demands assurances of his friendship, anxiously protests her commitment to him, implores him to write more often. She is jealous of a carnal attachment he is reported to have formed with Mme. de Montbazon, and orders him to give up this mistress. She is jealous of his devotion to Queen Christina of Sweden, and above all of Mme. de Sévigné. The young Mme. de La Fayette's friendship for Ménage is possessive and domineering and interwoven with an insidious coquetry.

Ménage reacted in kind. He addressed this poem to her:

> Dans l'empire amoureux
> Quand on est malheureux,
> Sans être criminel, on peut être rebelle,
> Et pour être inconstant, on n'est pas infidèle.
> Rien n'est si doux que la diversité;
> Le changement de fers tient lieu de liberté.
> D'un grand embrasement, d'un rigoureux servage,
> Il se sauve qui peut,
> Et vous, belle Doris, pour me faire un outrage,
> Vous m'accusez d'être volage.
> Hélas! Belle Doris, il ne l'est pas qui veut.[5]

> (In love's empire,
> when one is unlucky,
> one may rebel without being a criminal.
> And one can be inconstant without being unfaithful.
> Nothing is sweeter than diversity;
> a change of chains is almost as good as freedom.
> In the fires of passion, in the rigors of enslavement,
> It's every man for himself.
> And you, beautiful Doris, you do me wrong
> to accuse me of being fickle.
> Alas! Lovely Doris, if only I could be.)

This poem has a tailormade neatness, composed of wit, polish, and rationalized feelings. What exactly is Ménage admitting? That he has been "unfaithful" to his pupil, but is nevertheless still her slave?

But she has no claim on him, nor he on her. The witty conceit is addressed to the lady's *précieux* mask, and it clarifies her image (intelligent young woman beyond his reach) while it entertains and disturbs her. Such poetry can exist only in an environment emptied of everything but the ambiguous play of sentiments. The world in which Mme. de La Fayette and Ménage flirted with one another is an artificial, self-absorbed world wherein they can be totally occupied with the abstraction of love. The real world was the one in which she married La Fayette and secured for herself a place at court.

This friendship appears to have been a game of mutual sentimental blackmail, but it also produced Mme. de La Fayette's first literary efforts. Ménage formed her taste by introducing her to the novels of Mlle. de Scudéry. He helped her write a novella of her own, *La Princesse de Montpensier*, with a historical setting and a romantic plot about a lady unhappy in love. This book provides a point of comparison with her later masterpiece, and is in many ways a trial version of it.

She was terrified lest it be discovered that she was the author of this first work. She wrote angrily to a scholarly friend, Huet, who had revealed her authorship to his sister: "She will think I am trying to be a professional author, handing my books around like that!" This aristocratic recoil from professionalism was perhaps the more emphatic because her background was not as grand as her present position. She was to conceal her writing career carefully for the rest of her life, just as she concealed her private feelings.

For there is nothing in her youthful history that is known to us to compare with the devastations of her heroines—except for the intellectual flirtation with Ménage, which seems a far cry from the agonized plunge into love of Mme. de Cléves. Mme. de La Fayette toyed with Ménage's feelings in a way unthinkable to her high-minded fictional heroine. And yet—both she and her heroine seem more concerned for their own peace of mind than the man's. They both know that any man will always find some other woman if he cannot have her, but that she, if she were to allow herself to fall in love unwisely, would be trapped forever. The tidy mind of Mme. de La Fayette, contemplating the possibilities with Ménage, must have had a less elevated, more calculating set of thoughts than she gave to her amorous heroine Mme. de Clèves. She no doubt congratulated herself when she felt that he was more in love than she was. But from our selfish manipulations of other people we can learn of the dangerous beauties of self-giving. *La Princesse de Clèves* is a more noble story than the story of Mme. de La Fayette's tug-of-war with Ménage. But we can guess that the lady learned enough from this tantalizing relationship to use it for her book, transmuted though it is. Love is a menace. Best to avoid it. Woe is she who falls in.

It was much later, after she had finished her literary apprenticeship and the ambiguities of her friendship with Ménage were behind her, that Mme. de La Fayette formed her celebrated bond with La Rochefoucauld. This middle-aged association is a model of appearances, a triumph of *mondanité*.

It began fairly late in life for both of them. From 1667 when she was thirty-three and he fifty-four, and for thirteen years during which he was suffering from semiblindness and gout and she from internal disorders that dated back to her pregnancies, these two met and talked every day, wrote together, closeted in her study, sharing a circle of friends and an intellectual intimacy of a much higher order than Ménage could ever have offered. The taste of the day had grown more sedate, although the most popular literary subject was still love. Mme. de La Fayette embarked on her great novel with the cooperation of a very dour and weary La Rochefoucauld, whose disenchantment with the world was legendary, who knew all about the intricacies of the heart and the constant conflict of reason and passion. The two of them had all the leisure in the world to examine and refine their reactions to each other. Was this friendship? Was it perhaps love? Were they at least lovers? We will never know. We look in vain among his *Maximes* for this category of communion between man and woman. It looks like that very disinterested *"tendre amitié"* which was the aim of all precious women and which La Rochefoucauld professed he did not believe in.

We can see no connection between the frightened passion of Mme. de Clèves for her lover Nemours and the long-standing daily quiet pleasures of Mme. de La Fayette and La Rochefoucauld. It is nevertheless this friend who gave her a clear vision of the human condition as moral situation. This "classical" view, lifting man out of his contingencies in order to confront us with his essential moral being, was not new to French literature, but it was new to the novel.

In most other respects the book is a *précieux* document. Mme. de La Fayette had read her Scudéry well. Although she wisely suppressed the thousands of pages of windy prose and cut to the bone the complicated subplots of the *Cyrus*, there remained the hyperbolic style, the abstract psychological analysis, the sweetened portraiture. Mme. de La Fayette's *précieux* novel is often called the first novel of modern times. That is because in *Clèves* she added something of her own to Mlle. de Scudéry's hair-splitting analytical passion: Mme. de La Fayette brought to the genre, along with all her *précieux* baggage, the strength to look straight at a human dilemma —the despair of love—and follow it inexorably to its conclusion.

It was surely the relationship with La Rochefoucauld that gave her this strength. This was the artistic training that made all the difference between Mme. de La Fayette's great novel—the only *précieux* novel that is still read today—and all those that had gone before. It was this précieuse who, aided by her exigent friend, buried the *précieux* optimism under the implacable, bitter lucidity of classical art.

Upon La Rochefoucauld's death in 1680, the forty-six-year-old Mme. de La Fayette felt as bereaved as a widow. But she soon took up again with her old admirer Ménage, now turned sixty-seven. A twilight friendship, composed of nostalgia and kindness, it answers no questions but puts the final touch of enigma on a mysterious *éducation sentimentale* that is forever hidden behind a great book.

NOTES

1. Of the numerous works on Mme. de La Fayette we cite only C. Dédéyan, *Madame de La Fayette* (Société d'Edition d'Enseignement Supérieur, 1955) and Pingaud, *Madame de La Fayette par elle-même* ("Ecrivains de toujours" aux Editions du Seuil, 1960). Her own novels are collected in the Garnier edition, ed. E. Magne (1961).

Somaize calls her "Feliciane" (I, pp. 96, 205, 211).

2. Letter of September 1, 1656, *Lettres de Mme. de La Fayette et de Gilles Ménage*, p. 45.

3. Quoted in Somaize, I, p. 211.

4. Letter of September 18, 1654, *Lettres de Mme. de La Fayette et de Gilles Ménage*, p. 28.

5. Ménage, "Madrigal à Mlle. de La Vergne," quoted in: Mongrédien, *Les Précieux et les précieuses*, p. 247.

Conclusion

T HE WORLDLY women who circulated at the court of Louis XIV were different from the précieuses who had flourished in Paris in the 1650s, even when they were the same women. The difference was that they now belonged to a social system, whereas in the 1650s they had felt that they belonged only to themselves. The courtly figure is part of a complex display. The précieuse had been a gregarious individual. The courtly woman is knowing and disillusioned. The précieuse had been full of illusions and ignorant.

The *mondaines* who took over the vanguard of feminine fashion from the précieuses gave up all those wild notions about liberty. They knew that power for a woman now resided in support for authority. Who were the powerful women of the '60s, '70s, '80s? The royal mistresses. The royal sisters-in-law.

Those patterns of politeness designed by the Marquise de Rambouillet and intended as an alternative to an uncouth philistine court had now developed into a mechanism of courtly survival.

But when we look back to the beginning of the *précieux* experiment, we see that it was in the *chambre bleue* that the position of women had been elevated to such a degree of consideration that they could begin to think of expanding in other directions. The war of the Fronde was one. Women who had learned from the poets about their emotional power over men now set out to guide those men to victory. It proved to be a frivolous exercise, replete with vanity and self-indulgence. But after the Fronde, it seemed to many more women, of many classes and temperaments, that there was something to be gained in purely social mastery. The explosion of consciousness in so many women during the post-Fronde period, while it rested on the initial gains of Mme. de Rambouillet, was quite different in character from her placid social routines. The New Women were full of hope and energy. They were busy at last, with things to learn. They must learn how to read, how to think, how to write—above all, how to talk. And they must congregate. Solitary introspection was not their cup of tea. Civilization for them was discussion, not contemplation. Freedom was communication. They perched in their heavy damask beds, not to ponder within themselves but to reach out to their friends. When nobody came to see them they daydreamed fruitless circular daydreams that gave them a bellyache. Introspection was what a man did when he turned his back on a woman. They would have none of that. They went to bed to entertain. Privacy yes, solitude no.

They did not use their leisure wisely. When we read what they chattered about, we are embarrassed. The little parlor games, the enigmas, the metamorphoses, the sociable metaphors, the riddles, the amorous maps—these are a sorry monument. They were lazy and long-winded. They did not want to know about the *gouffre* of self-love that Pascal preached and La Rochefoucauld formulated. They would not look into themselves.

And they were vain and easily gulled. When the men wrote poems comparing them to crystals, to pearls, to the sun, they felt impervious and mighty: they became crystals, pearls, the sun.

The good aspects of *préciosité*, the affirmative, practical feminism, the resolute approach to the New, were hampered by the timidity of the women, ridiculed by their men, and finally terminated by the new vision of a closed universe which was classicism. Terminated? No, only submerged. For the *femmes savantes* endured into the eighteenth century, survived the classical period by turning their attention away from poetry and toward the sciences. Although the label *précieuse* was discarded, the précieuses themselves did not disappear at all. They became the admirers of an ex-poet and *bel esprit*, Fontenelle, who turned them from the played-out poetical themes of the fifties and got them interested in mathematics and Cartesian astronomy. Twenty years after *Les Précieuses ridicules*, ladies who had acquired a new set of heroes were taking up physics as passionately as they had once taken up the sonnet *Job*.

Women became involved in a curious intellectual dispute, the quarrel of the Ancients and the Moderns, in which the champions of women (Fontenelle, Perrault) looked to the future, believed in progress, evolution, the improvement of man. They were the Moderns. Their enemies, the Ancients—Boileau, La Fontaine, La Bruyère, antifeminists all—looked to the past, observed that the Greeks and Romans had already discovered all the truths and laws of human nature, and announced that there was little to add, for man was incorrigible and self-improvement a delusion. Boileau's bitter *Tenth Satire* attacks women not only for their vanity and selfishness, but also for their pretensions to change the world.

The Ancients had the advantage of being superior artists, but it was the Moderns, the champions of women, who won this end-of-century battle of the books. The quarrel of the old and the new was the end of the classical age. Poetry was the loser. It was now to be replaced by ideas, expanding, searching, active ideas that questioned the old order and refused the rigidity of Bourbon absolutism and—ultimately—the confining classical world view.

Thus, the précieuses were the spiritual grandmothers of a new set of ladies, the clear-thinking, well-educated women of the Enlightenment who would open their doors to intellectuals, not twittering alcovists now but serious philosophers. The brainy women who sat up in chairs to entertain Voltaire and d'Alembert a hundred years later did all the things the précieuses had dreamed of doing. Mme. de Lambert, Mme. de Tencin, Mme. du Châtelet, Mme. du Deffand, Mme. Geoffrin were never ridiculous. These ladies no longer suffered from sentimental confusion about chastity, or swooned over madrigals, or tried to draw the geometry of the passions. They talked as though they had always had the right to talk; they thought in ways that only men were supposed to be capable of. And their unhappiness came from knowledge, not ignorance.

The prudery had gone by now, too. Even when the eighteenth-century hostess is chaste, it is clear that she has chosen to be without consulting God, church, or society. The liberated morals of these famous women of the Enlightenment were in contrast to the affected prudery of the précieuses. But the difference is perhaps smaller than it seems. The précieuses, though cringing before social opinion, had little to do with official theological virtue either. The chastity of the truly devout woman is a sacrifice she makes to God's authority, a form of humility, a submission of personality. The prudery of the précieuse was, on the contrary, a demonstration of self-control, a form of pride, an expression of personality.

The précieuses had launched forth in many directions during their brief moment of glory, but the hallmark of the true précieuse, the cachet that identified them all, was a desire for personal freedom. That was the paradox of their predicament. Ideally, the précieuse had no parents, no husband, no children. Real women were hamstrung at every turn by fathers, brothers, husbands, public opinion, and their own emotions. But quite a few complained. They searched for solutions: birth control, temporary marriage, divorce. Their conversation was full of the heady alternatives to reality.

But it was all talk. They were not prepared to go out and padlock themselves to the gates of the Palais-Royal. They were not ready to let go of the charms and ruses of slavery. They settled for the mirage, the comedy of the alcovist, the spiritualization of love, the incoherent and lazy dabbling in literature. They wore the elegant mask.

They wore the mask of fragile femininity, decked out on the throne of their bed, framed in the safety of their heavy curtains. This theatrical display was a form of concealment, a hideout in a world where one's real self could become all too notorious. Society was small in the seventeenth century. In Paris it was very small indeed. Anonymity was not merely undesirable to the gregarious précieuse; it was impossible. *Préciosité* provided an official personage, behind which the real woman could study herself.

And within the small airless *ruelle* there was space for diversity and individual style. *Préciosité* was a social adventure. It helped to be noble, rich, of good reputation, but even without these any lady could set up for herself a *précieux* identity. *Préciosité* did not lower many social barriers in actual fact, but it did give to women of all classes a sense of belonging to a community of free individuals, of being a thing of value regardless of position, age, location, or even money.

But can we really speak of freedom in connection with these women? Were they not too vain, too conformist, too eager to enslave others? How could they be modernists and conformists at the same time, partisans of invention and order?

By being, alas, fashion mongers. This was the undoing of the précieuses as New Women. Their drive toward freedom was easily diverted into harmless channels, such as the dead end of modishness. For them, poetry—that most wonderful of all liberators of the imagination—was merely an object of fashion, as trivial as a bit of lace at the wrist. The urge toward originality was constantly curbed by the safety of the unoriginal.

In the domain of fashion, a balance is sought between the known and the unknown, as between Chanel and Courrèges. The lady of fashion wants to be noticed, but only within a framework of dress conventions. It is in subtle details, tucks and darts and cuff-buttons, rather than gigantic furbelows, that true originality shows.

Fashion poses a dilemma. The woman wishes to be distinguished and desired for qualities that, after all, are common to all women. The new look always produces the same woman cunningly wrapped, with two, not three, breasts. Fashion works best when it produces a perfect balance between banality and novelty. The successful précieuse is the one who has clothes sense, an eye for the right details of social behavior. The failed précieuse is the one who, like Angélique-Clarisse de Rambouillet, overdresses in her *précieux* personality. Modernity and classic decorum meet in the tact of the précieuse. And tact moves no mountains.

As the century wore on, conformity outweighed originality and became the only sure virtue. The précieuses were outmoded when their originality began to look odd, was isolated and laughed at. The reign of Louis xiv finished them off when it crushed individual style in favor of grandeur. Society became a magnificent fishpond in which everyone thrashed around in a welter of appearances. The self behind the mask dwindled. Individual destiny became ever more trivial. *Paraître*: to be on show, to be seen by one's contemporaries and receive their approval as a perfect reproduction of some preconceived paragon—that was the aim of courtly lives.

With the capitulation to conformity came cynicism and self-loathing. French moralists of the classical age grandly threw away all hope of generosity or humankindness and damned the race altogether. Lucidity in despair was their only remaining comfort.

But perhaps because they were second-class human beings, women could afford to disbelieve this. The précieuses had clung to a special form of freedom called change. They could be optimistic experimenters, keep their illusions, and go in for self-improvement. *Préciosité*, even though it promoted a shallow, conventional, dishonest literature designed for denying the unknown, was nevertheless on balance a yea-saying to the future. With all their self-indulgence and vanity, these women visualized a different life, and Boileau and Molière could not. Within the limits of their given, their imagination was more adventurous than that of the men of their time. They manifested their discontent with what *is*.

If it seems to us today that they made a poor job of it, it is because they could only see their situation *in terms of what they knew*. They could only desire that grace and power and self-determination that they thought men enjoyed. They did not dream that they would find nothing but more mountains on the other side of that mountain.

As literature, *préciosité* was insubstantial and of the moment. We might call *précieux* poetry art as an alternative to reality. The précieuses pathétically consumed this trivial art, overrated it, preferred it to the best. If it troubles our deep convictions about the serious artist—a Victor Hugo or a Racine—we must also see that the *précieux* poet simply had a different function in the lives of his readers. He was not supposed to be telling any sort of cosmic truth. He was playing. *Précieux* poetry was a game for the amusement of wretches. The underlying assumption is unassailable: a little superficial happiness can, in certain conditions, be just as valuable as truth.

Responding to the secret desire of the précieuse for private value for herself, this literature served her briefly and faded. The poet and the woman exploited one another and then parted company. Perhaps this was because the woman was not detached enough from her immediate problems to want a literature of real depth. All she needed—and she needed it to desperation—was something to keep her going, to warm her heart, however insincerely: to give her a name, above all, until history might catch up with her.

Has history caught up with her? So much has been earned by women in three hundred years of technical and social progress that we may well feel only pity for the hapless précieuses, with their crippled bodies and their blinkered thoughts. But now that the real human issues of womankind have come to the surface again, now that we can see that the problems are far more than a simple matter of birth control, votes, and jobs, we can remember those faraway ladies and their thirst for dialogue, their need to be interesting, with gentle affection and perhaps some qualified gratitude. We are their granddaughters, too, the inheritors of their verbiage and enthusiasm, and of their yearning toward self-knowledge.

Euphémie (II)

WHICH IS better, to be loved because one is always the same, or in spite of it?"

"Oh, surely," says Doralie, "it is better to be loved in spite of it. I would wish my lover never to know how plain and simple I am. Who among us does not long to be someone else? Who would wish to be loved for his unchanging, incurable mediocrity? Not I! I conceive love as an enchantment, a noble blindness to reality. Whoever loves me must love in the delusion that I am a creature of infinite variety. I would be a fleeting star in his sky, a snowflake, a drop of dew, a sunbeam dancing before his eyes. But alas, I wake every morning to find myself fixed forever in the sordid furrow of my lot—" Images, images of the monstrous acrobatics of her husband in that hot stifling rectangle she shares with him—

Agaride is shaking her head. "Doralie, you must come down to earth, and see that variety is not a delusion but a goal. We must see the world as it is, so that we can make it better. Fleeing reality, taking refuge in dreams, can only prolong our misery."

Bélise interrupts. "But what is the use of that? We cannot do anything. Here I am again—"

"Laid low by the lash of lawful love!" breathes Caliste, and Euphémie turns a brilliant smile of admiration on her.

"But my husband—"

"Very well, marriage is bad. We must improve it. Marriage is the butt of common jokes. It must be resanctified. Why not make the contract less permanent? A one-year trial, with the option on both sides to annul. Of course, it must be entered upon freely by both partners without pressure from their families."

Bélise is breathless. "And the woman should decide how many children she will have!"

Euphémie sighs at all this extravagance. "But is it better then to be loved because one is always the same?"

"Yes," says Agaride, "Yes, an unqualified yes. But in truth we are not always the same. We get worse. Love must expect this and go on loving. Love must worship at the shrine of the beloved, not because she is a snowflake one moment and a drop of dew the next, but because she is a woman, growing older, changing always for the worse, mortal—like all living things."

The bony cheeks, the flat chest, the crossed eyes, the enlarged knuckles of Agaride are transfigured by this idea, which possesses her like a refulgent angel.

"How wonderful you are, Agaride," Euphémie drawls. "How I would wish to be loved for my genuine self."

Florizel murmurs, "Surely you must know, Madame, that you *are* loved—for perfections that never change."

Corinne breaks in impatiently. "Oh, Florizel, it is all so monotonous. Love is impossible. Love consumes itself quickly, demands always fresh meat—"

Caliste upsets her lemonade. "Really, Corinne! Do you not mean that love is a butterfly flitting from flower to flower—?"

"I mean that love is a dreadful illusion. No one can fix a lover without assuming many faces. The beloved is constantly reinventing herself to please her lover. But in fact she is always the same and love is all based on trickery. As soon as the lover learns his beloved cannot change, his blindness is cured!"

Florizel gazes across at Corinne. "Neither my love nor its object will ever change!" She flings back, "Oh, Florizel, you mouth a lot of rubbish."

He smiles. "Only a cynic would quarrel with my certainty."

For a fleeting moment Euphémie wonders where Florizel and Corinne have met before. But Rodolphe interposes smoothly, "Well, as nobody wishes to be taken for a cynic, we will have to believe you. But I must say, the Clorises and Dorises of our poetry are very much the same—as each other. I suppose they are the many faces of one face—as Amidon says, the Muse. Because the Muse is one woman, and you love her for her sameness underneath her infinite variety of mortal incarnations. Twenty or thirty women may inhabit her in turn; but *she*, she whom we love with a constant burning flame never changes for the worse, never disappoints us because she is our own idea, of which each lovely lady is a momentary image."

Euphémie (II)

Euphémie is impatient. "But I am not talking about loving; I am talking about being loved. Amidon, what do you say?"

Amidon is ready. He clears the rattle from his throat. "Yes, love is a creature of many faces, a Proteus indeed. Of human love I distinguish nine categories, of divine six. The first and most elemental of human loves is that of a mother for her child. The child is constantly changing in its progress toward maturity, yet to the mother it is always the same. It is 'my child.' The second is the love of spouses, the third the love of country, the fourth the love of one's friend—"

Euphémie closes her eyes. After the nine categories of profane love must come the six categories of divine. Who will save them all?

Cathos. When Amidon stops to take out his large dirty handkerchief, Cathos, who has lost count of his categories, speaks out in a rush of words:

"I do think love is frightfully exciting, and wish I might some day be as perfect as all the ladies here, and loved because I will never change from being perfect. And I am going to try to be perfect like my aunt, because you cannot be loved unless you deserve it. And I think this is what Monsieur Amidon meant when he said my aunt was always the same. She will always be perfect. And so she will always deserve to be loved."

Cathos is beet-red and sweating. She is astonished at the ripple of approval that flows through the room.

Even Sophie makes a contribution at last. "That was well said, my dear. Let me put it another way. I wish to be loved for myself alone. I wish to be loved for not changing, in all my perfection. But in order to deserve this I must *be* perfect. Of course, none of us is. We are all the same not in perfection but in vice and vanity. If we could fix our fugitive virtues as firmly as our vices pin us down, then we would be lovable indeed. What are the truly lovable qualities? Beauty? Wit? Accomplishments? I wonder. These come and go; they are better or worse but never absolute. One quality only is absolute: the striving for perfection. If we could but choose ourselves, we would choose to be excellent. I myself believe in this choice, although the paradox is that it is nearly impossible to make. I believe in taking hold of one's self. The person who knows and possesses his own being is the person loved by all others, and loved always for being the same. The will to self-containment, definition, separation, distinction—call it what you will—this is what

298

the lover loves. For this is what makes us most human: our aware-
ness of our chosen self. What the lover loves, always and forever, is
the clear, sharp object which may be always the same but is nevertheless unique."

The ladies all sit a little straighter in their chairs. Even Euphémie
leans forward from her wrappings. "*Dear* Sophie!" is all she says.
She speaks for all the ladies present, to the little sparrow who has
captured the essence of the question and given it its answer, who has
shown them that the possibilities of their sameness are infinite, and
love will always be there to reward their belief in themselves.

Index

Index